MANAGING THE PSYCHOLOGICAL IMPACT OF MEDICAL TRAUMA

Michelle Flaum Hall, EdD, LPCC-S, is associate professor, Clinical Mental Health Counseling, Xavier University, Cincinnati, Ohio, and a partner at Hawthorne Integrative, LLC, a health care consulting and clinical counseling firm. Her scholarship about medical trauma and integrated health care has been published in such journals as *Nursing for Women's Health, ACA Vistas,* and *Journal of Interprofessional Education & Practice*. Dr. Hall has presented on the topic of medical trauma at local, state, and national clinical counseling conferences including the American Counseling Association Annual Convention; to students in advanced clinical mental health counseling courses; and to cancer survivors and their families. She has consulted with the California Maternal Quality Care Collaborative in the development of a national Postpartum Hemorrhage Toolkit, and has authored a tool to help medical professionals recognize the signs of acute stress disorder in the hospital setting. Dr. Hall currently participates in a work group for the national Council on Patient Safety in Women's Health Care to develop a safety toolkit focused on patient, family, and provider supports following a severe maternal event. Her clinical experience includes working with adults struggling with depression, posttraumatic stress disorder, and other anxiety-related disorders. Over the years, she has worked with numerous clients with complex reactions to life-threatening or life-altering medical diagnoses and procedures. Additionally, Dr. Hall works with seven health-related fields (especially nursing) across Xavier University to develop innovative interprofessional education experiences for future health care workers. She participated in IPEC (Interprofessional Education Collaborative), which is led by six health care associations including the American Association of Colleges of Nursing and the Association of American Medical Colleges. She is a Certified Master Trainer in TeamSTEPPS (Team Strategies and Tools to Enhance Performance and Patient Safety), an interprofessional, evidence-based communication training curriculum developed by the U.S. Department of Defense and the Agency for Healthcare Research and Quality, and has received training in mindfulness-based stress reduction from faculty at the University of Massachusetts School of Medicine.

    Scott E. Hall, PhD, LPCC-S, is associate professor, Counselor Education, University of Dayton, Dayton, Ohio, and a partner at Hawthorne Integrative, LLC, a health care consulting and clinical counseling firm. He has written on the topics of medical trauma and integrative health care and collaborates with health-related programs at the University of Dayton to develop wellness initiatives. His work has been published in *ACA Vistas, ADULTSPAN Journal, Journal of Workplace Behavioral Health, Journal of Contemporary Psychotherapy,* and *American Journal of Hospice & Palliative Care*. Dr. Hall has taught and created a wide range of courses at the University of Dayton, including all foundational courses in the mental health counseling program and specialized courses such as Counseling Men, Alternative Therapies, and Positive Psychotherapy. In his clinical practice, Dr. Hall counsels adults with depression, anxiety disorders, posttraumatic stress disorder (PTSD), and divorce-related concerns. In addition to his clinical experience working with medical trauma, he has also presented at national, state, and local professional conferences about PTSD-related topics in addition to medical trauma. He has also spoken about the mental and emotional impacts of a cancer diagnosis at the Cancer Support Community of Southwestern Ohio. Dr. Hall is a Certified Master Trainer in TeamSTEPPS and has received training in mindfulness-based stress reduction from faculty at the University of Massachusetts School of Medicine. He is a veteran of the United States Army.

MANAGING THE PSYCHOLOGICAL IMPACT OF MEDICAL TRAUMA

A Guide for Mental Health and Health Care Professionals

Michelle Flaum Hall, EdD, LPCC-S
Scott E. Hall, PhD, LPCC-S

SPRINGER PUBLISHING COMPANY
NEW YORK

Springer Publishing Company, LLC
11 West 42nd Street
New York, NY 10036
www.springerpub.com

Acquisitions Editor: Nancy S. Hale
Compositor: diacriTech

ISBN: 978-0-8261-2893-5
e-book ISBN: 978-0-8261-2894-2
Student Resources ISBN: 978-0-8261-2959-8

Student Resources are available from www.springerpub.com/hall

16 17 18 19 20 / 5 4 3 2 1

The author and the publisher of this Work have made every effort to use sources believed to be reliable to provide information that is accurate and compatible with the standards generally accepted at the time of publication. The author and publisher shall not be liable for any special, consequential, or exemplary damages resulting, in whole or in part, from the readers' use of, or reliance on, the information contained in this book. The publisher has no responsibility for the persistence or accuracy of URLs for external or third-party Internet websites referred to in this publication and does not guarantee that any content on such websites is, or will remain, accurate or appropriate.

Library of Congress Cataloging-in-Publication Data
Names: Hall, Michelle Flaum, author. | Hall, Scott E., author.
Title: Managing the psychological impact of medical trauma : a guide for
  mental health and health care professionals / Michelle Flaum Hall, Scott
  E. Hall.
Description: New York, NY : Springer Publishing Company, [2016] | Includes
  bibliographical references and index.
Identifiers: LCCN 2016014655 | ISBN 9780826128935
Subjects: | MESH: Patients—psychology | Stress, Psychological—prevention &
  control | Patient Care—psychology | Professional-Patient Relations
Classification: LCC RC552.T7 | NLM WM 172.4 | DDC 616.85/21—dc23 LC record available at
https://lccn.loc.gov/2016014655

Printed in the United States of America by McNaughton & Gunn.

*This book is dedicated to the countless patients
who have silently suffered the devastating
effects of medical trauma.*

The greatest mistake physicians make is that they attempt to cure the body without attempting to cure the mind; yet the mind and body are one and should not be treated separately.

Plato

CONTENTS

PREFACE

When Treatment Becomes Trauma

They would enter as a group at varying times, so I was never quite prepared for their arrival. I lay on a table under bright lights, without my clothes and only a thin cotton smock and polyester sheet to cover me. Multiple cords connected me to machines that spat alarming sounds and made movement from my position nearly impossible. I had not had water or food since the day before, and my requests for such were quietly denied.

My heart would race at the sight of them, for I knew what was about to unfold. Each time was the same: Two strangers dressed in pink smocks stood at my feet, forcing open my legs with enough power to overcome my strength and will to keep them closed. A third, someone I knew and trusted, pressed down upon my newly stitched abdomen with one hand while inserting an arm halfway up my body, scraping out my insides with the other. There was more blood than I had ever seen, even in the worst of horror films. I screamed and shuddered and tried desperately to cling to my humanity, which was slipping with every terrifying moment that passed.

After completing their task, the group left and I lay whimpering, trying in vain to soothe my ravaged body and wounded spirit. Yet just as I began to calm my wildly beating heart, the group would enter once again, beginning the Sisyphean process anew. As the hours passed, the apologies became more and more meaningless as I struggled to comprehend the magnitude of this trauma.

For the next several days I remained in this place while I recovered, with the same sights, sounds, smells, and people. It was an unspoken expectation that I should forget, or at least quickly forgive, what I had endured at the hands of people I had trusted. It was an unspoken expectation that I was to submit to care from the same people who enacted this trauma upon my body, my mind, and my spirit. Like all adults, I had given a silent consent to do whatever it took to save my life, even if it meant *torture*. If the same events had happened in an alley rather than in a hospital, I would have been whisked away to a safe place and expected to see the perpetrators in a police lineup or court of law, not every few hours or in a situation in which I needed to depend on them for my ongoing care and survival. While my mind could accept this double bind, my body and spirit were broken. In extreme cases of medical trauma, perpetrators are healers—they are our saviors—but when their work is done we are left to pick up the pieces of the life they have saved. Regardless of how noble the intentions, medical trauma exacts a toll that is not easily undone.

This story is my story, and I wish I could say it is wholly unique. The truth is, extreme forms of medical trauma like my childbirth experience happen every day, and have the potential to permanently scar the psyches of patients, their families, and staff long after patients' physical wounds have healed. Through the numerous conversations with former patients, family members, doctors, nurses, and administrators, I think it is safe to say that most are currently not prepared to meet the complex needs arising from medical traumas—but my hope is they will be.

My own experience of medical trauma was a double-edged sword in that I felt profoundly grateful toward my health care providers for saving my life following the birth of my daughter, and at the same time was deeply troubled that my emotional health was ignored throughout my entire episode of care. The posttraumatic stress that I experienced following this trauma was the first of many dominoes to fall, and it seemed that no life domain, no relationship, no corner of my mind or cell in my body was safe from the deeply felt memory of it all. To make matters worse, as a clinical mental health counselor I mistakenly believed that it was up to me to find my own way back (or forward) to a place of vitality, hope, and healing. This book is a stop along that journey.

Over the past decade, I have dedicated the life I nearly lost to helping others understand the nature and effects of trauma stemming from life-threatening medical events, chronic and life-altering illnesses, and even some everyday medical procedures. Through this work, I hope to impart insight about the psychological effects of *patient-hood*, including the impacts of vulnerability, decontextualization, and of receiving health care that is solely focused on the physical body.

Together with my husband and coauthor, Dr. Scott Hall, I invite you to consider how we can all become better stewards of patients' emotional health, especially when treatment becomes trauma.

Michelle Flaum Hall, EdD, LPCC-S

Note: The Appendices are available for download from Springer Publishing Company's website: www.springerpub.com/hall.

ACKNOWLEDGMENTS

I would like to begin by acknowledging the support I have received from friends, family, and colleagues, whose steadfast belief in me has been a powerful motivator and a reminder of the incredible strength of the human spirit. First, I would like to thank my mother, Barbara Andrews, who has been a consistently positive presence in my life and who first taught me that women can do anything they set their minds to do. I would also like to thank the following people for the support and inspiration they have provided: Nancy S. Hale at Springer Publishing Company; Emilia Ryan of eRpictorial, whose graphic design expertise has been much appreciated throughout the development of our clinical tools and protocols; Dr. Susan Schmidt, Director of the School of Nursing at Xavier University; interprofessional colleagues at Xavier who have played an important role in my professional development: Lisa Niehaus, Dr. Debra VanKuiken, Dr. Rick Browne, Dr. Jaylene Schaefer, Dr. Karen Enriquez, and Cathy Sacco; colleagues in counseling, including Dr. Brent Richardson, Diane St. Clair, Meredith Montgomery, Megan Lobsinger, and Rebecca Morra; Dr. Christine Morton at Stanford University and the California Maternal Quality Care Collaborative; Renee Byfield and the Association of Women's Health, Obstetric, and Neonatal Nursing; the Patient, Family, and Staff Support Workgroup with the Council on Patient Safety in Women's Health Care; Cynthia Ronan, Darcy Plunkett, and Regina Menza; my clients, colleagues, and students; and Dr. Scott Hall, my loving husband and capable coauthor. Last but certainly not least, I would like to mention my daughter Catherine, who every day models the perseverance, bravery, and compassion I aspire to embody. Thank you for being an amazing individual who makes motherhood more joyful than I ever imagined it could be.

Michelle Flaum Hall, EdD, LPCC-S

I would like to give thanks to the brave souls who were willing to share their insights and experiences regarding their own psychological struggles with medical trauma and their belief in the importance of this book. A special thanks to Tommy for allowing me as his friend to share in his struggle with illness. My gratitude also goes to my family, university colleagues, students, and clients who exemplify the effort to live life to the fullest, and to my children who inspire me with their own journeys of courage and resilience. My deepest thanks go to my wife and partner, Michelle, who demonstrates the essence of perseverance, unyielding compassion, and advocacy in her endeavor to shed light on the experience of medical trauma.

Scott E. Hall, PhD, LPCC-S

INTRODUCTION

A young woman nearly bleeds to death following the birth of her child. A man in his 40s with a career, wife, and two children is told: *You have pancreatic cancer.* A woman who has lost her mother and aunt to breast cancer gets a phone call: *We found something on your mammogram.* An athletic marathoner in the prime of his life injures his back and will never run again. A woman with a history of sexual trauma enters an OB/GYN's office for her first pelvic exam in 10 years. A heart attack, stroke, automobile accident, diagnosis of a chronic, life-altering disease ... the list of jarring medical experiences that can and do happen could easily take up the remaining pages of this book. In fact, for every *minute* you spend reading—in the United States alone—one person will have a heart attack (720,000 per year; Centers for Disease Control and Prevention [CDC], 2015a), nearly two people will have a stroke (800,000 per year; CDC, 2016b), 78 people will go to the emergency department (129.8 million per year; CDC, 2016a), three people will learn that they have cancer (1.67 million new cases in 2014; American Cancer Society, 2014), three people will learn they have diabetes (1.7 million new cases in 2012; American Diabetes Association, 2016), and for each hour that passes, nearly six women will suffer grave complications while giving birth (50,000 per year; CDC, 2015b). While the sheer numbers of medical experiences are certainly staggering, it can be downright overwhelming to think about the psychological implications of such traumas, emergencies, and life-threatening/life-altering diagnoses for patients and their families; more overwhelming is that for many, the emotional costs of medical experiences often go undetected, untreated, and unvoiced.

Why can the psychological impacts of medical traumas go largely undetected and initially untreated? There are certainly many theories:

- In the medical setting, the physical body takes precedence.

- Traditional health care teams are staffed by mostly medical professionals, so longer term emotional well-being is not on the radar.

- As adults, we are socialized to ignore or minimize the psychological impacts of medical traumas.

- Our health care system is in flux.

- Previous reimbursement models supported "sick" care rather than "health" care.

- Perceived need for mental health professionals is too narrowly defined.

While this list of potential factors is certainly not exhaustive, it does give us a glimpse at the many obstacles embedded within a health care system that has been charged with improving its operation along many fronts, including the quality and safety of care provided.

THE CURRENT STATE OF HEALTH CARE

Institute of Medicine and Quality Care

The Institute of Medicine (IOM) is a nonprofit organization that plays a prominent role in advising national leaders about the most salient matters in health care by convening scholars from around the country to provide guidance and innovative solutions to our most pressing health care challenges. One group of scholars, the Committee on Quality of Health Care in America, was assembled by the IOM and in 2000 published *To Err Is Human: Building a Safer Health System.* Findings in this report rocked the very foundation of the largest health care system in the world, sending tremors through the industry: Health care in the United States could not be considered safe, with as many as 98,000 people dying each year due to *preventable* medical errors, and with up to 70% of those attributable to ineffective communication (IOM, 2000).

Since the report was published, numerous health organizations and scholars around the country have grappled with the question of how to make health care safer. One answer to this problem, and an initiative that continues to gain momentum across the country, is the implementation of team-based communication skills training programs such as TeamSTEPPS®, developed through a partnership between the Agency for Healthcare Research and Quality and the United States Department of Defense to provide valuable tools to help interprofessional health care teams function more effectively

(Agency for Healthcare Research and Quality, 2016). Due in large part to its positive impact in the acute care or hospital setting, TeamSTEPPS has been modified for use in additional health care settings such as long-term care, primary care, and the dental setting. Its success is largely due to its focus and relevance: Health care is a team sport, and functioning effectively requires team-based communication skills. In sum, the health care system is taking great strides to reduce avoidable medical errors, thus making health interventions safer.

While it is critical that our health care be safe, safety does not necessarily equate to quality. In 2001, the IOM continued its work to improve health care in America by publishing *Crossing the Quality Chasm: A New Health System for the 21st Century*. In this reimagined conceptualization of health care quality, a new bar was set. For the first time, the IOM asserted that "health care should be safe, effective, patient-centered, timely, efficient, and equitable," which was a departure from previous conceptualizations of health care, which seemed to subordinate the patient in favor of the knowledge of health care providers (IOM, 2001, p. 40). For the first time, the patient was placed at the center of the quality initiative, thus giving birth to our focus on the patient experience.

Since these two publications, the health care system has been in a state of flux. As we move closer to operationalizing guidelines set forth by the IOM and in realizing care that is truly patient-centered, we grapple with how to retool for this new era in health care that requires that we be flexible, nimble, and wholly focused on the patient. While the IOM reports have been instrumental in helping health care systems improve patient care and outcomes, nothing has been quite as influential on the health care system as the Patient Protection and Affordable Care Act (PPACA).

A New Horizon: The PPACA

In March 2010, President Barack Obama signed a bill that would have wide-sweeping implications for the entire industry of health care in the United States: the Health Reform Bill, or Patient Protection and Affordable Care Act (PPACA). While many directives within the PPACA are outside of the scope of this book, there is one specific aim of the act that is clearly relevant, and that is improving health care *quality*. With the passing of the PPACA, an entirely new reimbursement structure was set forth in the industry, making *quality* rather than *quantity* the name of the game. According to the mandates found within the act, one way to improve health care quality is through innovations in the health care workforce.

What does the PPACA have to do with managing the psychological impacts of medical trauma? We believe the guidelines set forth in the act have the potential to set the stage for health care and mental health professionals to work together in new and innovative ways. Under Title V: Health Care Workforce, Subtitle B: Innovations in the Health Care Workforce, the PPACA lists as an "initial high priority" the "integrated health care work force planning that identifies health care professional skills needed and maximizes the skill sets of health care professionals across disciplines" (PPACA, p. 124, STAT. 596. A.1). Perhaps even more compelling is how the PPACA defines "health care workforce" and "health professionals"—while at one time this workforce could have been considered limited to physicians and nurses, the PPACA has been careful to expand this term to include mental health professionals as well (PPACA, p. 124, STAT. 598. 1).

The inclusion of *physical* health and *mental* health professionals in one umbrella term, *health professionals,* could be a jumping off point to realize a care system that is seamlessly and synergistically integrated. It seems that leading administrators, scholars, and practitioners around the country are coming to the same conclusion about health care, and the conclusion is this: In order to provide care of the highest quality, we must bring together professionals from multiple disciplines who can work effectively together to care for the whole person.

HEALTH CARE TRENDS RELEVANT TO MANAGING MEDICAL TRAUMA

We believe that there has never been a better time to broach the topic of medical trauma, given the climate emerging in the health care system today. With growing emphasis on the patient experience, patient-centered integrated care models, and holistic or whole-person care, it seems the industry is poised for exploring novel ideas about how to help people live healthier lives. If we can understand how medical experiences impact the whole person—and if the industry places value on whole-person care—then we are at a good place to consider innovative processes for prevention and intervention of the psychological impacts of medical trauma, and this requires the integration of mental health and physical health.

Integrated Care

Generally, integrated care has come to mean the connection between behavioral health care (mental health and substance abuse treatment) and general health care, specifically in primary care. The general aim of integrated care is to increase the quality of care for patients with both mental health and physical health care needs, recognizing that patients' holistic needs are best met when care providers work together. There have been numerous studies demonstrating the effectiveness of integrated care models, both in terms of quality and in terms of cost. Integrated care models vary as to the level of integration and can range from being loosely connected yet separate systems to being fully integrated systems of care (Doherty, 1995; Doherty, McDaniel, & Baird, 1996). The Substance Abuse and Mental Health Services Administration (SAMHSA) and the Health Resources and Services Administration (HRSA) have partnered to create the Center for Integrated Health Solutions (SAMHSA-HRSA Center for Integrated Health Solutions, 2013), offering training, technical assistance, and grant funding for community behavioral health care centers and community health centers that operate using an integrated care model. Thus, there are significant governmental agencies backing the model of integrated care. Many of the protocols we present in this book draw upon models of integrated care in order to meet the holistic needs of patients who experience medical trauma.

Holistic or "Whole Person" Care

Human beings are highly complex creatures with interconnected systems that work synergistically. By constructing separate systems of care—meaning general health care and mental health care—we have, in effect, deconstructed people in an attempt to simplify and streamline, fitting our patients into our own areas of expertise and systems of care. In a sense, whole-person care is about putting the pieces of the human puzzle back together again. It makes sense to us that the health care system should mirror those it serves. As mental health professionals, we are trained to see our clients as whole people or holistically, being sensitive to the psychological, physical, spiritual, and social dimensions of well-being; we use the term "holistic" to mean "whole." However, we recognize that within the general health care context, *holistic* care can indicate the use of alternative medicine practices such as homeopathy, chiropractic, energy healing, and faith healing, rather than conventional medicine. We want to be clear that in this book, we use the term *holistic* to refer to *whole person* care rather than limited to the use of alternative medicine over conventional medical practices. In managing the psychological impacts of medical trauma, using the holistic lens is critical in understanding and assessing effectively. How do we best intervene to meet the holistic needs of patients who experience medical trauma? We form knowledgeable, skilled, and effective interprofessional teams.

Interprofessional Education and Collaboration

National and even global organizations—the IOM, HRSA, Agency for Healthcare Research and Quality, and the World Health Organization, to name a few—have all recognized that in order to prepare the global health care workforce for the challenges of improving quality and safety in 21st-century health care, we need to revisit how we educate and prepare our workforce. If we expect practitioners to work and collaborate on teams comprised of professionals from diverse fields, it makes sense that we would want to prepare them for this experience. Thus, interprofessional education, or IPE, was born.

The expectation that health care professionals have training in the skills of interprofessional collaboration has found its way into the accreditation standards of all health care professional training programs, which we discuss later in this book. In addition, a national collaborative of six health professional school education associations (American Association of Colleges of Nursing, American Dental Education Association, American Association of Colleges of Pharmacy, Association of Schools and Programs of Public Health, American Association of Colleges of Osteopathic Medicine, and the Association of American Medical Colleges) called the Interprofessional Education Collaborative or IPEC, was formed to help encourage IPE efforts in order to improve team-based care and health outcomes. IPEC also helps support the efforts of educators who are working to design and offer innovative courses and programs to help prepare professions to work on interprofessional teams, and it is important for universities to explore how to bring the students of both general health and mental health training programs together to learn team-based skills.

At a recent IPEC Faculty Development Institute, a national meeting that brings together faculty from health professional programs, I (Michelle) was alarmed to find that of the over 150 participants in the room, I was one of only two mental health professionals—and the other mental health professional was a social worker from my university. While several of the faculty groups were grappling with how to bring together nursing, medical, and occasionally pharmacy students for interprofessional learning, it seemed that what we were attempting to do at my university was unique—designing IPE opportunities for students in eight health professional programs (including three mental health programs). Given what we health professionals are being called to do in this new era of health care, it seems evident that we need everyone at the table—and this includes representatives from the mental health profession. Noticeably absent from the list of IPEC's members are representatives from mental health professional education associations; hopefully this will change in the future.

A WORD ABOUT OUR PERSPECTIVE ...

The ideas promoted in this book are, in effect, ways to improve how we deliver health care to people who experience medical trauma. While it may make sense for mental health professionals, in our case clinical mental health counselors, to address the psychological impacts of medical trauma, it may seem less obvious as to our expertise in advocating for systemic changes in health care given that mental health professionals could be considered relative outsiders in this industry. Furthermore, given that clinical mental health counselors make up the smallest number of mental health professionals working in the health care industry, it might make even less sense that *we* would be writing this book. Some may even wonder, *how can an outsider possibly understand the system of health care or how to improve it?* To this I would say: It is all about perspective—or more specifically, the *outsider's* perspective. Perhaps Leonardo da Vinci said it best:

> Shadow is the obstruction of light. Shadows appear to me to be of supreme importance in perspective, because, without them opaque and solid bodies will be ill defined; that which is contained within their outlines and their boundaries themselves will be ill-understood unless they are shown against a background of a different tone from themselves.

As professional counselors, we bring a specific lens to the topic of managing the psychological impacts of medical trauma within the health care system, seeing patients as:

- Whole people, recognizing psychological, physical, spiritual, and social needs
- Being in context, understanding that we cannot truly understand behavior unless we view it contextually
- Capable of change, learning, growth, and improving well-being
- Possessing strengths, focusing on what is strong in addition to what is wrong
- Partners in a collaborative process, recognizing the value of a patient-centered approach

While the foundational views of our profession certainly influence our approach to the subject matter in this book, our valuable insights gained as patients—especially as patients *who also happen to be mental health professionals who study medical trauma*—play as significant a role in helping us develop unique approaches to managing the psychological impacts of medical trauma. For me (Michelle), this book is more than a professional endeavor; it is a calling. Over 12 years ago, I nearly lost my life to a postpartum hemorrhage following the birth of my only child. Experiencing this level of trauma through the lens of a counselor has yielded a perspective about medical care that I have sought to share with both the medical and mental health communities alike in an endeavor to influence how we care for patients. For Scott, experiences of medical trauma have also shaped his perspectives about health care delivery, and we weave these insights throughout the remaining pages of this book.

Speaking of Perspective—Is It Client or Patient? Behavioral Health or Mental Health?

Recognizing the multidisciplinary audience for this topic, we thought it might be helpful to clarify a few of the terms you will encounter throughout the remaining pages of this book. First, we use the term "patient" rather than "client" to refer to those we serve within the health care and mental health context. Newer terms such as "consumer" have become increasingly popular, but for the sake of clarity and universal understanding by multiple audiences we have chosen to use the traditional term used most widely within health care.

Conversely, we have deliberately chosen to use the title "mental health professional" rather than "behavioral health professional," the latter being more commonly used within health care settings. Why? While we understand the rationale for the term "behavioral health" within health care (e.g., focus on behavior—something that people can change; the newer term could have reduced stigma; it ties in more closely with the medical model in that behavior can be measured, assessed, and shaped to increase health and well-being), we want to emphasize *all* aspects of patients' experiences with medical trauma: mind, body, spirit, relationships, lifestyle, self-concept, and meaning-making. For us, the term "behavioral health professional" does not adequately represent the roles that mental health professionals can play in meeting the needs of patients who experience medical trauma.

From our work with colleagues from the mental health and health care professions we have learned the value of clarifying terminology in an effort to promote good communication. We understand that there may be additional terms we use throughout this book that may be less familiar to or seldom used by you and your profession, and in most cases we make every effort to clarify our meaning. It is a work in progress, this endeavor of interprofessional communication!

What This Book Is, and What It Is Not

Speaking of endeavors of interprofessional communication, we would like to take a moment to clarify what this book is and what it is not. First, this is not a book that details trauma techniques for mental health professionals. There are numerous books and resources written by trauma experts—mental health clinicians and researchers with decades of experience treating trauma—and we have included a resource list in Appendix A. Second, this is not a book that examines treatment protocols for managing the physical crises associated with medical traumas, as we are not medical professionals and have limited knowledge in this area. The true aim of this book is to build a bridge between mental health and health care professionals by exploring the emotional layer of the patient experience and how we can work together to improve the quality of care at every level for every patient. Further, this book also presents ideas on how to construct a safety net to ensure that fewer patients who experience medical trauma "slip through the cracks" of a health care system that can *sometimes* have a singular focus on caring for the physical body at the expense of all else.

One thing that became quite apparent to us during the months of research and preparation leading up to writing this book is that the pediatric health care system is doing a pretty good job of managing medical trauma. In fact, several years ago when we began our research, the only place we saw the term "medical trauma" being used was in literature published by the National Child Traumatic Stress Network on their website (www.nctsn .org). Given the inherent vulnerability in the pediatric population, many children's hospitals and pediatric treatment facilities have protocols in place to help children cope with receiving medical treatment and with the many effects of living with chronic illness. This book focuses primarily on helping adults manage the psychological and emotional effects of medical trauma; while many examples we provide depict life-threatening medical events, we should note that we do not focus on end-of-life care despite the many applications for medical trauma resources within hospice and palliative care models.

Book Overview

Managing the Psychological Impact of Medical Trauma: A Guide for Mental Health and Health Care Professionals serves as a supplemental text for use in mental health and health care professional training programs, and as a guide for currently practicing professional counselors, psychologists, social workers, nurses and nurse practitioners, physicians and physician assistants, nurse midwives, health care administrators, pharmacists, physical therapists, dentists, and any other practitioner who could serve on an interprofessional team within a medical setting.

In Part I, we define medical trauma and explain the unique characteristics, causes, and effects of this experience. In Chapter 1, we explore the concept of medical trauma, providing definitions and illustrations of how medical trauma is a unique form of trauma worthy of our attention. In addition, we introduce the many effects of medical trauma, from clinical diagnoses such as posttraumatic stress disorder (PTSD) and depression, emotional consequences such as grief and anger, and effects on relationships, identity, and lifestyle. While many readers are likely familiar with etiologies, contributing factors, and the myriad physical and psychological manifestations and effects of trauma, we invite you to apply what you already know to the context of the medical setting. In exploring the context of medical trauma, we use a framework called the *ecological perspective* (EP), which can aid in understanding the richly complex and multidimensional context of trauma. Using EP as a framework, we have created a model of medical trauma that incorporates four of the major contributing factors (the patient, diagnosis/procedures, medical staff, and environment) with a continuum of trauma experience.

Chapter 2 introduces the first factor in the model of medical trauma: the patient. From personality factors, styles of coping, and past history to the effects of the current support system and meaning-making, we explore the multidimensional patient and how his or her personal factors contribute to the experience of medical trauma. Additionally, we venture beyond the rarer clinical effects such as medical PTSD to examine the many crises patients can face following a medical trauma, from crises of personal identity, distress in relationships, disruptions in work or leisure, to spiritual and existential crises—patients' lives can dramatically change in the short term, long term, and indefinitely following a medical trauma.

In Chapter 3, we outline the many diagnoses, procedures, and medical experiences that can have dramatic impacts in patients' lives, including the IOM's top 15 priority conditions (IOM, 2001). In the model of medical trauma, we present these medical experiences in three levels: Level 1 Medical Trauma, or planned/routine medical interventions such as elective surgeries and in-office visits and procedures; Level 2 Medical Trauma, or life-threatening/-altering diagnoses and treatments; and Level 3 Medical Trauma, or unexpected, life-threatening medical events. We begin with Level 1 Medical Trauma by exploring planned or routine medical interventions that can, despite being anticipated, have psychological impacts on patients, especially when patients have preexisting mental health issues or a history of previous medical trauma. Level 1 Medical Traumas can include outpatient surgeries, office interventions (e.g., OB/GYN procedures), and other experiences in primary care. Level 2 Medical Traumas involve life-threatening or life-altering diagnoses such as cancer, cardiac disorders, pulmonary diseases, diabetes, and autoimmune disorders. In Level 3 Medical Traumas, we explore acute medical experiences that are often unexpected and in many cases life-threatening, such as obstetrical traumas, cardiac emergencies, and traumatic injuries from accidents.

Chapter 4 explores another important factor in understanding medical trauma: medical staff. An integral component of the overall treatment process, medical staff play a crucial role in the overall well-being of patients at all stages of the treatment process. We pay specific attention to the role of communication in the provider–patient relationship, as well as provider characteristics that can affect a medical trauma, such as staff members' styles of coping, personality factors, emotional intelligence, competence for and willingness to assess the psychological impacts of medical events, and competencies for team-based work.

In Chapter 5, we introduce the final factor in the model of medical trauma, which is the treatment environment. The environment can play a major role in how patients experience medical events, and provides more than merely a stage on which a medical trauma occurs. From elements of the physical environment (such as comfort, lighting, privacy, and noise) to characteristics of the organization (such as policies, procedures, and patient-centeredness), the medical environment is a critical component of the patient experience, *especially* when patients experience trauma in the medical setting.

Chapter 6 provides an opportunity to view three case studies that will illustrate three levels of medical trauma. The case of Keith highlights a Level 1 Medical Trauma, which is a planned lower back surgery. In the second case we meet Sharon, a woman undergoing treatment for breast cancer, or a Level 2 Medical Trauma. Last we present a Level 3 Medical Trauma in the case of Ann, a young woman who experienced a postpartum hemorrhage and hysterectomy at age 29. While all of these cases are constructed, they are aggregated details from our personal and clinical experiences of medical trauma.

In Part II, we present new models, protocols, and best practices for meeting the mental health needs of adult patients who experience medical trauma, and we explore prevention and intervention strategies that can be employed across the continuum of care. We highlight examples of health care systems and organizations that have successfully applied innovative ideas for treating the whole person as well as share ideas not yet tested but, we believe, worth pursuing. We have organized this section based on three levels of patient care: primary care (Level 1 Medical Trauma), specialist care (Level 2 Medical Trauma), and acute care (Level 3 Medical Trauma). While Part I focused on each individual piece of the medical trauma puzzle, Part II explores how the factors fit together and, more important, how professionals can improve integrated patient care across the treatment continuum. We revisit the three cases previously presented and explore how each scenario could have been different had some of the proposed protocols been followed. Part II closes with a discussion of the implications for the future of health care and a presentation of ideas for innovation and continued improvement of the patient experience.

We begin our examination of prevention and intervention strategies in Chapter 7 by focusing on the primary care setting and the most important factor in the model of medical trauma: the patient. We explore protective factors that contribute to strength, resilience, and healing—and the critical role of health care providers in assisting patients in self-efficacy and in mapping a future that promotes holistic well-being. A focal point of Chapter 7 is an exploration of integrated care models and how mental health professionals fit into the larger picture of primary care.

In Chapter 8, we revisit the common diagnoses and procedures we first presented in Chapter 3 and explore best practice models for meeting holistic patient needs that may be unique to each medical condition or experience. In addition to highlighting current practices, we explore new protocols for assimilating mental health professionals into existing models of care in order to promote prevention and intervention that meet patients' mental and emotional needs more effectively. Further, we illustrate best practices by highlighting organizations such as the Cleveland Clinic, Joslin Diabetes Center, and the Cancer Support Community.

Chapter 9 addresses the acute care setting and how medical staff can continue to evolve to meet the multidimensional needs of patients who experience medical trauma. We discuss the characteristics of highly effective interprofessional teams and how critical it is that teams receive formal training in communication skills, such as those presented in TeamSTEPPS. In addition, we explore the unique roles of mental health professionals on interprofessional teams, as well as how health care professionals can best leverage the help and support of such professionals. Further, we discuss the value of screening for specific psychological impacts of medical trauma and provide references for the many valuable assessment tools currently available, as well as original resources to help health care and mental health professionals identify such impacts. We also revisit the environmental factors most salient to the experience of medical trauma and address how we can actively intervene to promote comfort and healing in treatment environments within acute care. We introduce a global assessment tool, the Experience of Medical Trauma Scale, that can provide clinicians and staff with feedback about how the treatment environment influences the overall experience of patients who have suffered a medical trauma.

In Chapter 10, we travel to the edge of a new horizon in health care and consider the implications of continued innovation, especially as it relates to treating medical trauma. How can we use technology to further our efforts to prevent and manage medical trauma? How can IPE better prepare us for managing medical trauma and improving the overall patient experience? How can we use mindfulness-based interventions to prevent and heal from medical trauma? These are but a few of the questions we ponder as our discussion of medical trauma draws to a close.

REFERENCES

Agency for Healthcare Research and Quality. (2016). *TeamSTEPPS®: Strategies and tools to enhance performance and patient safety.* Retrieved from http://www.ahrq.gov/professionals/education/curriculum-tools/teamstepps/index.html

American Cancer Society. (2014). *Cancer facts & figures 2014.* Retrieved from http://www.cancer.org/acs/groups/content/@research/documents/webcontent/acspc-042151.pdf

American Diabetes Association. (2016). *Statistics about diabetes.* Retrieved from http://www.diabetes.org/diabetes-basics/statistics

Centers for Disease Control and Prevention. (2015a). *Heart disease.* Retrieved from http://www.cdc.gov/heartdisease/facts.htm

Centers for Disease Control and Prevention. (2015b). *Severe maternal morbidity in the United States*. Retrieved from http://www.cdc.gov/reproductivehealth/maternalinfanthealth/severematernalmorbidity.html

Centers for Disease Control and Prevention. (2016a). *Emergency department visits*. Retrieved from http://www.cdc.gov/nchs/fastats/emergency-department.htm

Centers for Disease Control and Prevention. (2016b). *Stroke*. Retrieved from http://www.cdc.gov/stroke

Doherty, W. (1995). The why's and levels of collaborative family health care. *Family Systems Medicine, 13*(3–4), 275–281. doi:10.1037/h0089174

Doherty, W., McDaniel, S. H., & Baird, M. A. (1996). Five levels of primary care/behavioral healthcare collaboration. *Behavioral Healthcare Tomorrow*, 25–28.

Institute of Medicine. (2000). *To err is human: Building a safer health system*. Washington, DC: National Academy Press.

Institute of Medicine. (2001). *Crossing the quality chasm: A new health system for the 21st century*. Washington, DC: National Academy Press.

Patient Protection and Affordable Care Act, 42 U.S.C. § 18001 (2010).

SAMHSA-HRSA Center for Integrated Health Solutions. (2013). *A standard framework for levels of integrated healthcare*. Retrieved from http://www.integration.samhsa.gov/integrated-care-models/A_Standard_Framework_for_Levels_of_Integrated_Healthcare.pdf

UNDERSTANDING MEDICAL TRAUMA

WHAT IS MEDICAL TRAUMA?

IN THIS CHAPTER, YOU WILL LEARN:

- *A definition of medical trauma, including its most prominent characteristics: medical trauma is subjective, biopsychosocialspiritual, on a continuum, contextual, and relational*

- *The basic psychophysiological effects of trauma*

- *How the ecological perspective of understanding human behavior can be applied to an understanding of medical trauma*

- *A model for understanding levels of medical trauma across three levels of care*

- *The psychological effects of medical trauma, including clinical disorders and secondary crises affecting all areas of life*

MEDICAL TRAUMA: A COMPLEX PHENOMENON

Health care and mental health professionals alike are quite familiar with the concept of trauma, having likely read about the topic, watched TV shows and movies depicting traumatic events, and consumed countless news stories about trauma experiences. If you have experienced trauma personally or vicariously, you have a visceral understanding of what trauma means, how trauma feels, and how trauma can have a lifelong effect after the ending of a distinct event. It seems the topic of trauma is omnipresent in the media, especially given horrific human experiences of war, terrorism, mass shootings, natural disasters, disease epidemics, and domestic violence. Contemporary life has certainly challenged us to find the most effective means of helping those who have experienced trauma; in fact, in recent decades numerous new therapies have emerged as having a unique efficacy in treating the effects of trauma; the most promising of such therapies address trauma using techniques that integrate the mind *and* the body, recognizing that trauma is a psychophysiological experience rather than a singular event happening to the mind *or* the body. It seems that finally we are abandoning the Cartesian perspective of mind–body dualism, due in large part to our growing understanding of neuroscience.

While there is currently a plethora of books, articles, and websites dedicated to exploring the effects of and treatments for trauma, it can be helpful to revisit simple definitions in order to get at the heart of the matter, as they say. According to Merriam-Webster's online dictionary, the term *trauma* was first used in the late 1600s and comes from the Greek word *traûma*, which means *wound*.

The dictionary defines *trauma* as

- A very difficult or unpleasant experience that causes someone to have mental or emotional problems usually for a long time
- A serious injury to a person's body
- An emotional upset

These characteristics of trauma may seem general, and in fact, they are. Who is to say what constitutes a difficult or unpleasant experience? What is meant by emotional problems? How serious does a *serious* injury have to be in order to be labeled a trauma? Definitions of *trauma* and *traumatic event* become more specific as we move into the realm of mental health. Consider these definitions:

The American Psychological Association defines *trauma* as

- An emotional response to a terrible event like an accident, rape, or natural disaster

The American Psychiatric Association (2013), in the *Diagnostic and Statistical Manual of Mental Disorders, Fifth Edition* (*DSM-5*), describes a *traumatic event* as one in which someone is

- Exposed to actual or threatened death, serious injury, or sexual violation
- "Exposure" means directly experiencing the traumatic event, witnessing the event, learning of a trauma happening to a close family member or friend, or being repeatedly exposed to aversive details about a traumatic event

The *DSM-5* definition of traumatic events forms the basis for the diagnostic criteria for posttraumatic stress disorder (PTSD), so it makes sense that these definitions are narrower with greater objectivity than the aforementioned dictionary definitions; however, it would be a mistake to limit our understanding of trauma to an objective set of criteria or list of checkboxes, for at the center of every traumatic experience is a person who derives meaning from that experience, and it is that meaning-making that becomes a key to appreciating the complexity of medical trauma.

Toward a Working Definition of Medical Trauma

When we first began researching patient experiences with medical trauma several years ago, we were struck by how little we saw the term "medical trauma" in the research and throughout the Internet. Most of the literature on trauma related to the medical setting has centered on "trauma medicine" and included topics such as specific clinical procedures and best practices for working with patients who have experienced various traumas *outside* of the medical setting (i.e., serious accidents). From countless conversations about medical trauma with health care professionals, we have realized that the idea that a patient could experience psychological trauma resulting from contact with the medical setting—the very place where people come to be healed—was intriguing to them at best and incredulous to them at worst, especially regarding trauma for adult patients. Despite the numerous research studies that focus on the effects of specific medical traumas (e.g., cardiac arrest) and that use the term "medical trauma," we have not seen a useful or descriptive definition of the phenomenon; therefore, given the absence of a general working definition of *psychological* medical trauma, we felt it important to draft one. Note that this definition and the model of medical trauma we discuss in this book refer to the emotional and subjective experience of trauma rather than the complex physiological responses to trauma. For a detailed review of how trauma affects multiple systems within the body, see Desborough (2000).

Definition of Medical Trauma

Medical trauma is a trauma that occurs from direct contact with the medical setting, and develops through a complex interaction between the patient, medical staff, medical environment, and the diagnostic and/or procedural experience that can have powerful psychological impacts due to the patient's unique interpretation of the event.

Let us break down this definition into its distinct components. First, in using the term **direct contact**, we attempt to initially define medical trauma for the *patient* (the phenomenon of vicarious medical trauma, in which family, friends, and medical staff can have a traumatic stress response to a patient's experience, is another important dimension worthy of attention but not a focus of this book). Second, medical trauma occurs through contact with the

medical setting. The term "medical setting" can refer to any aspect of direct experience with the health care system, from spending time in the hospital for treatment of an illness, injury, or procedure; visiting an ambulatory surgery center for an outpatient procedure; visiting an outpatient physician's office for ongoing treatment of a chronic or life-threatening illness, such as an autoimmune disease or cancer; visiting the dentist's office for the first time in 15 years; or getting an annual pelvic exam at an OB-GYN's office. These are but a few examples of the many health care experiences patients face on a daily basis at acute care (hospital) facilities, ambulatory surgery centers, testing centers, and outpatient medical and dental offices. Third, medical trauma develops through a **complex interaction** of multiple factors, including the patient, medical setting (including interactions with the staff and the environment), and the diagnosis or procedure. It is important to note that, while medical trauma is a subjective experience, the subject (patient) is not the only factor in the equation. In other words, a patient does not experience medical trauma simply because he or she has a predisposition for experiencing a medical event as traumatic: There are many characteristics of the medical environment, staff, and diagnoses/procedures that can influence a patient's response. Fourth, medical trauma can have powerful **psychological impacts**, from the development of clinical and subclinical mental health issues to affecting the health of relationships, sense of self, the body, work, leisure, and spiritual life. Lastly, the **patient's unique interpretation** of the medical trauma is a key to understanding the overall impacts of the experience. Meaning-making is at the heart of the medical trauma experience.

You might still be wondering how or even if medical trauma might differ from other forms of trauma, especially if we remove the context of the medical environment. Is the experience and maintenance of medical trauma symptoms any different from the traumatic stress response and ensuing psychological sequelae from other kinds of traumatic experiences? Donald Edmondson's (2014) work examining life-threatening medical events and PTSD has yielded the Enduring Somatic Threat model, a theory which differentiates medical trauma from nonmedical trauma in several compelling ways. First, Edmondson argues that nonmedical traumas and PTSD are in response to a discrete event in one's past, while medical trauma reactions endure because the threat (of disease, pain, and even death) is located in one's own body. Second, for many who experience a life-threatening medical event, ongoing medical care and monitoring are required in order to avoid subsequent events (e.g., heart attack and stroke). While many psychophysiological triggers of trauma could potentially be avoided in cases of nonmedical trauma, patients who experience life-threatening medical events can be retraumatized with ongoing medical care that can contribute to symptoms of hyperarousal, reexperiencing, and avoidance. Edmondson (2014) exemplifies this point when describing a patient's experience of cancer, suggesting that the trauma arises not because of a singular event, but rather from the emotional experience and vulnerability inherent in having this life-threatening disease. Third, Edmondson argues that a real and present danger associated with medical trauma is the influence of the traumatic stress response on subsequent health behaviors and overall health, as the perception of an ongoing threat can impact blood pressure, heart rate, sleep, and inflammation—all of which are risk factors for subsequent life-threatening medical events.

We revisit the concept of enduring threat and how it can maintain medical trauma symptoms in Chapter 3, but now we continue to build on our definition by addressing some of the characteristics of medical trauma that may exemplify its uniqueness as well as help us understand why it has in some ways been "off the radar" in terms of broader conversations about whole-person care. In order to deepen our understanding of medical trauma, we expand our definition to highlight that medical trauma is subjective for the patient; best understood as being on a continuum; biopsychosocial-spiritual in both the experience and in the effects; contextual; and relational.

Medical Trauma Is Subjective

While many trauma researchers study reactions from events universally thought of as traumatic, such as the effects of war, violence, or natural disasters, some contemporary scholars have turned their attention to trauma experienced in everyday life and the importance of subjectivity in the interpretation of the experience. Scaer (2005) and Levine (2010) both speak of their own traumas and how these experiences shape their perspectives and understanding of trauma as subjective. In *The Trauma Spectrum*, Scaer points to his experiences of medical trauma as a child as being particularly poignant, and argues that trauma exists on "a continuum of variably negative life events occurring over the life span, including events that may be accepted as 'normal' in the context of our daily experience because they are endorsed or perpetuated by our own cultural institutions" (p. 2). He continues by asserting that whether or to what degree these negative life events are perceived as traumatic depends upon how they are interpreted by the victim—in other words, if a person experiences an event as traumatic—*it is trauma*. These points strike at the heart of our understanding of medical trauma, for the subjectivity of this type of trauma is one of its most important characteristics.

In other words, medical trauma is not black or white, nor is it easily detected if we are not partnering with patients in order to understand their experiences. Because the interpretation of medical experiences as traumatic is not something we as clinicians can objectively ascertain without talking with the patient (i.e., we cannot objectively label a patient's experience as traumatic or not traumatic simply because they received X diagnosis or Y procedure), we should be careful to avoid attempts to characterize the effects of a medical experience without first understanding the patient's point of view.

Medical Trauma Exists on a Continuum

From the standpoint of assessment, we should approach medical trauma as if it could occur for patients at any point in the care delivery process. While we certainly cannot account for every patient's moment-by-moment emotional response to medical experiences, we can target specific kinds of medical experiences that are more likely to have psychological effects and intervene appropriately. In terms of building a model of medical trauma, we organize these specific kinds of medical experiences in three levels, moving along a continuum from greater to lesser threat to life: Level 3, or medical emergencies; Level 2, or life-threatening/life-altering diagnoses; and Level 1, or planned/ routine medical care. Although we discuss medical trauma in terms of these three levels or categories, we see these categories as being fluid and easily traversed. For example, a patient who has a heart attack (Level 3) and who has a traumatic stress response and ensuing, ongoing psychological effects could continue to struggle through his or her follow-up care (Level 2) to the point that every contact with the medical setting—even a trip to see a family physician for a sinus infection—could ignite acute reexperiencing and hyperarousal of the trauma (Level 1). We examine this model in more detail later in this chapter.

Medical Trauma Is Biopsychosocialspiritual

Through the work of trauma researchers and our increasing understanding of neuroscience and the brain, our body of knowledge about the complex effects of trauma is growing at a remarkable pace. From leading researchers on trauma, we understand what happens in the body and mind when the sympathetic nervous system, or more specifically the hypothalamic–pituitary–adrenal axis (HPA), is activated in response to stress and attempts to regulate the body, as well as what can happen if this activation becomes a patterned response to stressful stimuli. Further, we know the damaging effects of the traumatic stress response and excessive amounts of adrenaline and cortisol flowing through the body, especially in those individuals who develop PTSD.

Like other forms of trauma involving a direct connection to the body, medical trauma happens at multiple levels:

1. The body's integrity is compromised through illness or injury, and treatment is required to restore health or manage acuity.

2. A patient interprets this medical treatment, his or her suffering, and contact with the medical setting in a way that is unique to him or her

(in other words, the patient has a psychophysiological response to treatment).

3. A patient experiences a medical trauma socially, through ongoing interactions with medical staff and family.

4. A patient experiences the trauma spiritually, especially when facing his or her own mortality.

By viewing medical trauma holistically, we can improve our ability to assess how patients are experiencing their compromised health in the context of the medical setting. Given our earlier discussion of the subjectivity of medical trauma, we know that not everyone is going to experience a physical diagnosis or procedure as traumatic; in fact, the majority of people may not. For those who do, it is important to remember that the traumatic stress response can happen not only because of the patient's unique psychophysiological response, but also due to the qualities of the health care environment—or its context.

Medical Trauma Is Contextual

Studies of the effects of medical trauma often focus on specific factors of the patient: Preexisting mental health problems, past history of trauma, and personality factors are but a few topics addressed in the literature about medical trauma. It is important to remember that medical trauma, while subjective, does not happen in a vacuum. A medical experience is not traumatic simply because a patient has a vulnerability or predisposition to being traumatized; in other words, having been traumatized by a medical event does not denote weakness on the part of the patient. There are a number of other factors that can influence a patient's experience of a medical event as traumatic, one being the context of the medical environment. Qualities of the setting, such as lighting, unfamiliar or frightening objects, sounds, and scents, as well as uncomfortable furniture are but a few examples of how environmental factors can influence a patient's psychological response. Further, protocols within the medical environment that can increase a patient's feeling vulnerable—such as waiting for a procedure alone in a hospital gown without one's clothing—can heighten stress and leave someone susceptible to intense emotional reactions. How medical staff members communicate with patients and their overall sensitivity to the unique situation of the patient constitute other important factors in a patient's overall experience of a procedure or ongoing care with a chronic diagnosis. In sum, the environment and staff create a context for each episode of care that can either subtly or greatly impact patients' experiences.

Throughout this book, we explore the many factors that make up the context of medical trauma, and how characteristics within the medical setting can contribute to the experience of medical trauma. Beyond the medical environment, another contextual factor that is highly influential in a patient's experience is the context of the relationship between patients and providers.

Medical Trauma Is Relational

While some traumas occur outside of human relationships (for instance, a man sustaining injuries from a car accident caused by black ice or a woman who sustains serious injuries by slipping on rubble while hiking, causing her to fall several feet), medical trauma is often a relational trauma in that it occurs within the context of the patient–provider relationship. This is an important distinction and one that adds to the complexity of trauma experienced in the medical setting. The quality of the patient–provider relationship is foundational to the patient experience and rests upon the ability of a provider to build rapport, inspire and earn trust, and communicate care and respect. When a medical trauma occurs, the patient–provider relationship can become fractured; if a medical trauma remains undetected and goes unaddressed, the patient–provider relationship can suffer as a result.

The patient–provider relationship is a unique one. While much attention is paid to achieving a patient-centered health care experience, there is some debate about what that means and how to achieve it. Although we have made strides to move away from paternalistic care in favor of collaboration, regardless of our efforts a power differential always exists in a helping relationship. Despite the empowerment that can come from knowledge gained in this age of online information gathering, the fact remains that a patient submits himself or herself to the skill and expertise of a provider, especially in disempowering situations such as surgery or an invasive procedure. The fact also remains that in a helping relationship, there is vulnerability for the person seeking help and great responsibility for the person giving it.

Patient/Healer Relationship

Socialization

At a young age, we become socialized to accept medical treatment that will lead to our health and healing. There can be great fear for children who enter the medical setting: strangers asking questions, touching parts of their bodies that may be in pain, giving injections. Even for healthy children, these procedures can bring intense anticipatory anxiety. For example, my 11-year-old daughter has a great fear of getting tested for strep throat, given her ultrasensitive gag reflex and disdain for feeling overpowered or out of control. A few times when she was younger, she was held down by at least two nurses or medical assistants while a third swabbed the back of her throat, hoping to get a good enough sample for the test. On more than one occasion, my daughter vomited while getting swabbed, which further added to her discomfort, embarrassment, and fear. As a parent, it was difficult to watch and certainly triggered an inner conflict with the deeply held belief that I protect my child and never let anyone cause her harm. I remember the first time she struggled with the strep test. She was four, and as she was being held down to get the swab, she looked at me with panic and confusion. On the way home, she asked me repeatedly, "Mommy, why did you let them do that to me?" I tried (in vain) to explain to her that it was for her own good, and that we needed to know if she was sick so that we could get medicine to make her well again. Each time she has received a strep test, she has had strep throat—which has helped me reinforce to her how important medical testing can be, and has helped me socialize her into the role of being a patient. Because she is still a child, she has not yet been able to overcome her fear of getting this test, and regardless of my attempts to teach her how to better tolerate the procedure, her psychophysiological response takes over.

For children who have chronic illnesses or serious injuries, anxiety about medical treatment can be quite common given their frequent contact with hospitals and ongoing physical pain and discomfort. Thankfully, there are helpful resources through the National Child Traumatic Stress Network specifically developed to help children and their families manage the psychological impacts of medical trauma. Perhaps we have done a better job managing pediatric medical trauma because we recognize that children lack the ability to fully understand what may be happening to them, and given their vulnerable status they are more susceptible to fear regarding pain, suffering, and uncertainty. Adults have ostensibly had years of socialized acceptance of the inevitable discomfort that can accompany medical care; in effect, many of us give silent, lifelong consent to do what it takes to mend us, heal us, and save us. We submit ourselves to the procedures, the medication, the treatment—while often keeping our fears hidden and thus our psychological reactions to extreme medical events ignored.

Double Bind

In the preceding example of my daughter's first experience with the strep test, she talked about her thoughts, fears, and confusion with me on the car ride home. She needed to try to make sense of an experience that seemed to contradict what she had come to know of me and of our relationship, given my role as her primary protector, caregiver, and trusted parent. That I stood by and watched as people held her down while she was scared and defenseless did not seem to fit the paradigm of how she saw me. It was important that we had a long talk about this, even if she did not completely understand my rationale. Our open dialogue potentially thwarted the development of a *double bind*.

While much has been written about the "double bind" as it relates to the development of schizophrenia, the concept is interesting to explore as it relates to the experience of medical trauma. Gibney (2006) defines the double bind as "a communication matrix, in which messages contradict each other, the contradiction is not able to be communicated on and the unwell person is not able to leave the field of interaction" (p. 50). While the double bind is a rather complex interaction that was originally posited as a factor in the development of psychosis, it provides an intriguing lens through which to view medical trauma and the provider–patient relationship. The original double bind theory focused on parent–child communication, with the victim or receiver of the double bind being the child, and the sender, the parent. For the victim of a double bind, interactions with the sender create confusion and a lose/lose proposition; in many cases, there is no clear opportunity to address this confusion, and even if there were, there would be no validation in the exchange.

In the context of medical trauma—especially in cases in which extreme, painful, and even frightening measures are required to save a patient's life—a patient can experience the health care provider in complicated duality: In this case, the provider is a healer, yet also a perpetrator of a trauma. While we adults intellectually understand that medical staff perform required tasks to save and heal us, the pain inflicted on our bodies and the terror, confusion, and panic we may feel are not lessened because the intentions of doctors and nurses are pure; in fact, it may be precisely because of those pure intentions and our socialization to the medical setting that we often stay silent about this vulnerability and about the intense emotions we may feel. The double-bind concept is most relevant in cases where the threat to life is very real; emotions such as fear, terror, and uncertainty are intense; and patients experience their medical care as resembling torture.

Disenfranchised Trauma

As a result of the silent suffering experienced by some patients, medical trauma can be thought of as a disenfranchised trauma. For our purposes, we are using the term "disenfranchised" to simply mean unacknowledged. You might already be familiar with the term "disenfranchised grief," which is sometimes used to describe grief that a woman may experience after having a miscarriage or an abortion, or the grief following the death of a pet. When grief is disenfranchised, it is not discussed or acknowledged sometimes because the person grieving fears that people may not understand or that they may minimize the pain or suffering he or she is experiencing. For example, a few weeks ago I had dinner with a friend who shared with me the sad news that her cat had died. She told me the story of how she had to make the heart-wrenching decision to end her pet's life and then shared details of the experience. At the end of her story, she said that she had not told many people because she knew that most people "wouldn't understand" (and she knows how much I love my pets, and it probably did not hurt that I am a counselor, so she could at least expect an empathic response). It really struck me in that moment how vulnerable she was in her grief, and how disenfranchised some forms of grief can be. I thought back to the countless times clients would tell me—often with much trepidation—about abortions, miscarriages, divorces, and other experiences that are sometimes invalidated or minimized by others. Just as some grief can be disenfranchised, so too can trauma be invalidated or remain unacknowledged. Medical trauma can be one such trauma.

You might be wondering why we view medical trauma as being disenfranchised. The fact that we are well into the 21st century and, despite the abundance of books written about trauma, this is the first book dedicated solely to the topic of managing the psychological and emotional impacts of this unique trauma, is the first reason. Second, it has only been in the past few years that we have even seen the term "medical trauma" used; just a few years ago when Googling the term, I (Michelle) would consistently see resources related to trauma medicine, not medical trauma. The only exception to this was the National Child Traumatic Stress Network, which uses the term medical trauma, but only as it relates to children and their families. This was curious to me, and it would have given me pause to wonder if adult medical trauma actually existed, except for the fact that I experienced an extreme medical trauma and am still managing its effects over 10 years later. It is through this experience that my intense interest in researching medical trauma has grown, and it is from this experience and through countless conversations with others that I have learned that medical trauma is disenfranchised.

How does medical trauma go unacknowledged? There are many factors that can contribute to this, with patients, families, and providers playing roles in the issue. First, despite some efforts to provide more integrated services at primary care, specialty care, and hospital settings, the focus of care is overwhelmingly on the physical body: We see this in the information given at discharge, which often addresses only the physical implications of an episode of care; we hear it in conversations with providers and family members, who inquire about level of pain and physical discomfort; and we see how patients' emotional discomfort can become eclipsed by physical distress and pain. The result of this lack of acknowledgment of the psychological implications of medical treatment is that it remains off the radars of providers, family, and perhaps most seriously, the patients themselves. Furthermore, because the stigma for seeking mental health treatment is very much a reality in the lives of many patients, psychological distress and emotional consequences of medical trauma can remain unacknowledged, perhaps permanently.

UNDERSTANDING MEDICAL TRAUMA IN CONTEXT: THE ECOLOGICAL PERSPECTIVE

In growing our understanding of medical trauma, it is helpful to understand the complexity of the experience in order to design interventions that will lead to positive patient outcomes. From our earlier exploration of the characteristics of medical trauma, we can see that this trauma is not so simple to understand, in part because it is often not the product of a single factor. While it can be tempting to oversimplify the source of medical trauma as being located entirely within the patient and his or her predispositions, in doing so we are missing a large portion of the medical trauma puzzle. To help train our lens to see the broader landscape of medical trauma factors, we turn to the ecological perspective (EP).

What Is the EP?

When you see the word *ecology*, what comes to mind? For most of you, ecology has to do with the natural world, and more specifically, the *environment*. In basic terms, ecology is the study of relationships between living things and their environments. It seems logical that this would apply just as aptly to people as to animals, plants, and the like, and in the 1930s, psychologists borrowed the tools of ecology and began applying them to human behavior. Lewin (1935) did just that and created a formula, conceptualizing human behavior (B) as an interaction (f) between a person (P) and his or her environment (E), whereby indicating the complexity of interplay between the factors within a person (e.g., thoughts, emotions, traits, values, attitudes, personal history) and his or her context (i.e., the physical environment and sociocultural forces within the environment). The following is Lewin's now well-known formula or heuristic to represent the relationship:

$$B = f(P, E)$$

While the EP is an incredibly detailed and complex theory, we present it briefly here in order to illustrate a simple point: Behavior is contextual, and there are often multiple factors—both from a person and from his or her environment—that influence his or her thoughts, feelings, and actions.

Beyond Lewin's formula, there are other aspects of the EP relevant to our exploration of medical trauma. An example would be the conceptualization that our environment is composed of multiple systems (or contexts) of varying degrees of direct and indirect influence on our everyday lives. Bronfenbrenner (1979) first presented the concept of nested systems or environmental contexts using concentric circles, wherein the innermost circles represent environments more proximal, and therefore influential to an individual (such as school, workplace, or church) and the outermost circle represents more distal influences, such as mass media, the global environment, and other sociocultural forces. In this model, multiple systems make up the entirety of our environment (Figure 1.1).

At the center we see the individual, whose personal characteristics, including personality, physical features and health, development, history, thoughts, feelings, and behaviors interact to create each unique person. Moving beyond the person, we see the most proximate system of influence in his or her life, or the microsystem. The microsystem includes family and friends, place of work, school, the local community, and places of worship—and

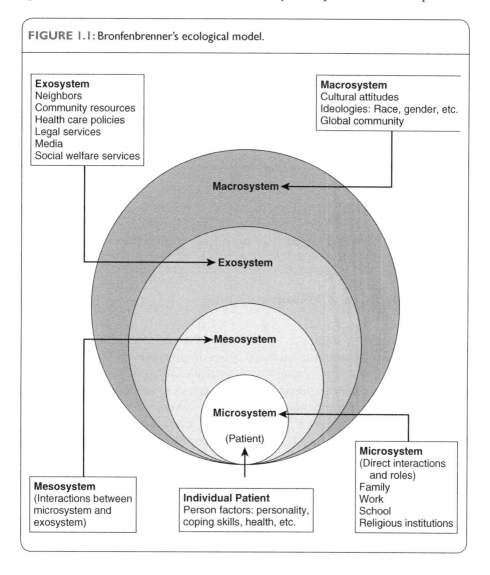

FIGURE 1.1: Bronfenbrenner's ecological model.

Exosystem
Neighbors
Community resources
Health care policies
Legal services
Media
Social welfare services

Macrosystem
Cultural attitudes
Ideologies: Race, gender, etc.
Global community

Macrosystem

Exosystem

Mesosystem

Microsystem

(Patient)

Mesosystem
(Interactions between microsystem and exosystem)

Individual Patient
Person factors: personality, coping skills, health, etc.

Microsystem
(Direct interactions and roles)
Family
Work
School
Religious institutions

represents the context in which individuals play multiple roles and engage in dyadic interactions (e.g., spouse, coworker, parent, and friend). Beyond the microsystem is the mesosystem, which represents the connections between elements in the microsystem. In the context of the medical setting, the mesosystem can be the interactions between family and health care providers. The exosystem represents a larger social system in which the individual does not directly participate but from which an individual can benefit or by which an individual can be affected. For example, the community and its resources, neighbors, local industry, and media are elements in the exosystem. Finally, the macrosystem includes the cultural context that is removed from the individual but still affects him or her, such as cultural attitudes or beliefs. The EP purports that people exist not in a single context but in multiple, nested systems much akin to the Russian stacked dolls where the smallest doll in the very center represents each person within his or her multiple, nested contexts of varying proximity and influence.

The EP provides a nice platform on which to build a model for understanding medical trauma due to the complex interactions between patients, staff, the medical environment, and medical experiences. The salient factors that exist within an individual patient, such as risk and protective factors, tolerance for the medical environment, and issues of identity (Chapter 2), as well as the many environmental forces at play, such as the physical environment of the medical setting (Chapter 3) and the medical staff (Chapter 4), create a complex interaction that influences how patients respond to a medical diagnosis, procedure, or event (Chapter 5). The EP reminds us that behavior is complicated, and that people exist in unique contexts that affect them and that are affected by them.

The Importance of Meaning-Making

In our earlier examination of the characteristics of medical trauma, we asserted that medical trauma is a highly subjective experience; in other words, a person's unique interpretation of his or her medical experience plays a central role in how that person thinks, feels, and acts in response to the physical sensations of an illness or intervention, behavior of staff, and aspects of the treatment environment. In terms of the EP, this subjective interpretation is understood to be a person's *meaning-making*. Each patient experiences the medical environment, diagnoses, procedures, interactions with providers, and adjustment following health care treatment in varied and unique ways, and it is really a person's meaning-making that drives his or her emotions, decisions, ability to cope, and behaviors throughout life.

In order to assess how a medical experience has impacted a patient, we must work to understand its meaning to them and for them. Later in this book, we present tools to help providers ascertain patients' meaning-making, or their unique interpretations of their diagnoses, treatment experience, and implications for their future health and well-being.

MODEL OF MEDICAL TRAUMA

While achieving a deeper understanding of the EP is well beyond the scope of this book, we wanted to give a basic description before presenting a model of medical trauma that we believe emphasizes the most salient contributing factors. With that basic understanding of the ecological framework achieved, we can now discuss a view of medical trauma that underscores the importance of viewing events, experiences, and reactions through a contextual lens. Recognizing that the experience of medical trauma is a complex interplay between the unique characteristics of the patient, the medical environment, medical staff, and the specific diagnosis and procedure(s)—and how the patient interprets the experience (meaning-making)—we can conceptualize it this way:

$$\text{Medical Trauma} = f\left(\frac{\text{Patient} \times \text{Diagnosis}}{\text{Procedures} \times \text{Medical Staff} \times \text{Medical Environment}}\right)$$

Another way in which to conceptualize the four factors of medical trauma is to place each factor in a nested system. Figure 1.2 illustrates the interactions among the four factors by placing the patient at the center, with the medical interventions being a shared experience between patients and staff—all happening within the context of the medical environment.

Four Factors of Medical Trauma

While we recognize the complexity of medical trauma and acknowledge the difficulty in simplifying the interactions among numerous contributing factors, we can at least begin by exploring the major categories within the formula that seem to account for the variables. While we explore each of these factors in detail in the next four chapters (Chapter 2, Patient Factors; Chapter 3, Diagnoses/Procedures; Chapter 4, Medical Staff; and Chapter 5, Medical Environment), we provide a brief introduction to each of the factors in the following.

Medical Trauma Factor: The Patient

We have already discussed the subjective nature of medical trauma, and how little we should assume about the unique experiences and interpretations

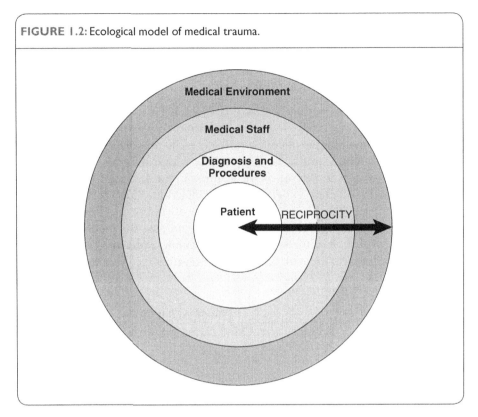

FIGURE 1.2: Ecological model of medical trauma.

of the patient. We learned about the importance of meaning-making within context, but what factors contribute to patients' interpretations of medical events as being traumatic? There are numerous variables we can explore regarding the uniqueness of each patient, but some factors seem to significantly influence a person's reactions to medical diagnoses/procedures, staff, and environment. From personality traits such as the Big Five (i.e., openness, agreeableness, conscientiousness, extraversion, and neuroticism), past history of trauma, and preexisting mental health conditions, patients' predispositions and histories can increase the likelihood of their experiencing a significant medical event as traumatic; conversely, patients bring protective factors to the equation, be it their resilience, hopefulness, strength, and/or optimism.

Medical Trauma Factor: Diagnoses/Procedures

While it is true that a patient could experience any diagnosis, procedure, or medical event as traumatic, some circumstances could be considered more likely to trigger a traumatic stress response. For the purposes of this book, we focus on diagnoses that can have chronic, life-altering effects or that can be life-threatening, as well as emergency procedures and events that can present a threat to life and well-being. Recognizing that some patients can be predisposed to having a traumatic stress response to even routine medical care, we suggest providers view medical trauma as being on a continuum with various levels according to the specific medical experience and the unique interpretation of the patient. Along that continuum we can plot three distinct levels of medical trauma, recognizing the interrelationship between all levels.

Level 1: Planned or Routine Medical Procedures

In a Level 1 Medical Trauma, patients can experience psychological distress as a result of medical procedures or office visits that are planned (e.g., a scheduled outpatient surgery or in-office procedure such as a pelvic exam). While the actual threat to life or well-being may be extremely low to absent in these circumstances, patients can interpret such experiences as threatening or stressful, especially with prior history of traumatic medical experiences. Whether they are triggered by some aspect of the setting, the actual procedure, fear of pain or discomfort, prior history of trauma, or by any number of other risk factors, patients' unique interpretations are important for providers to understand because they can impact overall health in many areas of life. Furthermore, in many cases the real effects of a Level 1 Medical Trauma do not manifest until after patients leave the medical setting, making follow-up care that much more critical. In Chapter 6, we present the case of Keith who experienced a Level 1 Medical Trauma.

Level 2: Life-Threatening/-Altering Diagnoses

Level 2 Medical Traumas, which include life-threatening diseases and/or chronic, life-altering diagnoses, can have a profound effect on patients' lives and psychological well-being. The Agency for Healthcare Quality and Research has labeled 15 of these conditions as a "top priority" because they "affect many people and account for a sizable portion of the national health burden and associated expenditures" (Institute of Medicine [IOM], 2001, p. 10). The 15 top priority conditions that make up Level 2 Medical Traumas are:

Cancer

Diabetes

Emphysema

High cholesterol

HIV/AIDS

Hypertension

Ischemic heart disease

Stroke

Arthritis

Asthma

Gallbladder disease

Stomach ulcers

Back problems

Alzheimer's disease and other dementias

Depression and anxiety

Of these 15 top priority conditions, we would venture to guess that only the last disorders in the list—depression and anxiety—are *consistently* treated using an approach that integrates mental health professionals into the health care treatment team and vice versa. There are great opportunities to improve how we care for the whole person with respect to these chronic and potentially life-threatening diseases, which we explore later in this book. We present an example of a Level 2 Medical Trauma in the case of Sharon in Chapter 6.

Level 3: Medical Emergencies

Level 3 Medical Traumas are perhaps the most obvious medical events that could trigger a traumatic response, given their critical nature. Most objective observers would readily understand how and why a patient may have a traumatic stress response to a medical crisis, especially one that is life-threatening. Events such as heart attacks, strokes, accidents, emergencies requiring surgery, and childbirth traumas (e.g., postpartum hemorrhage), during which a patient is cognizant of the potentiality of his or her death and conscious while experiencing life-saving procedures that may be painful, can be traumatic for patients, their families, and even providers. Regardless of how obvious the traumatic nature of an event may be to patients, families, and providers, this awareness does not always translate to ensuring that patients are assessed for psychological distress and that they receive mental health intervention. We explore a Level 3 Medical Trauma in Chapter 6 through the case of Ann.

While the levels of medical trauma include many kinds of health care experiences, it does not necessarily mean that patients who have these conditions or who experience these events will necessarily have a traumatic stress response or even that they will struggle to adjust following the experience. Figure 1.3 illustrates the continuum of medical trauma, plotting each level of trauma according to the actual threat to life and well-being and the patient's subjective interpretation of the experience. Notice the diagonal line of intervention, which suggests mental health intervention for medical trauma, and prevention and wellness for patients who experience less psychological distress.

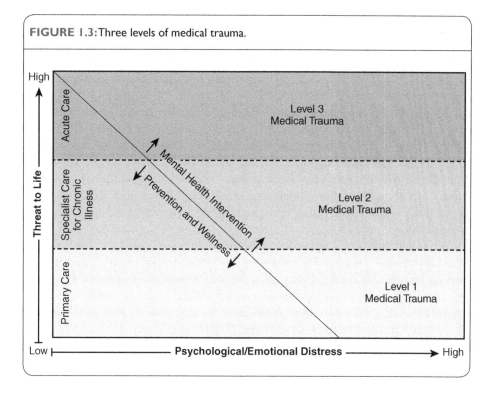

FIGURE 1.3: Three levels of medical trauma.

It should be noted that patients can experience trauma at each point on the care continuum, depending on his or her unique medical history. Consider a patient (John), who suffers his first heart attack (Level 3 Medical Trauma) and who has a traumatic stress response to the event. Following a brief hospital stay, John is discharged from the hospital with the knowledge of his diagnosis: coronary artery disease. As a result of his life-threatening medical diagnosis (Level 2 Medical Trauma), John is now living with the possibility of having additional heart complications and feels a looming threat with regard to his physical health and safety. John will have to continually monitor his health, which will require regular visits to his physician and cardiologist. Given his acute experience and the ongoing challenges of living with a life-threatening disease, even visits to his primary care physician (Level 1 Medical Trauma) trigger an intense psychological response.

Most research on medical trauma has explored the effects of specific medical events and diagnoses on various psychological domains and on the development of PTSD, sometimes isolating certain risk factors and qualities of the patient. Although fewer studies have examined characteristics of medical staff and how providers can influence the psychological state of patients, we feel it is important to examine such characteristics and how they contribute to the patient experience of medical trauma.

Medical Trauma Factor: Medical Staff

There is no doubt that the medical staff plays a central role in the patient experience. From the first contact with a receptionist to the weeks and months of follow-up care and ongoing communication, the rapport and relationships built with patients in many ways create the foundation for eventual patient outcomes; furthermore, the quality of care provided by staff and the level of sensitivity, empathy, and caring present in communication and in the manner in which providers perform procedures can influence how patients interpret and respond to their health care experience. Factors that contribute to health care providers' abilities to provide empathic care include their own communication styles, emotional intelligence and ability to perform tasks while maintaining awareness of patient emotions, and personal stress-management style.

While sensitive and empathic care is important in every health care interaction, also relevant are health care providers' attitudes about and competency with integrating mental health professionals into treatment teams when necessary. This integration requires ongoing training for both health care and mental health professionals to learn how to function on interprofessional teams with mutual respect and synergy. High-functioning interprofessional teams create a safety net for patients who experience medical trauma and can ensure that patients are getting the holistic care they need. Interprofessional teams can also work to manage aspects of the medical environment that can contribute to the experience of the medical setting as traumatic.

Medical Trauma Factor: Medical Environment

Think back to the discussion of the EP, specifically with respect to the concept that we all live, think, feel, and behave within specific contexts. For health care professionals working in the hospital setting, this context is completely normal to them; they have become habituated to this environment. While they were not always habituated to this environment, with time and experience they became increasingly more comfortable operating within it. They grew into their roles as physicians, nurses, medical assistants, and specialists, and they function within this environment in ways that are congruent with their identities as professionals. In other words, when health care professionals enter into health care environments, they are *contextualized*.

Now, think about the experience of the patient. Patients are often not habituated to the health care environments they enter. They enter with their names and health histories and become increasingly *decontextualized* as processes unfold. Patients must adjust to a consistent stream of new faces, communication styles, questions, directives, procedures, equipment, and environments—all while managing the vulnerability that seems built-in to the patient role. For some patients, being decontextualized and disempowered can contribute to their experiencing a medical event as traumatic. While the medical environment is likely not going to be the sole cause of a medical trauma, it can certainly add fuel to an already burning fire.

Up to this point, you have learned about the characteristics unique to medical trauma, the four factors that contribute to an ecological understanding of medical trauma (patient, diagnosis, medical staff, and medical environment), and the three levels of medical trauma. Before exploring each of the four factors in more detail in the next several chapters, we first want to explore how medical trauma impacts the patient, from the emergence of clinical mental health disorders to various secondary life crises.

THE EFFECTS OF MEDICAL TRAUMA

Much of the literature related to the effects of medical trauma focuses on specific medical events or diagnoses and the occurrence of PTSD (e.g., the occurrences of PTSD following cardiac arrest). While PTSD is certainly one possible psychological response to medical trauma, it would be a disservice to patients if we were to limit ourselves to only discussing this severe disorder and other *DSM-5* clinical disorders: Medical trauma can have other wide-ranging and long-lasting effects (we call them secondary crises) that may not meet diagnostic criteria but that may be life-changing nonetheless. That said, following a brief review of some possible clinical reactions to medical trauma, we explore secondary crises that can result from the trauma experience.

Trauma and Clinical Disorders

Anxiety and PTSD

Over the past several decades, scholars have worked to increase our collective understanding of the prevalence of PTSD in response to various medical crises, including obstetrical trauma, cardiac emergencies, stroke, and serious autoimmune disorders such as HIV. In studying these medical traumas and their effects, we have achieved a greater understanding of psychological risk factors and contextual characteristics that contribute to the development of this debilitating emotional disorder. In Chapter 3, we review current research regarding anxiety and PTSD related to the 15 priority conditions. While it seems obvious to focus our efforts on understanding the development of acute stress disorder and PTSD as they relate to medical trauma, it is important to note that patients can experience other clinical disorders, the effects of which can equal PTSD in their intensity, severity, and impact on well-being. One such disorder is depression.

Depression

Like other mental disorders, depression exists on a continuum, or from what would be considered nonclinical, transient depression to grief to clinical depression that can be mild, moderate, or severe. As we have already discussed, the experience of a medical trauma can be a shock to patients' sense of well-being, equilibrium, and mortality. For some patients who receive unanticipated diagnoses such as cancer, heart conditions, or diabetes, it is not uncommon for them to feel sadness and dismay in addition to fear, anxiety, and a myriad of other intense emotions. For some, a life-altering or threatening diagnosis can represent an ending that becomes very painful emotionally; whether it is an end to good health, quality relationships, certain lifestyle activities, or even to life itself, serious diagnoses can trigger grief and depression that is sometimes not immediately recognized by patients and their families. In Chapter 3, we explore depression and grief as they relate to specific physical diagnoses and procedures.

In addition to the many clinical reactions some patients can develop as a result of medical traumas, traumatic medical experiences can also lead to significant impairment in nearly all areas of life, affecting relationships, work, development, sense of self, spirituality, and even identity. The following is a brief discussion of these secondary crises, which we revisit in Part II of this book when discussing how to screen patients for medical trauma.

Consequences of Medical Trauma: Primary and Secondary Crises

In addition to the subclinical and clinical mental and emotional responses to medical trauma, patients can also experience crises as a result of medical conditions and procedures. We organize these crises in two levels: primary crises, which are immediate physical and emotional effects of a medical trauma; and secondary crises (Hall & Hall, 2013), which result from primary crises and develop through patients' meaning-making and unique context. In our personal and professional experience, many primary and secondary crises of medical trauma can often be overlooked—by medical providers, patients, families, and even mental health professionals who will likely recognize the crisis but may or may not make the connection to the patient's medical experience.

The following section introduces these crises and provides brief examples of how they might manifest in different levels of medical trauma. We have conceptualized these primary and secondary crises according to categories of wellness, recognizing that medical traumas can compromise wellness in all areas of life: A life-threatening or chronic diagnosis can have dramatic impacts on our bodies, emotions, spiritual well-being, relationships, development, identity, work, leisure and lifestyle, finances, and sense of self. We explore each of these in this section, as well as in Chapter 6 through case studies. We begin with the physical crisis, which can become the first domino in a cascade of crises in a patient's life following the experience of a medical trauma.

Physical Crisis

Perhaps the most obvious crisis for the patient, the physical crisis refers to the destabilization of physical health and well-being both during and after a medical event, or throughout a patient's experience with a serious diagnosis. This destabilization can include pain, wounds, altered physical abilities, difficult side effects from medication, and other changes in the physical state of the body. Health care providers most readily anticipate the physical crisis of a medical trauma, attending to pain management, medication management, and wound care while regularly monitoring signs of physical health and distress. When patients are discharged from a hospital stay, resources and instructions often focus solely on the ongoing management of the physical crisis; directions for the administration of medication and care of wounds, as well as guidelines for addressing disruptions in the expected healing process are the most commonly covered topics in discharge materials following a medical procedure or hospital stay.

Whenever the body is sick, injured, or procedurally cut/manipulated, a physical trauma occurs. Given the model of medical trauma and understanding of the deeply contextual nature of the experience, each patient's reaction to this destabilization within the body can be as unique as the patient is. For some patients who experience medical trauma, the physical crisis of illness, lingering pain, and/or healing can lead to emotional distress and, subsequently, disruptions in other life domains.

Emotional Crisis

As we learn in greater detail in Chapter 2, the unique characteristics of the individual patient make up a significant factor in the experience of medical trauma as being emotionally distressing. Personal factors such as personality, distress tolerance, coping skills, and optimism can influence how a patient adjusts to temporary or more permanent disruptions in functioning due to medical conditions or procedures. Some patients can develop clinical reactions to a medical trauma (such as anxiety, PTSD, or depression) while others may experience emotional distress that is subclinical yet still significant. It is normal for patients to have emotional reactions to medical experiences: For example, patients may feel scared about the pain of an upcoming procedure, worried about the healing process and how they will cope with physical limitations, or angry about a miscommunication or medical mistake. While these examples certainly do not adequately cover the range of emotional responses patients can have before, during, or after a medical procedure, they remind us of how normal it is to have feelings about the state of our physical health and well-being.

When patients experience emotions that grow in intensity and get caught in a loop to the point of creating a disruption in their normal levels of functioning, we could say that they are experiencing an emotional crisis. Sadness, anger, worry, irritability, fear, and even apathy—when unabated—can lead to secondary crises in the lives of patients. When patients are destabilized and experience emotional dysfunction, one of the first areas of life to be affected is relationships.

Relational Crisis

When we say that no medical trauma exists in a vacuum, we are also implying that no patient exists in isolation of his or her context—which ultimately means the social context of family, friends, coworkers, and neighbors. When operating at peak health and wellness, our patients are fathers, mothers, sisters, brothers, husbands, wives, daughters, sons, aunts, uncles, grandparents, coworkers, and friends; when our patients are sick or injured, they obviously do not shed these roles. Due to the sometimes extreme emotional distress and physical limitations that can accompany a medical trauma, patients can be challenged to function in these roles to the levels in which they—and everyone else—have become accustomed. Given this, relationships can change—and suffer—as a result of a medical trauma.

For example, Lana was diagnosed with uterine cancer at age 28 and had a complete hysterectomy in order to remove several tumors. While she felt her treatment team was very competent and caring, Lana still experienced great emotional distress while in the hospital. After receiving the news that she was now cancer free, Lana found it difficult to relax and engaged in constant worry about her health. In addition, she became more irritable, and little squabbles with her husband Jeff seemed to erupt into arguments that would last for days. Having lost her uterus and ovaries, Lana was now taking hormones to keep her body functioning properly and it seemed she was always struggling to keep her emotions regulated. Jeff struggled to understand Lana and be patient with her fluctuating moods, and Lana began to resent Jeff for not being more understanding of her situation. Because Lana was having difficulty working through her anxiety about having sex after surgery, as well as her chronic struggle to regulate her hormones and mood, her physical relationship with Jeff suffered. With a lack of physical intimacy, little emotional understanding, and difficulty communicating, Lana and Jeff's marriage began to crumble. They divorced within 2 years of Lana's surgery. While Lana's experience provides an example of a relational crisis, given her age at the time of her surgery, a developmental crisis could be on the horizon for Lana as well.

Developmental Crisis

A developmental crisis could be defined as a disruption in what could be considered the normal course of development in the life span of the patient, as defined by his or her social and cultural context. Some medical traumas, especially Levels 2 and 3, can destabilize a patient enough to alter when, how, or whether he or she meets life development milestones. In the aforementioned case of Lana, the experience of cancer (Level 2 trauma) and subsequent hysterectomy altered Lana's plans to someday give birth to children of her own. While she certainly could plan for adoption or use of a surrogate, her dreams for biological motherhood ended abruptly with the surgery to remove her cancer and reproductive organs. At 28, Lana could not help but compare her own circumstances to those of her peers—many of whom were getting married and having babies while Lana battled a life-threatening disease, lost her ability to reproduce, and eventually ended her marriage.

Medical traumas can lead to many developmental disruptions, from delaying reaching specific milestones to requiring temporary or permanent interruptions in school, work, and the regular interactions within a patient's social world. While some patients are resilient to such interferences and life course changes, others experience emotional distress when faced with redefining roles and remapping the direction of their lives.

Identity Crisis

Sometimes accompanying a developmental crisis, a crisis of identity is a dysregulation in how people perceive themselves—their roles, abilities and self-efficacy, life course, goals, and even self-worth. During an identity crisis, we struggle to bridge our past with our potential future, especially when we reject some aspect of our current circumstances. In Lana's case, her identity crisis centered around her struggle to redefine herself as a woman, having lost her ability to reproduce and her role as a wife—both of which, for her, were significant in the forming of her identity. Lana grew up in a family and culture in which the most prized roles for women were those of wife and mother, therefore Lana would understandably experience some struggle around these issues.

Some patients who experience a crisis of identity related to medical trauma can feel confused about how to proceed in their lives. Serious illness and injury can derail our life plans and require that we learn to accept new circumstances despite strong emotions, such as sadness, disappointment, fear, and anger. For those who struggle to find peace and acceptance of the state of their health, a medical trauma can prompt a crisis of faith, a spiritual crisis, or an existential crisis.

Spiritual/Existential Crisis

Anger and confusion can sometimes lead us to question *why*. When faced with the uncertainty and fear that often accompany a medical crisis or trauma, patients will often lean on their faith to give them strength and courage to get through the procedure or course of treatment. Hospitals often employ chaplains and pastoral counselors to support the spiritual health of patients and their families, and these spiritual advisors are often called upon for support during a medical trauma when the outcome is gravely serious, such as the certain death of the patient. For patients who experience medical trauma, survive the ordeal, and have ongoing difficulty accepting new circumstances, they can question their faith, even losing faith in the higher power they previously called upon for protection and comfort.

A patient's interpretation of a medical trauma is often at the core of a spiritual or existential crisis. *What does this experience mean to me? For me? How will I go on, given these new changes I now have to deal with? Why did this have to happen to me?* This last question is a quintessential one, often at the heart of a patient's spiritual struggle with medical trauma. Harold Kushner (1981) grappled with this very question in his classic book, "When Bad Things Happen to Good People," and while this book and others like it are full of insights, it seems that each of us must struggle with this question, whether alone or within our faith communities. Some patients unable to heal emotionally from a medical trauma can continue to struggle spiritually, maintaining anger toward God and an inability to accept this experience as part of their life stories.

Avocational/Leisure Crisis

We use the term "avocational/leisure crisis" to refer to other aspects of a patient's life that might become altered as a result of a medical trauma, from the disruption of normal routines to the inability to participate in loved activities. While at first glance this kind of crisis could seem minor compared to other crises listed earlier, the inability for people to live their lives as they wish can become a central crisis with devastating effects. In many cases, a lifestyle crisis can lead to other, potentially more serious crises because leisure activities (or how we choose to spend our time when we are not working, going to school, or cleaning the house) can protect us from depression and anxiety, and can add a sense of purpose and meaning to our lives.

Consider the case of Jim Miller, a beloved father and husband in the prime of his life who experienced an injury that required that he stop running, an activity he excelled in and cherished for most of his life. As a result of his inability to run, Jim lost his chief coping skill to help him handle stress and ward off depression. Still functioning at work and at home, Jim masked his increasing struggle until the day he decided to end his own life. In an article published by the *Cincinnati Enquirer* about Jim's death, the author says of Jim's injury: "It deprived him of the place he said had made him feel free" (Ramsey, 2014). While this is an extreme example of the effects of medical trauma on lifestyle, it is important that we remember that this example depicts a Level 1 trauma (orthopedic injury)—which can easily remain off the radar of health care and mental health professionals with regard to psychological effects.

Financial Crisis

The financial crisis is another challenge patients can experience as a result of a medical trauma, and it can be both a cause and an effect of other secondary crises. For some, a medical trauma such as cancer, heart attack, or severe birth trauma can have devastating financial consequences that only serve to exacerbate a struggle to heal and can lead to other secondary crises. We hear the term "mounting hospital bills" and understand that for many patients, medical treatment for serious health issues can lead to financial hardship that can feel unsurmountable. For many, financial stress is one of the most significant and damaging forms of stress in their lives, and can have devastating effects on relationships, physical and emotional well-being, and a healthy self-concept. Given that many patients will face work disruptions as they heal from medical trauma, this only serves to exacerbate financial stress, leading to more debt and financial crisis.

Over the years, we have worked with many individuals who developed depression, anxiety, and/or difficulty handling anger as a result of the effects of medical trauma on the ability to engage in loved activities—especially when the activities contribute to wellness. In Chapter 6, we explore three case studies depicting the psychological impacts of medical trauma, from clinical disorders to the complex interactions among secondary crises.

SUMMARY

In this chapter, you have become acquainted with the concept of medical trauma, exploring the many characteristics that make trauma from contact with the medical setting unique. Medical trauma is a subjective, relational, contextual, and psychophysiological trauma that is best understood through the lens of the EP, recognizing that medical trauma develops through a complex relationship between the patient, his or her diagnosis and procedures, medical providers, and the medical environment. Depending on the nature and severity of patients' diagnoses, a medical trauma can be labeled a Level 1 (routine/planned procedures), Level 2 (life-threatening/-altering diagnoses), or Level 3 (emergent medical events) Medical Trauma. Lastly, you have learned that medical traumas can have psychological impacts ranging from the development of clinical disorders, such as PTSD and depression to the experience of secondary crises that affect all areas of life and functioning.

REFERENCES

American Psychiatric Association. (2013). *Diagnostic and statistical manual of mental disorders* (5th ed.). Arlington, VA: American Psychiatric Publishing.

Bronfenbrenner, U. (1979). *The ecology of human development: Experiments by nature and design.* Cambridge, MA: Harvard University Press.

Cook, E. P. (2012). *Understanding people in context: The ecological perspective in counseling.* Alexandria, VA: American Counseling Association.

Desborough, J. P. (2000). The stress response to trauma and surgery. *British Journal of Anaesthesia, 85*(1), 109–117.

Edmondson, D. (2014). An enduring somatic threat model of posttraumatic stress disorder due to acute life-threatening medical events. *Social and Personality Psychology Compass, 8*(3), 118–134.

Gibney, P. (2006). The double bind theory: Still crazy-making after all these years. *Psychotherapy in Australia, 12*(3), 48–55.

Hall, M. F., & Hall, S. E. (2013). When treatment becomes trauma: Defining, preventing, and transforming medical trauma. *VISTAS Online, 73*, 1–15.

Institute of Medicine. (2001). *Crossing the quality chasm: A new health system for the 21st century.* Washington, DC: National Academy Press.

Kushner, H. S. (1981). *When bad things happen to good people.* New York, NY: Schocken Books.

Levine, P. (2010). *In an unspoken voice: How the body releases trauma and restores goodness.* Berkeley, CA: North Atlantic.

Lewin, K. (1935). *A dynamic theory of personality.* New York, NY: McGraw-Hill.

Ramsey, K. (2014). Loving response to beloved coach's life lost to suicide. *Cincinnati Enquirer.* Retrieved from http://www.cincinnati.com/story/opinion/columnists/krista-ramsey/2014/08/14/krista-ramsey-helping-families-deal-suicide/14093989

Scaer, R. (2005). *The trauma spectrum: Hidden wounds and human resiliency.* New York, NY: W. W. Norton.

2 | MEDICAL TRAUMA FACTORS: THE PATIENT

IN THIS CHAPTER, YOU WILL LEARN:

- *The importance of recognizing how patient factors can influence the experience of medical trauma*
- *Specific risk factors relevant to the trauma experience: personality, coping skills, past trauma history, preexisting mental health issues, previous medical experiences, lifestyle factors, life stressors, support system, existential factors, resilience factors, and meaning-making*
- *How the process of decontextualization can contribute to the experience of medical events as traumatic*

As you may recall, in Chapter 1 we presented a model of medical trauma as being the result of several factors that converge to create a unique experience for each patient; those factors represent the significant influences within the medical environment, relationships with medical staff, the actual medical procedures or diagnoses, and, of course, the patient. The most significant factor, the patient and his or her many characteristics, will be the focus of this chapter as we seek to unpack the influential variables in the medical trauma experience.

In Chapter 1 we highlighted the subjectivity of medical trauma, and how meaning-making influences a person's ultimate interpretation of his or her medical experience. In this chapter, we continue our examination of medical trauma using the ecological lens to explore how a patient's unique traits, characteristics, and history contribute to his or her interpretation of a medical experience. We begin this examination by taking a closer look at risk factors.

PATIENT FACTORS: RISK FACTORS

We know that traumatic events can overwhelm a person physically, mentally, and emotionally, leaving him or her feeling like the world has been turned upside down without any direction on how to move forward. This can be frightening, confusing, and frustrating to say the least. We also know, however, that not all events that might objectively be considered traumatic will be experienced as such by everyone (Storr, Ialongo, Anthony, & Breslau, 2007). While there are a number of factors that shape a traumatic experience, we begin with the patient and the factors or predispositions that he or she contributes to the medical trauma equation, because they can be largely influential in how a patient adjusts to a specific procedure or diagnosis. We call these factors or predispositions *risk factors* because their presence can increase the likelihood that patients may experience traumatic stress responses and subsequent clinical disorders and secondary crises. Risk factors can be individual, family related, social, economic, and environmental and are usually in some combination (Hosman, Jane-Llopis, & Saxena, 2005). There are many factors related to the onset of mental disorders, yet each plays a unique role in a person's profile and susceptibility to trauma. The risk factors that we explore include personality, coping skills, past trauma history, preexisting mental health issues, previous medical experiences, lifestyle factors, life stressors, support system, and existential factors.

Although much has been written regarding potential risk factors for posttraumatic stress disorder (PTSD), there still remains no definitive way to determine who will experience trauma and recover with or without PTSD symptoms (Heinrichs, Wagner, Schoch, Soravia, Hellhammer, & Ehlert, 2005; National Institute of Mental Health [NIMH], 2011). As a result, research and speculation continue with the list of potential factors growing. New thoughts have emerged that are channeling research toward biological, existential, and social dynamics, all in an effort to gain better clarity on who is most at risk for PTSD and how to adjust services to minimize a traumatic outcome. One of the most prominent risk factors to emerge in the research is aspects of a person's personality.

Personality Factors

Each of us has a personality that shapes how we participate in the world, relate to others, and think of ourselves. There are many patient factors that can be understood in relation to the ecological model, perhaps the most significant of which is personality traits, which have been defined as "dimensions of human individuality" (p. 207) that are consistent in thought, feeling, and behavior across situations and time (McAdams & Pals, 2006). Basically, we each have temperaments and dispositions that are unique to us and noticed by others, and these temperaments appear to become established in youth (Klimstra, Hale, Raaijmakers, Branje, & Meeus, 2009) and are influenced by neurobiological functioning (Roberts & DelVechio, 2000). For example, a child who is friendly and interested in leading an active life will likely continue to be so throughout his or her life. Likewise, a moody child whose emotional states seem unpredictable and who chooses to devalue new experiences will most likely retain these traits in at least some form. It is important to note, however, that an individual's early temperament does not exist in isolation from his or her environment. Parents or caregivers can either directly or indirectly (through modeling behavior) influence and reinforce a child's early temperament so that personality traits become fairly consistent throughout adulthood (Roberts & DelVechio, 2000). Even then, personality can influence and be influenced by how a person cognitively processes life events and experiences environmental expectations.

For example, 11-year-old Marcus watches his father consistently belittle other drivers with flashes of road rage every morning on the way to school, to the point that Marcus has come to expect and can almost predict when his father will yell. The underlying message to Marcus, unfortunately, is that there is to be no patience with other people. This realization creates anxiety in Marcus because he, too, has experienced his father's judgment and unfair expectations. Herein lies the internal aspect of personality trait influence. Marcus's ability to cognitively process his father's actions, or any life events for that matter, is an emerging pattern that begins to shape coping mechanisms, self-identity, and relationships. The lessons that Marcus has learned from his father find their way into how others know Marcus. At school Marcus presents as a moody child who has trouble making friends and is quick to blame others for his own frustrations and problems. A child will often practice what he or she knows, even to his or her own detriment.

This is an everyday scenario that shows elements of modeling behavior and emotional reactions to life. As Marcus tracks through adolescence and adulthood, he carries forth such events, which add to the consistency of his own temperament. Let us unpack this example by examining temperament through the lens of the Big Five personality traits and how they influence people's experience of medical events.

The Big Five

There are five independent personality traits (termed the Big Five) that influence behavior and are consistent across time, settings, and cultures (Caspi, Roberts, & Shiner, 2005; Kotov, Gamez, Schmidt, & Watson, 2010). These traits are extraversion, openness to experience, neuroticism/negative emotionality, conscientiousness, and agreeableness (Caspi et al., 2005; Soto, John, Gosling, & Potter, 2011). This five-factor personality model stipulates that the traits describe cognitive, emotional, and behavioral differences in people (Weiss et al., 2009) with each trait viewed on a continuum. In an attempt to further understand differences in the human experience, research has emerged that explores personality *styles*, or how an individual is understood from a two-trait interaction (Funder, 2001). For example, how a person who is low on agreeableness and high on extraversion might fare in stressful situations. First we examine each trait independently, and then explore how these traits can influence patients' experiences of medical events.

Extraversion

A person who scores high on the extraversion trait is usually outgoing and social with an assertive energy about them. They look forward to talking with others and connecting through shared activities as opposed to working alone (McCabe & Fleeson, 2012). An extroverted person, for example, might be more inclined to spend an evening with friends instead of staying home to read or engage in other solitary activities. They also like sharing thoughts verbally rather than processing them internally. Because of this outward orientation to the world and others, extroverts tend to be high participants in work groups and meetings. If not leading the group, they will most certainly be asking questions and contributing to conversation. An extroverted patient may be inclined to engage in conversation with medical staff, and will more than likely verbalize many of his or her questions or concerns.

A person who reflects the opposite of this outgoing profile could be considered an introvert. While extroverts derive their energy from human interaction, those who are more introverted may favor alone time to recharge their internal stores of energy. If around groups of people for too long, introverts may feel as if their energy is depleted. Reenergizing for the introvert comes from solitary activities while an extrovert gets a boost from human connection or multiple tasks going at once. Patients who are more introverted may be less likely to engage freely in conversation with staff, may be less likely to verbalize questions or concerns (either because they do not feel comfortable or because they need more time to process their thoughts), and may become more tiresome of ongoing interaction with medical staff during a medical procedure or hospital stay.

Now that you have a basic understanding of extraversion and introversion, consider how this trait contributes to shaping a medical experience.

Patient Profile: Low in Extraversion. Forty-year-old Alexander was fit, friendly, quiet, and seemed to live life in a low-key sort of way. He experienced little stress in his life other than his awareness that midlife was approaching and that he was becoming more of a mentor at work, which required more interaction with his subordinates. Alexander had been a distance runner since junior high school. Running was his way of centering himself and becoming reenergized when life got too busy or meetings became too frequent. At least three times per week Alexander would run at the track in his employer's fitness center.

Given his fitness regimen, coworkers were surprised to hear that Alexander was rushed to the hospital with reported chest pains and the discovery of a heart valve blockage requiring two stents. With little knowledge about his condition, Alexander began gathering information from multiple sources including the Internet and books. Given how overwhelmed and shocked he felt about his recent medical experience, Alexander had difficulty verbalizing his thoughts and feelings about his newly diagnosed heart condition and new-found fears about running. The challenge with Alexander being low on extraversion was his reluctance to reach out and develop a support network during his recovery, as well as his tendency to ruminate with negative thoughts about his mortality.

Openness to Experience

People who are high on the "openness to experience'" trait have a curiosity about life and a willingness to try new things such as different foods, new places to vacation, hobbies, music, or friends. For them, variety is important and so is having an appreciation for creativity, adventure, and emotion. A person high in this trait may look at having security as becoming complacent especially if there is no room for new learning. Not being very open to experience might also show in a person's unwillingness to accept new models of care, or it could contribute to a patient's discomfort in being out of his or her typical environment. This trait could also manifest in response to a medical procedure, a patient's openness to hear about and allow for an intervention, or even in the willingness to participate in healthy post-op care. The idea of change can be frightening to someone not comfortable with uncertainty, which is most assuredly common with serious medical diagnoses. Further, someone who is high on openness to experience could have difficulty with the monotony and boredom that can accompany a lengthy hospital stay, possibly leading to depression or anxiety.

Patient Profile: Low in Openness to Experience.   An example of a person who scores low on openness to experience is Richard. Richard always orders the same thing at the same restaurant and then returns home to watch the same show while reclining in his favorite chair. His morning rituals are the same, eating the same breakfast and engaging in the same order of tasks prior to leaving for work. Routine is part of every facet of Richard's life. No surprises, if he can help it, and certainly not radical explorations into the unknown. Keeping a predictable routine keeps anxiety down for Richard. He likes it that way and through choice avoids the kind of experiences that might challenge how he has come to know himself and the world.

Now imagine if Richard went in for a routine annual checkup that indicated a high cholesterol count and increase in weight gain. Upon further exploration, Richard's doctor learns that Richard does not exercise and maintains a diet of fried eggs with bacon in the morning followed by high-fat snack foods throughout the day. Watching TV is a daily activity for Richard, as he says it relaxes him after a tough day behind the computer screen (sitting all day). Richard also has a family history of poor health and at 45 years old, he has been encouraged by his doctor more than once to change some habits. Lifestyle had to change and Richard knew it, yet at the same time he was good at convincing himself that he would just cut back on some bad habits. Progress with a patient like Richard can be slow. Unfortunately, in Richard's case, it took a mild heart attack before he began to change patterns toward healthy living. Many people are like Richard to varying degrees, which can be a risk factor in their willingness to understand and participate in a good quality of life, especially if that means doing things differently; further, any disruptions in routine for people who are not open to change can exacerbate the stress of medical procedures and ongoing medical treatment for chronic diagnoses.

Conscientiousness

Conscientiousness shows in how organized, self-disciplined, and methodical a person is. Being efficient in planning and reaching goals is also notable while having a careless attitude is not. Furthermore, conscientiousness, or lack thereof, has implications for other quality-of-life issues. Think of the employee who is tasked with meeting deadlines and ensuring that the work they do is without error (e.g., intensive care nurse). This would make for a difficult profession for someone low on conscientiousness. Roberts, Kuncel, Shiner, Caspi, and Goldberg (2007) reviewed 175 studies published between 1980 and 2007 and noted that a low score on conscientiousness was linked to psychopathology and was also the greatest personality predictor for mortality and factors related to poor health. You can imagine then how this attribute can influence one's ability to bounce back from difficult life circumstances or to do what is required to maintain good health.

Patient Profile: Low in Conscientiousness. Jerome, who is low in conscientiousness, believed in the idea of *good* health and decided to talk with his family practitioner about how to improve his cholesterol and blood pressure. His doctor shared that improving his health would require sticking with a structured plan that included a balance of a healthy diet and exercise. Reaching his goals would require that Jerome cut down on junk food, which had become a big part of his diet, and develop a consistent exercise routine, which Jerome had typically struggled to maintain. While this sounded fine to Jerome in theory, his challenge would be to implement it on a daily, weekly, and monthly basis. Some people will stick to such a plan with an unwavering commitment. Jerome, on the other hand, lacked the determination and follow-through to see any consistent improvement. This scenario plays out en masse each year as New Year's resolutions create a spike in gym attendance in January, only to drop off by February or March. To succeed in such plans necessitates a certain level of conscientiousness that many people lack.

Agreeableness

To be agreeable means to be friendly and helpful toward others and can also present as an easygoing and warm disposition. Cooperation versus competition is partly what builds trust with this type of person, along with empathic communication. Furthermore, people high in agreeableness have a level of compassion that matches their even-tempered disposition. People who are low in agreeableness, however, can be suspicious and judgmental while having little interest in helping others. Have you ever been around a person who simply disagrees for the sake of disagreeing? Not a very pleasant experience to say the least. In the health care setting, it can be difficult to create an alliance and positive provider–patient relationship with patients who are low in agreeableness. When you add illness, pain, discomfort, and decontextualization to the experience of someone already low in agreeableness, the result can be poor relationships with staff and poor patient outcomes.

Patient Profile: Low in Agreeableness.   Lora was very adamant that her doctor's suggestion for her to have a colonoscopy was more about the health care system trying to make extra money than about prevention. She also did not agree that simply turning 50 was reason enough for the procedure. Lora relented; however, the night before the colonoscopy she became more agitated. Each sip of the prescribed, bitter colon cleanse was a reminder that she really did object to the whole process and the reason for it. Lora arrived several minutes late to her appointment with no apologies and with an attitude that was less than friendly. She was on autopilot with her opposition and continued to make it difficult for herself and everyone around her. As much as the staff tried to be supportive and caring, Lora would have none of it. She left that day with no change in opinion and a plan to find a different family physician before her next appointment. Being low in agreeableness does not always present as rigid in thought as it did with Lora. It does, however, require a level of patience and "letting down the guard" for progress to be made.

Neuroticism

Neurotic people are often characterized as being sensitive to life in ways that trigger emotional instability, as well as having low impulse control in managing emotions. People who score high on the neuroticism scale can easily "fly off the handle" and become quickly agitated. They also do not typically present a confident and secure image (Hatcher, Whitaker, & Karl, 2009), which in turn can influence rumination in negative ways about an experience, thereby exacerbating trauma symptoms (Broadbridge, 2014). Furthermore, neuroticism was found to be higher in women than men, and girls struggled with anxiety and depression more than boys (Donnellan & Lucas, 2008). This trend could partly be influenced by social expectations, gender stereotypes, and biological influences during early adolescence (e.g., Stice & Bearman, 2001). However, based on a cross-sectional sample of over 1 million children, adolescents, and adults, differences between neuroticism, depression, and anxiety lessened between males and females as they moved into adulthood and middle age (Soto et al., 2011).

Patient Profile: High in Neuroticism. Nicole scores high in neuroticism, yet has worked diligently over the years to learn how to better self-regulate emotions and cultivate a more optimistic outlook on life. She recalled how at a young age she was considered by her parents and teachers to be a "sensitive" child. Teachers would say that any feedback Nicole received seemed to spark an emotional reaction that was a mix of frustration, defensiveness, and blame. Many people would say they "walk on eggshells" when around Nicole. Her neurotic disposition was an unfortunate limitation for her and contributed to her unhealthy lifestyle. Exercise and diet were less than ideal and friendships were difficult to maintain because Nicole was such an emotional drain on anyone willing to spend any time with her. Of course, as others pulled back, Nicole felt more isolated and blamed them for it. It is not difficult to imagine how a person like Nicole might handle difficult medical situations, such as receiving an unwanted diagnosis, dealing with inefficient or ineffective medical treatment, or experiencing a medical trauma.

Now that we have considered each of the Big Five personality traits and how they may manifest in people when they become patients, let us continue the discussion by taking a closer look at how these traits can influence the experience of trauma.

Influence on Trauma

Certain personality dispositions have been identified as having a direct influence on the development of PTSD symptoms following trauma. Seeing life through a negative lens (neuroticism) along with being highly self-critical are orientations that can not only make it difficult to handle trauma, but also can prolong the emotional effects of trauma long after a traumatic event has occurred. Further, people who have a difficult time accepting the reality of their situation (agreeableness) may also find traumatic experiences difficult to overcome. Hatcher et al. (2009) noted this trend with persons experiencing posttraumatic stress following a spinal cord injury, and that being highly self-critical along with negative views of the world further contribute to stress symptoms (Agar, Kennedy, & King, 2006).

Psychological inflexibility (Hayes, Luoma, Bond, Masuda, & Lillis, 2006; Plumb, Orsillo, & Luterek, 2004) is also an influence to psychopathology and is related to one's lack of openness to new experiences. In the case of trauma, an unwillingness to let go of a conceptualized past, a poor self-knowledge mixed with a poor self-concept, and fear about the future can severely hinder healthy progress (Plumb et al., 2004). These characteristics reflect a dysfunctional cognitive pattern that has most likely been integral to the patient's personality prior to the trauma. Also, because trauma has as much to do with emotions as the actual experience and thoughts about it, being able to identify, separate, and manage emotions is critical. Persons who struggle to do this are less likely to accept their trauma and hence have a more difficult time healing from it (Hatcher et al., 2009).

In a study of potential risk factors for PTSD in children and adolescents ages 6 to 18, Trickey, Siddaway, Meiser-Stedman, Serpell, and Field (2012) analyzed 64 studies ($N = 32,238$) and found that variables during and after the traumatic experience seemed to have a greater influence on the development of PTSD symptoms than did pretrauma variables. Subjective experiences of the trauma as being life-threatening along with low social support were major factors. Also significant were comorbid psychological problems, poor family functioning, and social withdrawal. Patients who were quick to blame others, suppress thoughts, and look for distractions did not fare well in preventing PTSD symptoms. These findings lead us to our next variable in understanding patient factors of medical trauma: methods of coping.

Coping Skills

From time to time, we are all challenged with life's demands in ways that might feel like we are just hanging on, barely maintaining a balance to our lives; other times, we are able to handle great difficulty without much distress. How we cope with life is in many ways dictated by our personality, temperament, and the influence of our role models.

Coping styles are the predisposition someone has toward difficult life events. For instance, Garssen (2007) noted that a coping style characterized by a person's attempt to inhibit negative thoughts or feelings about a situation is a way to preserve their positive self-image. This approach has proven effective with cancer patients in dealing with pain and depression (Prasertsri, Holden, Keefe, & Wilkie, 2011) as it reflects an adaptive method for handling the difficulty of a situation. To avoid one's own negative thoughts or emotions is often far easier said than done and requires an opposite yet equal desire to remain optimistic about oneself or a situation. If unable to do this, a person can experience thoughts and feelings that the situation will not improve, which can lead to despair.

Coping strategies are specific ways in which a person attempts to deal with a specific stressor. Common strategies might include cognitive and behavioral methods to reduce or simply tolerate the discomfort (Keefe, Rumble, Scipio, Giordana, & Perri, 2004). Challenging cognitive distortions (e.g., using positive self-statements) can help bypass the thinking traps that catastrophizing or overgeneralizing can create. Likewise, without effective behavioral strategies (e.g., exercise, specific goals, or positive relationships) stress can increase and one's ability to cope can plummet, leaving one with a feeling of being out of control. Feeling out of control can also be influenced by a lack of information about a diagnosis or how life might change as a result; not knowing can create and fuel anxiety. Information, however, serves as an antidote and can clear the way to set goals and then implement appropriate coping strategies.

Perception

Our perception can motivate the way we think, feel, and behave. As such, coping strategies we utilize can be influenced by how we perceive or appraise a situation or experience. Perception is subjective and leads two people who experience the same event to have different interpretations, which in turn lead to different emotional reactions. Psychological coping, which hinges upon perception, is also a key factor in adjusting to the challenges of chronic diseases (Goretti, Portaccio, Zipoli, Razzolini, & Amato, 2009) and can directly impact a patient's quality of life. Furthermore, in a review of research between 2000 and 2009 it was found that a number of psychological risk factors directly contribute to people's reactions to living with chronic pain (mainly musculoskeletal) and the negative impact on work disability (Nicholas, Linton, Watson, & Main, 2011). Also contributing to people's perceptions of illness or injury are stress and distress (along with anxiety and depression), and belief patterns of fear/avoidance and catastrophic thinking. Likewise, poor coping strategies that are passive in nature (e.g., not initiating social support or simply waiting for others to offer assistance) correlated with poor outcomes (Linton, 2000).

Perception and Decontextualization

Of special concern to us as we seek to understand medical trauma is the patient's perception of being decontextualized while in the medical setting. When you think about your niche, or typical environment, you likely think about your home and workplace since you spend most of your time in these locations. You feel comfortable there, and likely feel a sense of power over many aspects of your life within these environments. For those who are not used to being in a medical setting, the experience takes them out of their zone of comfort and can exacerbate discomfort and distress. Patients who perceive that they are powerless in their medical situations, yet who are used to having much control in their lives (e.g., work, relationships, time) may be particularly troubled and find coping difficult. Such people might also base their worth and self-understanding on the *context* of how they are known by others (e.g., the boss or the spouse who always provides); in other words, the roles we play help define us. The environment that supports this identity (e.g., the workplace and home) could be considered a place of safety because there is a certainty and familiarity about them. This, in turn, minimizes the anxiety of the unknown.

Suppose such a person were admitted to the hospital for an emergency procedure that required a short-term stay. The context and environment of this person's world is now different and he or she is not viewed in the same way as at work and home. The factors have now changed. This person is not being asked to fix problems, delegate responsibilities, or to be a provider to others. All control, information, and the task of caring rests with the hospital and staff. Feeling *decontextualized* like this can be disorienting, disempowering, and frustrating—even despite excellent care from medical staff. Being forced to temporarily let go of one's identity in this manner can leave a person vulnerable to stress and to experiencing medical events as traumatic. We will explore these concepts further in the case studies in Chapter 6.

Past Trauma History

Reexperiencing trauma and triggers from a previous traumatic event have more to do with sensory impressions than with discernable thoughts. The five senses are heightened during traumatic events and record the event, along with the sensory response, in the implicit memory system of the brain (Ehlers & Clark, 2000). Our sight, for instance, might notice and record objects that were in the periphery during a traumatic experience. The light of the day might be noticed. Was it early morning light, midday, or dusk? Other light sources, for example, flashlights or even the overhead surgical lights designed to help during an operation, are perceived. Noises, too, are acutely filed in our memory only to serve as triggers for recall at a later time. Seemingly random noises such as rain ticking against the window or the distinct sound of small metal instruments being shuffled on a tray can create a ripple effect of energy through one's body at the precise moment the sounds are perceived and unconsciously connected to a prior traumatic experience. Smells, tastes, and physical sensations are also powerful modalities for recall and can likewise trigger intrusive memories.

Consider the case of Jennifer, who at 15 was out with some friends one Friday night on their way to a party. Jennifer was one of five passengers in a small car that was driven by a classmate who received his driver's license only 2 months prior. The driver and another friend had been drinking before picking up the others. Even with the music blaring, Jennifer could hear the driver mention that he had a little bit too much to drink, but was okay because he had driven this road "a million times" before. The combination of the loud music, talking, and laughing—mixed with alcohol, a fast speed, and inexperience—became the perfect storm. Jennifer could feel her anxiety rising as her control seemed to disappear, and she thought of what her parents would think if they saw her in that moment.

Jennifer did not remember anything after that thought, and remained unconscious until her mother's touch and a beeping monitor awoke her the next day. A friend had died and several others were in the hospital as a result of the accident. As Jennifer lay in the hospital bed, she realized that even though she had been transported to a safe place, she felt no different. The common experience of having no control frightened her and left an indelible imprint in her psyche. It took months of physical therapy and counseling for Jennifer to begin healing from the physical and emotional scars of that night. In this case, the trauma Jennifer experienced may predispose her to experience future life events in which she has little control as being traumatic, making the recovery process even more challenging. Prior traumatic experiences and how they are processed are components of just one risk factor to be considered in our understanding of variables that contribute to medical trauma. On a related note, it is also important to understand how previous medical experiences can color perceptions of medical events.

Previous Medical Experiences

Patients who enter the medical setting are likely not strangers to the environment; they may have experienced any number of interactions with doctors and nurses in practice offices and even hopsitals over the years. Routine office checkups, quick outpatient procedures, or lengthy hospital stays could all be part of a patient's past medical history. Whatever their medical history, chances are that patients have opinions regarding their experiences, as well as judgments about the effectiveness, patient-centeredness, and success of each episode of care. When patients enter the medical setting for each appointment, assessment, and procedure, they bring their own medical histories as well as the histories of those close to them—all contribute to patients' expectations, demeanor, emotional state, and perceptions throughout a medical encounter. When patients have past negative medical experiences, whether due to the care they received, the uncertainty they experienced, or simply because they were in a lot of pain, they can become primed to experience future care as negative, too. This is human nature: For every bad experience we have, it takes five good experiences to override the negativity and trepidation we feel.

Let us look at an example. Ian was a 40-year-old father of two who received an annual dermatology checkup, and during his latest checkup a melanoma was discovered. This prompted Ian to think about his father, who had skin cancer with serious complications. Ian remembered the ongoing doctor visits, long waits, mounting bills, and financial strain that his father endured, and his own annual checkup triggered a cascade of memories about his father's experience. What he observed years ago had now become his reality. Ian knew that he needed to move forward with his own treatment because to do otherwise posed too great a risk. At the same time, he experienced mounting anxiety regarding how much his experience would parallel his father's.

Building on the case of Ian, we know that persons who were previously exposed to life-threatening illness or medical complications themselves were found to be more at risk for future traumatic experiences (Kutz, Shabtai, Solomon, Neumann, & David, 1994) and PTSD symptoms, holding true for patients who had experienced prior difficulties such as strokes (e.g., Merriman, Norman, & Barton, 2007), traumatic childbirth (Bailham & Joseph, 2003), survivors of ICU treatment (Bienvenu & Neufeld, 2011), spinal cord injury (e.g., Hatcher et al., 2009), and heart disease (Spindler & Pedersen, 2005). In these examples, patients appraised those early medical crises as times when they felt helpless and hopeless, in pain, and at risk of losing their own lives. This retrospective appraisal also set a baseline belief about what to make of future related events. Overall, Bienvenu and Neufeld (2011) noted that there is a similarity in risk factors for PTSD in general and medical illness-related PTSD.

Preexisting Mental Health Issues

Anxiety and depression are known to be risk factors for PTSD symptoms, and they can predispose individuals to negative evaluations of life events (e.g., Hapke, Schumann, Rumpf, John, & Meyer, 2006). Persons who have depression will commonly view past situations in ways that cast them as helpless, hopeless, or disappointing—all of which can worsen depression and also lead to anxiety. Further, an anxious person can easily self-generate fear and worry over what is to come, asking "What if?" about how situations might unfold. Their thinking can quickly escalate an upcoming surgical procedure, for instance, into an unmanageable and debilitating experience. Depression and anxiety can also correlate to a person's overall quality of life before and after medical events, and can shape how a person decides to cope during a medical experience. Goretti et al. (2009) found this to be true in a study of 104 patients with multiple sclerosis who indicated the negative impact that depression and anxiety had on their avoidance of others and difficulty practicing positive cognitions and coping strategies.

Higher levels of hostility, lower intelligence levels, and low self-efficacy have also been identified as risk factors for developing PTSD symptoms (Heinrichs et al., 2005). Depression can accompany these factors (Benight & Bandura, 2004) and can sometimes manifest as being on edge, having a short temper, or showing anger. To judge others in a negative way or to blame others for one's misfortune can also fuel anger and potential hostility. Emotional self-regulation is challenging for such individuals and can leave them ill-equipped to cope with health issues in adaptive and neutral ways. Unfortunately, what can result from this lack of self-regulation is a cycle that moves from hardship to blame to anger toward self and others, which reinforces a poor self-concept. This cycle can have detrimental consequences in the medical setting. Take for example the anxious patient who undergoes surgery to repair a torn meniscus. Recovery was not as timely as expected and frustration turned to blame. "It must have been a botched job," this patient claims, which fueled animosity toward the medical staff. Online surveys and blog sites became an outlet to vent frustration. It was easier to blame others than to work on engaging in healthier, more adaptive ways of coping with the ongoing pain and disappointment.

Lifestyle Factors and Stress

There are numerous influences in life that can lead to significant stress: A chaotic home life where kids are yelling, appliances are not working, pets needing more food, and clothes needing cleaning are the kinds of everyday events that show up in the lives of most adults. Add to that a career that does not meet financial or personal needs (e.g., autonomy, recognition), poor relationships with people who matter, little-to-no time for leisure activities, and possibly a lack of health and wellness, and you have a recipe for significant strain on an individual and his or her family. How a person chooses to live and make decisions in life says a lot about the *quantity* and *quality* of life roles that person juggles as well as the overall balance (or imbalance) among them. It is not only the events or lifestyle issues that create stress (such as a poor diet and the biological effects this has on mood and energy level; Schneiderman, Ironson, & Seigel, 2005), but also how a person *perceives* such issues. Each of us therefore has an opportunity to choose how we interpret our experiences. If we are pessimistic, we tend to have a negative view of these stressors and in turn we will expect negative outcomes (Luger, Cotter, & Sherman, 2009). Having a pessimistic outlook has also been linked to negative health outcomes for patients with everything from cardiac issues (Bennett & Elliot, 2005) to osteoarthritis (Luger et al., 2009). Pessimism diminishes the quality of life satisfaction and contributes to poorer psychological health throughout the patient population and even among hospital doctors (Clarke & Singh, 2005).

Some people might pride themselves on having a pessimistic outlook, suggesting that it keeps them from being blind-sided by life. Always waiting for the "other shoe to drop" when things are good can also diminish the full enjoyment of life when it seems to be going right. This anticipation of stress relates to the worry of when the stress will occur, what it will actually be, and how it will be handled. Our quality of life is affected by how we handle stress before, during, and after life transitions; further, there are a number of such transitions or experiences that are considered to be troubling at the very least. The top 10 life event stressors that have the greatest mental and emotional impact for adults are the death of a spouse, divorce, marital separation, imprisonment, death of a close family member, *personal injury or illness*, marriage, dismissal from work, marital reconciliation, and retirement (Rahe & Tolles, 2002). As this list reinforces, having an illness or requiring medical treatment can be highly stressful.

Support System

Having a support system means having connections to others, to resources, and to organizations with whom we can feel safe and vulnerable. This can include our partners, family members, close friends, coworkers, or a trusted counselor. These are people we can turn to and trust in times of need and who provide a sense of security that can be critical in times of illness. They might lend a hand in watching the kids or provide a meal when an illness or medical procedure precludes us from caring for our loved ones. Simple acts of care remind us that we do not have to be alone in life. There is also reassurance in this knowledge as we feel better equipped to handle life's challenges. For some people it may take years to cultivate the kinds of relationships that constitute a support system. For others, it may seem like the system was always in place.

There is an old adage that says "You never know who your true friends are until the going gets tough." Tough times can appear in the form of unexpected tragedy or trauma catching us off-guard and wondering what to do next. Depending on the circumstances, support systems have to decide how they will participate in helping a person move forward. Unfortunately, just because a support system might be available, this does not guarantee that the traumatized person will engage with it. If connecting with others seems intimidating and too vulnerable, then social isolation can occur, which can further compound psychological symptoms of trauma (e.g., Schumm, Briggs-Phillips, & Hobfoll, 2006).

Existential Factors

Having goals in life gives us a sense of meaning and purpose. Achieving those goals takes a level of self-discipline and determination, and often a willingness to connect with others; however, social isolation coupled with unclear direction is often a recipe for depression and low self-esteem, which, as we have discussed, is a precursor to PTSD symptoms following a traumatic experience. Existential risk factors are those areas of our lives that center on having little meaning; feeling isolated from ourselves, others, and the world; not having a sense of freedom; and death or other endings (Yalom, 2008). No one is immune from experiencing existential issues, yet how and when those issues arise and how we handle them is sometimes a mystery. Take the case of Rita. A few months ago, Rita moved out of state because the job she held for 12 years ended abruptly and she needed to find employment fast. Feeling betrayed by her previous employer, Rita accepted a position with a new company out of state. After moving, she felt completely alone in her new surroundings. After all, Rita's friends resided in her home state, and making friends was not something she did easily.

The timing could not have been worse as Rita was in the early stages of battling breast cancer that was diagnosed 3 months earlier. These transitions triggered several existential concerns for Rita. First, she had no control over her job ending or of the diagnosis she had received. Second, leaving her previous company felt like a part of her identity was lost, as working there gave her value and self-confidence. The medical interventions further challenged Rita's self-confidence and identity as a woman. Third, she felt isolated from her friends, isolated from herself ("I just do not know who I am anymore"), and isolated from the world (wondering how she would fit in with the new organization and residence). A deeper existential concern challenged how she made meaning of these changes and how new meaning could be found. After all, Rita's previous company had a philanthropic mission that she believed in, and her lifestyle followed suit. She took pride in the active role she played in that mission through all of her volunteer efforts, and she felt good about the energy she expended to help others. Just 3 months ago, her life seemed to click with a united theme. The new transitions, however, seemed to send everything in a tailspin. Rita's new task was to find meaning along with some degree of control in connecting with others and herself, while managing the changes she experienced.

Making meaning of one's life and relationships has a direct impact on wellness (Seligman, 2012). Unfortunately, Rita's initial beliefs (schema) regarding her job loss and cancer diagnosis were irrational and self-defeating, thus compromising her well-being. Her interpretation of events left her feeling as if others cannot be trusted and that life is unfair no matter how hard she tries—an unfortunate new core belief (thinking like this encourages a pessimistic view of the past and sets up a negative bias toward the future). Rita's way of making meaning of her transition made it difficult for a new beginning to take hold and flourish.

There are three essential tasks that are accomplished through meaning-making (Cook, 2012). One, as humans we are able to *communicate* with others about the world and how we experience it. Likewise we can express how we feel and think, as well as share our needs and desires. Being vulnerable with our private world (support system) helps connect us at a deeper level with those we love and with ourselves. It teaches us to risk knowing who we are and to learn about trust through conversation. Communication, however, is reciprocal: Developing the ability to listen to another's story and to show genuine empathy is just as important as our willingness to share our own story.

The second task is that meaning-making helps us *understand* the world and how we function in it. Meaning comes from learning about things in context. Sometimes another person's understanding or interpretation of an event could be very different from our own. We then have to decide which meaning to endorse or how to reconcile the differences. For instance, suppose a patient experiences recovery from surgery as a painful, long-standing event, prompting him or her to doubt the worth of having the surgery at all. The surgical staff, however, views the outcome as a complete success and that the procedure was necessary for the patient to have a better quality of life. Who is right? It depends on whom you ask. Understanding the meaning someone derives from an event helps us decide how to respond. By listening to the patient's concerns, the medical staff is better able to respond in empathic ways. Further, when a patient experiences an illness or procedure as traumatic, *it is trauma*.

The third task of meaning-making is that it helps us *predict* what might happen in the future. Although we may not be right in our predictions, we can at least feel that some of the mystery of what lies ahead is minimized. Knowing how our experiences will unfold can also help lower anxiety, which often comes from *not* knowing. For example, a patient who has an upcoming surgery to repair a torn ligament is told about the process and how it will affect mobility for the next few months—frustrating news for someone who plays several sports and takes pride in the ability to get around and be independent! Having the information, though, provides this patient with the facts necessary to create meaning and to exercise some control in how he or she chooses to think about, feel, and behave regarding the effects of the surgery. For this patient, life moves along in a modified way with the knowledge that these restrictions are temporary. The real difficulty is when change is permanent and not to our liking.

The meaning patients make of medical trauma can have direct impacts on identity and how they see themselves. Identity that is tied to feeling competent (that they are good at something), worthwhile (that they matter), and accepted (that they belong) promotes a positive self-concept (Hall, 2006). If any of these three components are lost, then one's identity can change. Suppose Amanda went for a regular checkup only to discover that she had a degenerative disc disease that would require a lifestyle change and prescription medicine. Playing field hockey would need to be replaced with an activity less jarring with minimal lateral, twisting moves. Amanda had been playing field hockey since eighth grade and was considered a top player on her college team. Being so talented is how she defined herself and how others knew her. She was competent, important to the team, and belonged. It was her identity. The news was traumatic as it forced her to redefine who she was at her core. Exploring meaning-making would be the task at hand and an important step in moving forward in positive ways.

The identity of *being* a patient can also have implications for meaning-making. Those who over identify as a patient might see themselves as having limited power regarding their treatment and they may be okay about that. They might automatically access the medical system for their well-being and let go of self-responsibility for prevention and personal care. Such persons could often be quick to visit the doctor or hospital emergency department at the slightest sign of pain or illness.

Compare this profile to persons who reject being a patient. They do not like being sick or ill any longer than necessary (most of us do not!), and hospitals and operations are things to avoid if they can help it. These settings are not part of their context and are unfamiliar to them. Because the environment is not of their choice, such patients may feel decontextualized. The medical setting is not the context that brings feelings of competence, being worthwhile, or belonging. Instead, feelings of not being in control arise along with uncertainty and vulnerability, which can contribute to anxiety and a traumatic stress response.

Resilience Factors

We would be remiss if we ended this chapter on patient factors without at least mentioning that patients can bring just as much strength as risk factors to their medical experiences. While we explore resilience factors to trauma, or protective factors, in more depth in Chapter 7, we wanted to at least give a nod to these influences because that can have a powerful effect for patients who experience medical trauma. Protective factors include such qualities and strengths as a positive support network, optimistic attitude, healthy lifestyle with exercise, and quality relationships. Resiliency is reflected in a person's character, personality, and coping ability (Agaibi & Wilson, 2005) in overcoming high levels of stress in traumatic events so that a healthy mental and emotional state is maintained (Bonnano, 2004). Character strengths are also protective factors that can boost resilience and well-being, as well as happiness, mental and physical health, and satisfying relationships (Peterson & Seligman, 2004). There are 24 strengths (categorized under six virtues: wisdom, courage, humanity, justice, temperance, and transcendence) that have been identified as consistent across cultures and gender. As we discussed earlier, risk factors to medical trauma and PTSD symptoms often reflect the very things that influence one's ability and degree of resiliency. The presence of character strengths can act as protection and offset the effects of a traumatic experience.

SUMMARY

Medical trauma is shaped by numerous factors that play a role in a person's experience and recovery. Personality traits of neuroticism, inflexibility, high judgment, and a careless attitude are the very dispositions that can influence a person to have a traumatic stress response. Also relevant are poor coping skills that are fueled by cognitive distortions (e.g., catastrophizing) along with an absence of significant goals coupled with unhealthy behaviors such as poor diet and a limited exercise routine. Life stressors and lifestyles that are difficult to manage also create risk for a traumatic stress response to medical experiences. Furthermore, previous life traumas pose a risk for future trauma, as do previous medical experiences that were perceived as negative or created a level of anxiety or fear resulting in psychological and emotional triggers. If previous or ongoing mental health issues are a factor, risk is compounded. Having, or simply perceiving to have, minimal support systems can leave a person feeling isolated from others, which is also a risk factor for trauma. This and other existential issues of meaninglessness, lack of freedom, and endings can burden a person in ways that challenge his or her sense of self and identity.

Risk factors of the patient typically do not exist in isolation and are known to be multipliers in a person's susceptibility to medical trauma. How these factors are considered by staff and patients alike will be critical in ensuring the trauma from medical experiences remains minimal. The mental and emotional strains of a traumatic event along with resulting symptoms of PTSD need to be considered when we plan for a patient's discharge following difficult medical events and for the ongoing treatment of a chronic disease. Likewise, there are identified patient risk factors that heighten the possibility of a traumatic stress response and should be assessed by appropriate staff, namely mental health professionals, as part of interprofessional teams.

REFERENCES

Agaibi, C., & Wilson, J. (2005). Trauma, PTSD, and resilience: A review of the literature. *Trauma, Violence, & Abuse, 6*(3), 195–216.

Agar, E., Kennedy, P., & King, N. (2006). The role of negative cognitive appraisals in PTSD symptoms following spinal cord injuries. *Behavioural and Cognitive Psychotherapy, 34,* 437–452.

Bailham, D., & Joseph, S. (2003). Posttraumatic stress following childbirth: A review of the emerging literature and directions for research and practice. *Psychology, Health & Medicine, 8*(2), 159–168.

Benight, C., & Bandura, A. (2004). Social cognitive theory of posttraumatic recovery: The role of perceived self-efficacy. *Behaviour Research and Therapy, 42*(10), 1129–1148.

Bennett, K., & Elliott, M. (2005). Depressive symptoms and health among cardiovascular disease patients in cardiac rehabilitation programs. *Journal of Applied Social Psychology, 35*(12), 2620–2642.

Bienvenu, O. J., & Neufeld, K. J. (2011). Posttraumatic stress disorder in medical settings: Focus on the critically ill. *Current Psychiatry Reports, 13*(1), 3–9.

Bonnano, G. A. (2004). Loss, trauma and human resilience. *American Psychologist, 59*(1), 20–28.

Broadbridge, C. (2014). The role of memory, personality, and thought processes in posttraumatic stress disorder. *Dissertation Abstracts International, 74*(12-B[E]), 1–133.

Caspi, A., Roberts, B., & Shiner, R. (2005). Personality development: Stability and change. *Annual Review of Psychology, 56,* 453–484.

Clarke, D., & Singh, R. (2005). The influence of pessimistic explanatory style on the relation between stressful life events and hospital doctor's psychological distress. *Social Behavior and Personality, 33,* 259–272.

Cook, E. P. (2012). *Understanding people in context: The ecological perspective in counseling.* Alexandria, VA: American Counseling Association.

Donnellan, M. B., & Lucas, R. E. (2008). Age differences in the Big Five across the life span: Evidence from two national samples. *Psychology and Aging, 23,* 558–566. doi:10.1037/a0012897

Ehlers, A., & Clark, D. M. (2000). A cognitive model of posttraumatic stress disorder. *Behaviour Research and Therapy, 38,* 319–345.

Funder, D. C. (2001). Personality. *Annual Review of Psychology, 52,* 197–221.

Garssen, B. (2007). Repression: Finding our way in the maze of concepts. *Journal of Behavioral Medicine, 30*(6), 471–481.

Goretti, B., Portaccio, E., Zipoli, V., Razzolini, L., & Amato, M. P. (2009). Coping strategies, psychological variables and their relationship with quality of life in multiple sclerosis. *Neurological Sciences, 31*(2), 227–230. doi:10.1007/s10072-010-0372-8

Hall, S. E. (2006). Developing character identity: A new framework for counseling adults in transition. *ADULTSPAN Journal, 5,* 15–24. doi:10.1002/j.2161-0029.2006.tb00010.x

Hapke, U., Schumann, A., Rumpf, H. J., John, U., & Meyer, C. (2006). Posttraumatic stress disorder: The role of trauma, preexisting psychiatric disorders, and gender. *European Archives of Psychiatry and Clinical Neuroscience, 256,* 299–306.

Hatcher, M., Whitaker, C., & Karl, A. (2009). What predicts posttraumatic stress following spinal cord injury? *British Journal of Health Psychology, 14,* 541–561.

Hayes, S. C., Luoma, J. B., Bond, F. W., Masuda, A., & Lillis, J. (2006). Acceptance and commitment therapy: Model, processes and outcomes. *Behaviour Research and Therapy, 44*, 1–25.

Heinrichs, M., Wagner, D., Schoch, W., Soravia, L. M., Hellhammer, D. H., & Ehlert, U. (2005). Predicting posttraumatic stress symptoms from pretraumatic risk factors: A 2-year prospective follow-up study in firefighters. *American Journal of Psychiatry, 162*, 2276–2286.

Hosman, C., Jané-Llopis, E., & Saxena, S. (Eds.). (2005). *Prevention of mental disorders: Effective interventions and policy options.* Oxford, UK: Oxford University Press.

Keefe, F. J., Rumble, M. E., Scipio, C. D., Giordano, L. A., & Perri, L. M. (2004). Psychological aspects of persistent pain: Current state of the science. *Journal of Pain, 5*(4), 195–211.

Klimstra, T., Hale, W., Raaijmakers, Q., Branje, S., & Meeus, W. (2009). Maturation of personality in adolescence. *Journal of Personality and Social Psychology, 96*(4), 898–912.

Kotov, R., Gamez, W., Schmidt, F., & Watson, D. (2010). Linking "big" personality traits to anxiety, depressive, and substance use disorders: A meta-analysis. *Psychological Bulletin, 136*(5), 768–821.

Kutz, I., Shabtai, H., Solomon, Z., Neumann, M., & David, D. (1994). Posttraumatic stress disorder in myocardial infarction patients: Prevalence study. *Israel Journal of Psychiatry and Related Sciences, 31*, 48–56.

Linton, S. J. (2000). A review of psychological risk factors in back and neck pain. *Spine, 25*(9), 1148–1156.

Luger, T. M., Cotter, K. A., & Sherman, A. M. (2009). It's all in how you view it: Pessimism, social relations, and life satisfaction in older adults with osteoarthritis. *Aging and Mental Health, 13*, 635–647.

McAdams, D., & Pals, J. (2006). A new Big Five: Fundamental principles for an integrative science of personality. *American Psychologist, 61*(3), 204–217.

McCabe, K. O., & Fleeson, W. (2012). What is extraversion for? Integrating trait and motivational perspectives and identifying the purpose of extraversion. *Psychological Science, 23*(12), 1498–1505.

Merriman, C., Norman, P., & Barton, J. (2007). Psychological correlates of PTSD symptoms following stroke. *Psychology, Health & Medicine, 12*(5), 592–602.

National Institute of Mental Health. (2011). *Post-traumatic stress disorder (PTSD) risk prediction.* Retrieved from http://www.nimh.nih.gov/research-priorities/scientific-meetings/2011/post-traumatic-stress-disorder-ptsd-risk-prediction/index.shtml

Nicholas, M. K., Linton, S. J., Watson, P. J., & Main, C. J. (2011). Early identification and management of psychological risk factors ("yellow flags") in patients with low back pain: A reappraisal. *Physical Therapy, 91*(5), 1–17.

Peterson, G., & Seligman, M. E. P. (2004). *Character strengths and virtues: A handbook and classification.* New York, NY: Oxford University Press.

Plumb, J. C., Orsillo, S. M., & Luterek, J. A. (2004). A preliminary test of the role of experiential avoidance in postevent functioning. *Journal of Behavior Therapy and Experimental Psychiatry, 35*(3), 245–257.

Prasertsri, N., Holden, J., Keefe, F., & Wilkie, D. (2011). Repressive coping style: Relationships with depression, pain, and pain coping strategies in lung cancer outpatients. *Lung Cancer, 71*(2), 235–240.

Rahe, R., & Tolles, R. (2002). The Brief Stress and Coping Inventory: A useful stress management instrument. *International Journal of Stress Management, 9*(2), 61–70.

Roberts, B., & DelVecchio, W. (2000). The rank-order consistency of personality traits from childhood to old age: A quantitative review of longitudinal studies. *Psychological Bulletin, 126*(1), 3–25.

Roberts, B. W., Kuncel, N. R., Shiner, R., Caspi, A., & Goldberg, L. R. (2007). The power of personality: The comparative validity of personality traits, socioeconomic status, and cognitive ability for predicting important life outcomes. *Perspectives on Psychological Science, 2*, 313–345. doi:10.1111/j.1745-6916.2007.00047.x

Schneiderman, N., Ironson, G., & Siegel, S. D. (2005). Stress and health: Psychological, behavioral, and biological determinants. *Annual Review of Clinical Psychology, 1*, 607.

Schumm, J., Briggs-Phillips, M., & Hobfoll, S., (2006). Cumulative interpersonal traumas and social support as risk and resiliency factors in predicting PTSD and depression among inner-city women. *Journal of Traumatic Stress, 19*(6), 825–836.

Seligman, M. E. P. (2011). *Flourish: A visionary new understanding of happiness and well-being*. New York, NY: Free Press.

Soto, C., John, O., Gosling, S., & Potter, J. (2011). Age differences in personality traits from 10 to 65: Big Five domains and facets in a large cross-sectional sample. *Journal of Personality and Social Psychology, 100*(2), 330–348.

Spindler, H., & Pedersen, S. (2005). Posttraumatic stress disorder in the wake of heart disease: Prevalence, risk factors, and future research directions. *Psychosomatic Medicine, 67*(5), 715–723.

Stice, E., & Bearman, S. K. (2001). Body-image and eating disturbances prospectively predict increases in depressive symptoms in adolescent girls: A growth curve analysis. *Developmental Psychology, 37*, 597–607. doi:1037/0012-1649.37.5.597

Storr, C. L., Ialongo, N. S., Anthony, J. C., & Breslau, N. (2007). Childhood antecedents of exposure to traumatic events and PTSD. *American Journal of Psychiatry, 164*, 119–125.

Trickey, D., Siddaway, A. P., Meiser-Stedman, R., Serpell, L., & Field, A. P. (2012). A meta-analysis of risk factors for post-traumatic stress disorder in children and adolescents. *Clinical Psychology Review, 32*(2), 122–138.

Weiss, A., Sutin, A. R., Duberstein, P. R., Friedman, B., Bagby, M., & Costa, P. T. (2009). The personality domains and styles of the five-factor model are related to incident depression in Medicare recipients aged 65 to 100. *American Journal of Geriatric Psychiatry, 17*(7), 591–601. doi:10.1097/JGP.0b013e31819d859d

Yalom, I. (2008). Staring at the sun: Overcoming the terror of death. *The Humanistic Psychologist, 36*(3–4), 283–297.

3

MEDICAL TRAUMA FACTORS: DIAGNOSES AND PROCEDURES

IN THIS CHAPTER, YOU WILL LEARN:

- *The psychological impacts of Level 3 Medical Traumas, including prevalence for posttraumatic stress disorder (PTSD), depression, and secondary crises*
- *The varied psychological responses to Level 2 Medical Traumas and how unique characteristics of specific life-threatening or altering diagnoses can impact all aspects of patients' lives*
- *How planned or routine medical procedures (Level 1 Medical Traumas) can lead to a traumatic stress response in patients*

We began our discussion of the multiple factors that contribute to medical trauma in Chapter 2 by surveying the numerous patient factors that can influence people's medical experiences; risk factors can color our perceptions, affect our reactions to pain and discomfort, and impact our outlook regarding healing and recovery. Beyond the factors patients bring to each medical experience, perhaps the next most influential factor in the medical trauma equation is the diagnosis, procedure, or treatment itself. In Chapter 1, we first presented these diagnoses and procedures according to levels of medical trauma: Level 1 Medical Traumas, or anticipated medical interventions that may not readily be perceived as having the potential to trigger a traumatic stress response; Level 2 Medical Traumas, which include serious diagnoses that can threaten patients' lives or severely alter their lifestyle; and Level 3 Medical Traumas, which are those unexpected, life-threatening medical events most objectively identified as being traumatic.

In this chapter, we explore each level of trauma by highlighting unique characteristics of specific diagnoses, procedures, and medical events. Additionally, we present the latest research from studies examining the incidence and prevalence of mental health implications (e.g., PTSD and depression) of these medically induced traumas. For comparison purposes, the prevalence for PTSD within the lifetime in the general population is 7.8% according to the National Center for PTSD, while the prevalence for depression (within the last 12 months) is 6.9%, according to the World Health Organization.

We begin our examination of diagnoses and procedures with Level 3 Medical Traumas, as they are the most serious medical experiences readily recognized as having the greatest potential for provoking a traumatic stress response. In this section, we explore birth-related traumas, vascular emergencies, and accidents.

LEVEL 3 MEDICAL TRAUMA: UNEXPECTED, LIFE-THREATENING MEDICAL EVENTS

According to the Centers for Disease Control and Prevention (CDC), approximately 136 million people visit hospital emergency departments or trauma centers in a given year (CDC, 2016b). While we could presume that a healthy proportion of these visits is for treatment of non–life-threatening illness and injuries, many are serious enough to require hospitalization (11.9%; CDC, 2016b). Acute, life-threatening, and unanticipated events such as heart attacks and strokes, as well as severe injuries from automobile and other accidents, are commonplace in daily life, while other critical medical events such as obstetrical traumas often occur while patients are in the hospital. Regardless of where each type of crisis begins, there is a common thread running through them all: They are unexpected, they present a very real and present threat to patients' lives, and they have the potential for serious, life-altering physical and psychological consequences with long-term effects.

We begin our exploration of such crises with what some may consider the most harrowing of medical traumas because it occurs at a time of great vulnerability for the patient and can affect not one but two lives: obstetrical or childbirth-related traumas.

Obstetrical Trauma

Some could argue that childbirth, more than any other physical phenomenon, has the potential to rouse the broadest range of human emotions. The birth of a child is a vulnerable time—for mothers, infants, fathers, and families—and it is within the context of this vulnerability that patients have their childbirth experience. It should be noted that for a large number of women, even "normal" childbirth without any notable complications can be traumatic with up to 1.7% to 3% meeting the criteria for PTSD up to a year postpartum (Czarnocka & Slade, 2000; Wijma, Soderquist, & Wijma, 1997). While the largest percentage of women experience childbirth without any complications, there is a growing number of women, both in the United States and globally, who endure unimaginable pain and suffering during and following the birth of a child. Some women experience what is termed *severe maternal morbidity* (SMM), which is considered to be the most severe complications of pregnancy (such as postpartum hemorrhage, venous thrombotic embolism, and cardiac disorders) and which can lead to increased medical costs, lengthy hospital stays, and prolonged recovery. According to the CDC, the most common indicators of SMM include blood transfusion, heart failure, and hysterectomy—all serious, unanticipated complications of childbirth (CDC, 2015b).

The following are sobering statistics regarding childbirth in this country, according to the CDC: For every 10,000 births, 163 women are hospitalized for SMM, and for a rising number of women in the United States, childbirth exacts the ultimate toll—death (17.8 for every 10,000 births in 2009–2011). When we examine global figures of maternal mortality from the World Health Organization (2015), that number becomes almost mind-boggling: 289,000 women die in childbirth every year. Considering our perception that quality of medical care only advances over time, it may be surprising to learn that SMM is actually rising in the United States at double the rate of occurrences in Western Europe (Council on Patient Safety in Women's Health Care, 2015). In response to such an alarming rise, national women's health care organizations (e.g., collectives, such as the Council on Patient Safety in Women's Health Care; American Board of Obstetrics and Gynecology [ABO+G]; Association of Women's Health Obstetric and Neonatal Nurses [AWHONN]) and state collaboratives (e.g., the California Maternal Quality Care Collaborative [CMQCC]) made up of physicians, nurses, midwives, and researchers have been working together to create bundles of clinical tools to help promote safety and positive clinical outcomes, and such toolkits are becoming more inclusive of mental health resources (learn more about such initiatives in Chapters 8 and 9). In addition to the obvious physical implications of SMM, health care professionals are recognizing the psychological implications as well. In the following section, we examine such implications, which range from PTSD and depression to secondary crises affecting nearly all aspects of patients' lives.

PTSD and Gynecological/Obstetrical Trauma

SMM has another name, which in itself evokes the precariousness of the experience: *near-miss*. For many women who experience obstetrical traumas that can be categorized as near-misses, they have come as close as possible to their own deaths without actually dying—a sobering, terrifying, and life-changing incident. A maternal near-miss can have jarring emotional consequences for women, with fear for their own lives and the well-being of their babies figuring prominently in the experience: "During the emergency, a time women described as being between life and death, women not only feared for their lives, they feared for the lives and futures of their babies, their partners, and other members of their families" (Elmir, Schmied, Jackson, & Wilkes, 2012, p. 230). For some, the result of this intense fear from such a harrowing birth experience is PTSD: Prevalence of postpartum PTSD ranges from 1.7% to 9%, with women meeting criteria for the disorder up to 6 months postpartum (Beck, 2004; Beck, Gable, Sakala & Declercq, 2011; Czarnocka & Slade, 2000; Engelhard, van den Hout, & Arntz, 2001; Menage, 1993; Wijma et al., 1997).

Many studies of gynecological and obstetrical trauma include an examination of patient risk factors that may contribute to the experience of a procedure as traumatic. For example, preexisting mental health diagnoses, previous traumas including sexual traumas and rape, poor support from family or significant others, and conflict or poor relationships with staff are but a few risk factors that can contribute to a traumatic stress response and development of PTSD (Czarnocka & Slade, 2000). While patient risk factors are certainly important when attempting to understand gynecological and obstetrical trauma, it should also be noted that patients can have a traumatic stress response to childbirth-related traumas *without* having preexisting risk factors. Menage (1993) studied the emotional effects of obstetric and gynecological procedures in 500 women and found that one fifth described the procedure as being "terrifying" or "very distressing" (p. 221). Furthermore, 30 women met the criteria for PTSD, with nearly half reporting no *prior history of trauma or additional risk factors* often associated with this population. The mean score on the PTSD-I for this group of women was 78, compared to the mean score of a group of Vietnam War combat veterans, which was 76 (Mengage, 1993). As this sample suggests, for some women, visiting the OB/GYN can be quite traumatic.

While some patients who experience birth trauma certainly do meet the full criteria for PTSD, many more do not; having said this, it is critical that we view the trauma response on a continuum rather than dichotomously (Ayers, Joseph, McKenzie-McHarg, Slade, & Wijma, 2008), recognizing that patients experience many complex emotions worthy of our attention. One such experience is depression, given its comorbidity with anxiety and PTSD (Ayers et al., 2008) and its multifaceted effects on the lives and well-being of patients.

Depression and Gynecological/Obstetrical Trauma

According to the American Psychological Association (APA), it is estimated that 9% to 14% of women will experience depression postpartum, regardless of their childbirth experience (APA, 2015). Acute stress, including childbirth trauma and other life stressors, can play a role in exacerbating depression symptoms. Sequelae of birth traumas such as hysterectomy and other surgical interventions can often lead to depression as women are tasked with processing intense emotions, such as grief, sadness, pain, and deep disappointment (Elmir et al., 2012).

Secondary Crises and Obstetrical Trauma

The experience of an obstetrical trauma can set in motion a series of crises in nearly all domains of life. For SMM events, such as postpartum hemorrhage, patients must process the terror and existential effects of coming close to their own mortality, the disappointment and grief arising from the birth experience, and the physical implications of the hemorrhage (which could include massive blood transfusions, hysterectomy, and other surgical procedures)—all while functioning as a mother, partner, sister, daughter, coworker, and so on. The emotional, physical, and spiritual consequences of birth trauma can lead to crises in all areas of life, especially if the patient is not receiving follow-up care that integrates mental health into the process of physical healing.

To illustrate how birth trauma can lead to multiple secondary crises, consider my (Michelle) story:

> Eleven years ago I entered the hospital to give birth to my first and only child. I entered the doors at the stroke of midnight, full of hope and anticipation for a peaceful and fulfilling birth experience. Instead, I endured a level of trauma unimaginable to me: a placental abruption, emergency C-section, uterine atony, Stage IV hemorrhage, life-saving hysterectomy, ICU stay, and pneumonia.
>
> The interventions used to save my life and my uterus exacted a stiff psychological toll in that they bordered on torture, requiring endurance of mind-numbing pain, massive blood loss (10 liters required to save my life), and awareness of being precariously close to death. When I was discharged from the hospital a week later, I was given detailed instructions for wound care, medication management, and caring for the health of my newborn infant—basically, the ordinary information for the most extraordinary of circumstances.
>
> While in the hospital, my health care team didn't notice the many signs of acute stress disorder, which can sometimes follow a traumatic experience. It was almost as if my emotional experience wasn't on anyone's radar. I wasn't suicidal, homicidal, or psychotic—so no mental health professional was called to consult during any point in my hospital stay.

My traumatic stress reaction—which included being in a stupor or daze, hypervigilant, having a racing heartbeat, having a poor appetite, having difficulty sleeping, and needing to be alone— was described in my chart as "cooperative, quiet, and calm." At discharge, my nurses and doctors knew that I was going home to a supportive environment with ample financial resources, so there was ostensibly no need to plan for follow-up with a mental health professional.

Throughout the months following my daughter's birth, I had the challenge of assimilating all that had transpired while I was in the hospital. I had to grieve the loss of my ability to give birth to another child; I had to accept the limitations of my new body, which included starting hormone replacement therapy and dealing with symptoms of menopause at age 29; I had to redefine what it means to be a woman, having lost my reproductive organs; I had to process the trauma of coming so close to my own death; I had to work through the existential crisis that accompanies this kind of loss, which included a temporary loss of faith in God; I had to come to terms with the loss of my entire blood supply, and the strange effect that this can have on identity and physical well-being; I had to learn how to manage my newly developed anxiety and depression, which included short trials of antidepressant and antianxiety medications; I had to learn how to cope with my conflicted feelings about my doctor, who had become both my savior and the perpetrator of this trauma; I had to learn to interact with my then-husband, who was not inclined to deal directly with strong emotion; I had to manage many of my family members' reactions to my experience and their insistence that I take legal action against my physician and the hospital; and I had to learn how to live with PTSD. In sum, I had to work through the physical, psychological, personal, existential/spiritual, and relational crises that accompanied the experience of this trauma, all while learning how to be a new mom.

I encountered many challenges in the months and years following my daughter's birth. Within 2 years, my marriage fell apart, due in part to our inability to heal from this trauma together; we divorced shortly after my daughter turned three. I also ended my relationship with my physician, in part because she had become a symbol of my trauma. Due to the extreme physical trauma to my body and my developing PTSD, I stopped going to OB-GYNs altogether: It took me 10 years to work up the courage to visit a new specialist.

As you can see from this example, a Level 3 Medical Trauma, while often a single event, can lead to numerous life-altering challenges that can span many years. Birth traumas have the potential for setting in motion damaging effects in all areas of life: The trauma can affect relationships and sexual health, identity and well-being, spirituality, lifestyle, and developmental milestones. For women who experience obstetrical trauma on the day of their baby's birth, they have the added, ongoing challenge of defusing their trauma experience from the joyous event of bringing a child into the world. Children's birthdays are also anniversaries of another sort, and women work to manage conflicting emotions that may arise (Beck, 2004).

While most obstetrical emergencies are certainly unexpected, some occur while patients are already receiving care at a hospital or other medical facility, which can increase chances of a more favorable outcome (i.e., survival of baby and mother). The next Level 3 trauma we examine is vascular emergencies (i.e., heart attacks and strokes), the shocking, life-threatening, and disempowering nature of which can readily initiate a traumatic stress response.

Vascular Traumas

Cardiovascular and cerebrovascular traumas, or heart attacks and strokes, are considered to be among the most unexpected and serious of medical traumas, requiring visits to the emergency department and often leading to hospital and ICU stays. While these traumas begin as discrete medical events, they require ongoing monitoring and treatment in order to decrease likelihood of subsequent medical crises—and this treatment can become complicated when patients develop PTSD or other psychological consequences.

Heart Attack

I cannot breathe, my chest is tight, like it is being squeezed in a vice grip. My arms are numb. Life passes by in the blink of an eye, and the terror of reality sets in: I am having a heart attack, and I might die. If you have ever witnessed someone experiencing an acute cardiac event, then you know how terrifying the situation can be. For the purposes of our discussion about cardiac events, we focus on acute coronary syndrome (ACS), which includes myocardial infarction (heart attack) and unstable angina (lack of blood flow and oxygen to the heart). When considering the psychological impacts of ACS, we should underscore that these impacts, namely PTSD, can have adverse effects on the physical health of patients; people diagnosed with ACS *and* medical PTSD are twice as likely to suffer a subsequent cardiac event, and they are twice as likely as those who did not develop PTSD to die as a result of the condition (Edmondson et al., 2012). Further, in their meta-analysis of 24 articles (N = 2,383) examining prevalence rates of PTSD induced by ACS, Edmondson et al. (2012) found an aggregated prevalence rate of 12% or roughly 168,000 people who may struggle with the psychological disorder.

In a study of 171 patients following heart attack, 45% met the criteria for either major or minor depression immediately following the attack, and 33% met the criteria 3 to 4 months later (Schleifer et al., 1989). In their meta-analysis of studies examining comorbidity of mood disorders and medical illness, Evans et al. (2005) found prevalence for depression and cardiac diseases to fall between 17% and 27%. Given the existential threat present for people who experience heart attacks, it is understandable that such a jarring event has the clear potential for triggering a wide range of psychological responses—especially anxiety and depression.

Stroke and TIA

Like heart attacks, strokes are acute medical events that cause sudden, debilitating, and frightening physical changes that can potentially lead to permanent disability or death. Strokes are caused by either a clot that blocks blood flow to the brain (ischemic) or bleeding in the brain (hemorrhagic), and they require immediate emergency medical assistance due to the potential lethality. Strokes can cause abrupt and serious symptoms such as: numbness in the face, extremities, or a large part of the body; loss of senses, such as vision or hearing; loss of speech or the ability to understand speech; loss of balance and other motor disruptions; severe headache; and loss of consciousness. While these symptoms are alarming in the short term, what is perhaps most devastating about strokes is the propensity for long-term and even permanent incapacity.

A less severe but equally menacing cerebrovascular event is the transient ischemic attack (TIA), which is a ministroke that often lasts up to 24 hours; people who experience a TIA typically return to normal physical functioning, but are faced with the prospect of a full-blown stroke at some point in the future—a recipe for anticipatory anxiety and the potential for developing PTSD.

Several studies examining the prevalence of stroke and TIA-induced PTSD have been conducted, but due to the heterogeneity of samples and differences in timing of when PTSD measures were taken relative to the stroke, we are left with a broad range of 3% to 37% (Edmondson, Richardson, et al., 2013). In their meta-analysis of nine studies ($N = 1,138$) investigating the prevalence of PTSD in patients who suffered a stroke or TIA, Edmondson, Richardson et al. (2013) found an overall rate of 13%, with 23% diagnosed with PTSD within the first year of the stroke and 11% diagnosed at some point after the first year. The authors' calculation of the number of people living with stroke- or TIA-induced PTSD is staggering: 297,850 people in the

United States alone. Prevalence for depression among those who suffered a stroke or other cerebrovascular event is even higher, at 14% to 19% (Evans et al., 2005).

Given the suddenness and severity of cerebrovascular traumas such as TIA and stroke, it is evident how such an experience fits the category of Level 3 Medical Trauma; further, because a stroke or even TIA is rarely an isolated event without permanent ramifications, the experience can lead to a chronic traumatic stress response in the patient and secondary crises that can impact all areas of life.

Accidents

Accidents rank clearly among other Level 3 Medical Traumas due to the shocking manner in which they can occur and to the sometimes devastating physical consequences that can result. Beyond the frightening experience of the event itself and intensity with which rescuers work to connect a patient to medical care, accidents often require painful and invasive treatment in order to save a patient's life. Depending on the nature of the accident, patients may experience permanent injuries, chronic pain, and disabilities that can affect their lives in many ways, including the development of PTSD and depression. As the leading cause of death of people in the first half of life, accidents are worth our attention; beyond the mortality rates, we should also note that about 29 million Americans receive treatment for accidents each year, with 2.8 million requiring hospitalization for their injuries (CDC, 2015a). Since the number, severity, and types of injuries people can sustain from accidents and violence can vary greatly, we focus more broadly on the prevalence of PTSD and depression comorbid with traumatic brain injury (TBI) and other physical injuries.

Traumatic Brain Injury

TBI occurs when an external force to the head causes injury to the brain, including damage to cells, brain structures, bleeding, and clots that can cause coma, seizures, nerve death, and a staggering number of intellectual, behavioral, and social problems. Approximately 5.3 million Americans are living with disabilities stemming from a TBI, and TBIs are the leading cause of death for people ages 1 to 44 (Brain Trauma Foundation, 2015). According to the Mayo Clinic, the most common causes of TBIs include falls, vehicle accidents, violence, sports injuries, and blast-/combat-related injuries—all of which could have the potential to trigger a traumatic stress response. While TBIs occur outside of the medical setting, they are a medical event worth including because of the potential for developing PTSD and depression, as well as the heightened risk of suicide. Research has found that patients with comorbid

PTSD and TBI have a 3.3 times greater likelihood of attempting suicide as those with a TBI alone (Brenner et al., 2011); even in cases of a mild TBI, research has shown a complex interplay between PTSD and suicidality suggesting that TBIs exacerbate psychiatric symptoms and leave patients with increased vulnerability to attempt suicide (Barnes, Walter, & Chard, 2012). In addition to the prevalence of PTSD and depression in people who experience a TBI, studies also show a reduction in overall wellness, perceived wellness, ability to manage stress, and physical fitness as measured by BMI (Braden et al., 2012).

Other Physical Injuries

Traumatic injuries can have lasting and even lifelong consequences for patients. While TBIs could be considered one of the more severe injuries given its many effects, other physical injuries have the potential to trigger intense psychological reactions and profound changes in life functioning depending on patients' subjective interpretations of the accident and the severity of injuries. Research has demonstrated a positive association between perceived threat to life, the severity of injuries, and level of distress with the development of posttraumatic stress symptoms (PTSSs; Irish et al., 2013). In one study of automobile accident survivors, Ehlers, Mayou, and Bryant (1998) found prevalence for PTSD at 16% within a year of the accident. Even for those who do not meet the full criteria for PTSD, PTSSs can have severe implications for overall health. Studies have also shown that a traumatic stress response leading to PTSS can have health implications several months following a motor vehicle accident (Baranyi et al., 2010; Irish et al., 2013). Baranyi et al. (2010) also found differences in vitality and mental health between paired samples with and without PTSD, with those suffering from PTSD showing more dysfunction in these areas.

In the next section, we examine Level 2 Medical Traumas or the trauma response stemming from life-threatening/-altering diagnoses. While these experiences do not have the alarming force of a Level 3 Medical Trauma, they can lead to a crescendo of psychological distress nonetheless. Earlier we discussed a compelling model that differentiates medical trauma from other forms of trauma—the Enduring Somatic Threat (EST) model (Edmondson, 2014). You will recall from our discussion of the EST model (see Chapter 1) that the very nature of medical trauma stemming from an acute, life-threatening physiological crisis is such that the threat exists within a person rather than from an external source, and that this internal locus of threat is central to the maintenance of trauma symptoms following a Level 3 Medical Trauma because the threat endures after the acute trauma has passed. In this case, a Level 3 Medical Trauma leads to Level 2 trauma as patients attempt to adjust to living with a chronic illness that has a very real potential to threaten life.

LEVEL 2 MEDICAL TRAUMA: LIFE-THREATENING/-ALTERING DIAGNOSES

Cancer, diabetes, cardiac disorders, and asthma are among the many Level 2 Medical Traumas. While some of these conditions begin as shocking and traumatic events, others reveal themselves over time following extensive testing and observation; for those who experience the latter, the shock comes when a worst-case scenario is confirmed: You have X disorder. Despite the many ways in which patients learn of their diagnoses, one common denominator among them all is the requirement of sustained medical intervention in order for them to live their lives fully—or more precisely—to live, *period*. The disorders we have mentioned are but a few of the disorders listed among the Institute of Medicine's top priorities, and for good reason: The high cost for patients, their families, our communities, and the nation is indeed staggering. While such costs are often calculated in terms of dollars and cents, the emotional toll of these and other serious diagnoses can be equally alarming. In this section, we explore the life-threatening and life-altering diagnoses that can have dramatic psychological effects for patients. While some Level 2 Medical Traumas can stem from Level 3 Traumas (e.g., a first heart attack that indicates ACS, a chronic condition), others are diagnosed after careful assessment of symptoms. While some Level 2 Traumas do not begin as dramatically as Level 3, the physical and psychological consequences of such illnesses can be equally as startling and grave. We begin with perhaps one of the most terrifying of such diagnoses: cancer.

Cancer

The term *neoplasm* comes from two Greek words: neo, meaning "new" and plasma, meaning "creation." At first glance, the word neoplasm seems to promise something hopeful, but when viewed in the context of cancer and accompanied by the word *malignant* or *malignancy* (which, incidentally, sounds a lot more like what it is—*mal* or bad), it holds a different meaning altogether. Conceivably one of our greatest collective fears is hearing the words "You have cancer" being spoken to a loved one or to ourselves, as we understand this diagnosis to mean that medical intervention will be required in order to avoid certain death. While many of us have had some form of experience with cancer, this experience does little to lessen the blow of a diagnosis, and certainly does not protect us from the psychological sequelae of this kind of medical trauma.

The experience of cancer often means confronting one's own mortality; submitting to ongoing and sometimes debilitating medical treatments while tolerating significant time spent within the medical setting; experiencing extreme pain, nausea, and fatigue; adjusting to social isolation; reorganizing one's lifestyle to accommodate treatment; and managing grief, depression, and anxiety. Cancer is a trauma to the body, mind, and soul that can create immense distress for patients and their families. An important contributing factor to the traumatic nature of cancer is the experience of the medical culture and the stark contrast between the intimate, lived experience of the patient and the matter-of-fact, clinical experience of medical staff (Leal et al., 2015). The qualitative study of Leal et al. (2015) also sheds light on other aspects of people's lived experiences with cancer, noting how the prospect of being monitored for the rest of their lives contributed to patients' distress. Indeed, for patients with chronic, life-threatening diseases such as cancer, the lengthy treatments, and lifelong monitoring can lead to a destructive loop of anxiety and depression in addition to affecting the quality of everyday life.

From quantitative research examining the prevalence of clinical disorders comorbid with cancer, we know that anxiety, PTSD, and depression are commonplace as patients fight to survive and live with a terrifying threat harbored within their own bodies. In one study examining depression, anxiety, and quality of life in cancer patients, of the 405 participants surveyed, 309 were found to suffer with depression, with 135 also having comorbid anxiety (Brown, Kroenke, Theobald, Wu, & Tu, 2010). In another study, comorbid depression was found with nearly all forms of cancer (18.5% of $N = 7,749$), and an even higher prevalence found in patients suffering with pancreatic cancer (28.8% of $N = 304$), a highly lethal form of cancer and the fourth leading cause of cancer-related deaths (Clark, Loscalzo, Trask, Zabora, & Philip, 2010). Overall prevalence for comorbid depression and cancer is 22% to 29% (Evans et al., 2005). When patients' mental health is affected by living with cancer, overall quality of life can suffer. It has been found that comorbid breast cancer and PTSD contribute to a decrease in overall quality of life, including mental and physical well-being (Shelby, Golden-Kreutz, & Andersen, 2008). Clearly, for some patients the experience of cancer includes not only the physical implications but also significant emotional effects that can alter all aspects of life.

Diabetes

In the United States, approximately 29 million people live with diabetes, and almost 86 million are considered prediabetic (American Diabetes Association, 2016). It is a disease that clearly affects a great number of people, from children to older adults, and it is a ubiquitous presence in the lives of those who have it. Diabetes requires vigilant monitoring, administration of medication multiple times a day, and careful dietary and activity planning. While many people with diabetes are able to lead healthy and productive lives, they do so under the looming presence of this chronic, life-altering, and life-threatening disease. Through meta-analytic studies, we know that people with diabetes have a higher likelihood of developing depression than do nondiabetics (Hasan, Mamun, Clavarino, & Kairuz, 2015); Evans et al. (2005) list the prevalence rate for self-reported depression at 26%. Over the past several decades, numerous studies have examined comorbidity of diabetes (Type 1 and Type 2) with depression and anxiety in an effort to understand how mental health issues impact adherence to treatment regimens and influence management of the disease (Gavard, Lustman, & Clouse, 1993). Of particular interest in our discussion are those studies that elucidate the mental health effects of living with diabetes, and how the rigor of managing the disease, coupled with the deadly consequences of failing to do so, can have severe psychological consequences.

Similar to the experience of cancer patients and the effects of treatment on mental health, people living with diabetes are reminded multiple times per day of the precarious nature of their own health and survival, which can lead to health anxiety and more seriously, to PTSD. Claude, Hadjistavropoulos, and Friesen (2014) found a prevalence of 24.1% when examining health anxiety in a sample of 414 people living with Type 1 and Type 2 diabetes, and noted that this anxiety was related in part to fear of diabetes complications, in addition to trait risk factors and poor adherence to treatment regimen. In a study of 90 participants with Type 1 diabetes that required intensive regimens, 25.5% met the full criteria for PTSD, with many more meeting criteria for specific clusters of the disorder: 65.5% for reexperiencing cluster, 31.1% for avoidance cluster, 54.4% for arousal, and 95.5% reported at least one life domain impacted by the disease (Myers, Boyer, Herbert, Barakat, & Scheiner, 2007). Results from the Myers et al. (2007) study show that two variables, perceived death threat from hypoglycemia and fear of hypoglycemia, significantly predict PTSSs, which underscores the importance of subjectivity and perception in the experience of medical trauma.

Cardiac Disorders

Cardiac disorders are often identified following an acute medical event such as a heart attack, or when plaque builds up in the arteries feeding the heart to the point that a clot forms, cutting off vital blood flow and oxygen to the heart muscle. The buildup of plaque can take place over a long period of time preceding a heart attack, during which time a person may be unaware that they have coronary artery (or heart) disease; however, following a heart attack, patients become acutely aware of the condition that caused their brush with death—to the point of developing clinical anxiety, depression, and even PTSD. Heart disease makes its way onto our list for good reason: It is the number one cause of death for both men and women in the United States, and as such it can have severe implications (physical *and* emotional) for those receiving the diagnosis.

Living with coronary artery disease, like other chronic and life-threatening illnesses, requires vigilance regarding lifestyle and stress management. Recent studies have demonstrated how excessive stress can lead to exacerbation of symptoms, future heart attacks, and readmissions to the hospital, with as much as a threefold increase in risk for readmission (Edmondson, Green, Ye, Halazun, & Davidson, 2014). Given what we know about the effects of stress on physical health, it is easy to see how psychological well-being plays a crucial role in the overall health and quality of life for people who live with heart conditions; beyond that, psychological well-being can literally mean the difference between life and death. For example, patients exhibiting symptoms of PTSD and who have heart conditions have demonstrated a significant delay in going to the hospital when experiencing an acute event. Newman, Muntner, Shimbo, Davidson, and Shaffer et al. (2011) examined the length of time it took 241 people experiencing an acute cardiac event to go to the hospital, and found that people who exhibited symptoms of PTSD directly related to having a heart condition (17.8% of the sample) took an average of 178% longer to present at the hospital than those without PTSD symptoms (25.8 hours versus 10.7 hours). In a situation in which every second counts, this time difference is staggering to say the least—and prompts us to consider the heavy price of untreated medical trauma.

Pulmonary Disorders

Pulmonary disorders, or diseases that involve the lungs and breathing, are prevalent across age, sex, and every other demographic. Diseases such as emphysema, chronic bronchitis, and asthma, along with acute events such as a pulmonary embolism (blood clot in the lungs), can have a significant impact on people's quality of life and psychological well-being. While some pulmonary diseases are the direct result of lifestyle or environmental factors and develop later in life, such as chronic obstructive pulmonary disease or COPD, others can develop early, requiring lifelong vigilance and monitoring. Asthma is one such chronic disease, and there have been numerous studies examining the psychological impacts of living with asthma.

Asthma

According to the CDC, 18.7 million adults and 6.8 million children currently live with asthma in the United States (CDC, 2016a). According to the (Asthma and Allergy Foundation of America, 2015) nine people die from asthma every day, while 4,700 visit emergency departments each day. As a Top 15 Priority Condition, asthma is clearly on the radar of the health care industry due in large part to the mounting costs of the disorder, both economically and personally. From the standpoint of medical trauma, asthma has the potential for triggering a traumatic stress response because of the ever-present possibility for an asthma attack. During an attack, the airways become swollen and bronchial tubes narrow, making breathing progressively more difficult. Although some asthma attacks can be minor and easily managed with medication, some can become life-threatening and require immediate medical attention—an event that for some can lead to PTSD.

Kean, Kelsay, Wamboldt, and Wamboldt (2006) found that 20% of adolescents who suffered a severe asthma attack met the full criteria for PTSD, and in a sample of 156 college students with asthma, 3% met the full criteria for PTSD and 44% met partial criteria for the disorder (Chung, Rudd, & Wall, 2012). Like other life-threatening and chronic disorders, asthma is a direct contributor to the development of clinical mental health disorders as well as to other secondary crises. In their study of college students living with asthma, Chung and Wall (2012) found that those with asthma had significantly more physical problems, relationship dysfunction, and depression compared to a control group, and were five times more likely to develop a psychiatric disorder. Some studies have examined how a known contributing factor to developing PTSD, alexithymia, might play a role in cases of comorbid PTSD and asthma. As you may know, alexithymia is the inability to recognize and name emotions within one's self, and it can affect one's ability to process complex emotion following a traumatic event. In the case of the Chung and Wall (2012) study, alexithymia predicted the development of general psychiatric disorders independent of a PTSD diagnosis.

As with other chronic and life-threatening medical illnesses, depression is prevalent in asthma sufferers and can impact disease management in serious ways. In one study examining work-related asthma, participants with asthma were significantly more likely to have depression than those without asthma, and when both conditions were present there was a higher likelihood of adverse asthma outcomes (Mazurek, Knoeller, & Moorman, 2012). Just as depression can exacerbate asthma, asthma can lead to depression. In their study of asthma sufferers ($N = 91$), Yonas et al. (2013) found a higher incidence of depression, lower quality of life, and poorer asthma management compared to the control ($N = 36$). It seems as if depression creates a vicious cycle for those suffering with chronic illnesses: It contributes to poor management of the physical symptoms, which leads to acute, life-threatening events, which lead to more depression, and so on.

Autoimmune Disorders

Of all the chronic, life-threatening/-altering disorders we have discussed thus far, this category perhaps best exemplifies the internal threat posed by disease; indeed, when a person has an autoimmune disorder, the body turns on itself, attacking healthy tissue and leaving people vulnerable to debilitating symptoms and profound changes to quality of life, vitality, and even longevity. There are numerous distinct types of autoimmune diseases (over 25) we could discuss, but we limit our brief review to only a few, namely, HIV/AIDS and rheumatoid arthritis (RA) (note that Type 1 diabetes, technically an autoimmune disorder, was addressed in its own category earlier).

HIV/AIDS

The HIV and the final stage of the infection, AIDS, are human diseases that became newsworthy in the 1980s and remained in the headlines, in part because of the devastation wreaked by the disease in the United States and globally. Although strides have certainly been made regarding treating the disease and prolonging life, there is still currently no cure; depending on the resources available to patients, the diagnosis may not necessarily mean a death sentence, but like many other Level 2 traumas, survival requires sustained medical intervention.

There have been numerous studies examining the psychological impacts of receiving an HIV diagnosis and living with HIV/AIDS. More specifically, researchers have sought to understand the traumatic stress response in this population, as well as the prevalence of HIV-related PTSD. A challenge in conducting this research, and more specifically in understanding the primary causes of PTSD, is that many research participants are coming from environments in which there are several confounding variables that make it difficult to draw clear conclusions. Some populations with high rates of HIV/AIDS, such as those in parts of Africa, are also plagued by poverty, famine, war, and other atrocities that can certainly contribute to trauma-induced disorders such as PTSD. Given these challenges, researchers are careful to discriminate between lifetime PTSD and HIV-related PTSD. In one such study, researchers differentiated between lifetime PTSD and HIV-related PTSD and found incidence rates of 54.1% and 40%, respectively, suggesting that receiving an HIV diagnosis and living with HIV are traumas that can lead to serious mental health diagnoses (Martin & Kagee, 2011). In another study sampling 61 homosexual and bisexual men, results showed that 30% had developed PTSD within 4 years of receiving a diagnosis of HIV (Kelly et.al., 1998), while a study of 67 African American women yielded a PTSD rate of 35.3% between 12 and 14 months following their first positive HIV test. Additional qualitative studies show chronic PTSD in patients living with HIV (Howsepian, 1998). In sum, receiving an HIV diagnosis and living with the threat of AIDS represents a trauma in the lives of many sufferers, with a significant proportion developing PTSD in response to this disease.

Depression is also common for people living with HIV and AIDS, affecting twice as many of those who have the disease than those who do not, according to one study (Ciesla & Roberts, 2001). Meta-analyses of comorbidity of depression and HIV/AIDS show prevalence between 5% and 20% (Evans et al., 2005). While there are many confounds to studies examining depression and HIV/AIDS, researchers strive to control for as many variables as possible as they seek to understand the lived experience of patients with this disease.

Rheumatoid Arthritis

RA is a chronic inflammatory disease in which the body attacks tissue and joints primarily in the hands and feet, and in some cases multiple organs throughout the body, such as the skin, blood vessels, and lungs. RA can cause significant deformity over time and can have dramatic impacts on people's quality of life and ability to perform basic tasks. While the many physical ailments associated with RA can lead to secondary crises in all life domains, the disease has also been linked to depression and anxiety. In one study examining protective factors for patients living with RA, over half of the 117 participants scored above the threshold for anxiety and depression using the Hospital Anxiety and Depression Scale (Dirika & Karancib, 2010). While most studies give a snapshot of psychological functioning at one point in time, longitudinal data give us a better picture of the longer term emotional effects of chronic illness. In a study of 1,117 participants diagnosed with RA, measurements taken over 18 years showed 25.2% suffered with intermittent depression, while 9% were chronically depressed (Morris, Yelin, Panopalis, Julian, & Katz, 2011); rates for depression in RA patients were similar in the Hyphantis et al. (2013) study at 25.1% of participants living with the disorder. Studies such as these, which also examine quality of life factors and health-related implications of psychological disorders, reinforce the importance of treating the whole person when helping people manage chronic illness.

Before moving on to the psychological implications of Level 1 Medical Traumas, let us examine a few additional chronic disorders and their emotional and life-altering effects.

Other Disorders

Alzheimer's Disease

A diagnosis of dementia can devastate an individual and his or her family, for it means that profound changes in cognitive ability and overall health are on the horizon. According to the Alzheimer's Association, approximately 80% of dementias are caused by Alzheimer's disease while the remaining are vascular dementias caused by stroke. As one might imagine, there is significant comorbidity with dementia (Alzheimer's disease) and depression, with the prevalence ranging from 30% to 50% (Evans et al., 2005). Dementia can lead to a cascade of secondary crises, negatively impacting identity, relationships, career, spirituality, and lifestyle while simultaneously affecting close family and friends who must watch as their loved one's functioning deteriorates. We see this process vividly in the film, *Still Alice*, in which the main character, once a prominent professor at Columbia University, is diagnosed with early-onset Alzheimer's and experiences profound decompensation in nearly every aspect of her life. The dramatization of this topic resonated with moviegoers and members of the Academy of Motion Picture Arts and Sciences, who awarded leading actress Julianne Moore an Academy Award for her performance in 2015.

Parkinson's Disease

Parkinson's is a degenerative disorder of the central nervous system, with the most obvious symptoms being psychomotor agitation, shaking, muscle rigidity, and a slowing down of motor activity. Beyond gross and fine motor movement disruptions, Parkinson's can lead to sleep and emotional disturbances, with depression being prevalent in many cases. In a meta-analytic study of the prevalence of comorbid depression and Parkinson's, results ranged widely from 4% to 75% (Evans et al., 2005). Dementia is also possible in advanced stages of Parkinson's disease. Given the pronounced disruption in motor skills, people with Parkinson's experience significant obstacles to engaging in many loved activities which can have dramatic impacts on lifestyle, emotional health, and identity; furthermore, symptoms can lead to social isolation, which can exacerbate mood disturbances and decrease quality of life.

Epilepsy

According to the Epilepsy Foundation, approximately 2 million people have been diagnosed with epilepsy in the United States. A neurological disorder, epilepsy causes disruptions in the brain's electrical activity which leads to seizures. Epilepsy can be found in children, adolescents, and adults and can be genetic or caused by an injury such as a TBI. Similar to those with heart conditions, diabetes, and asthma, people with epilepsy live daily life with the possibility of experiencing an acute medical event, namely, a seizure. Given this, it is not surprising that some may develop a traumatic stress response to this acute event, which can have serious emotional effects. Studies examining the prevalence of comorbid depression show a range of 20% and 55% when examined meta-analytically (Evans et al., 2005). Regarding seizure-induced PTSD, Chung, Allen, and Dennis (2013) studied 71 people with epilepsy and found that 51% of men and 22% of women met the criteria for PTSD, which also strongly correlated with alexithymia in this case.

In addition to the powerful emotional effects in patients, there can also be serious psychological impacts for parents and partners of those with epilepsy. For example, in their study of 80 parents of epileptic children, Iseri, Ozten, and Aker (2006) found 31.5% met criteria for both PTSD and major depressive disorder, while the vast majority met the criteria for the PTSD symptom clusters of reexperiencing and arousal (88.8% and 80%, respectively). Regarding partners of people with epilepsy, Norup and Elklit (2013) found a prevalence of 7.7% for full PTSD, and 43.9% for subclinical PTSD in a sample of 614 respondents.

While this review was certainly not exhaustive regarding chronic disorders and their myriad effects, it provides a snapshot of the psychological impacts of these types of medical traumas. Now we turn to the last level of medical trauma, which can easily fall off the radar of health care and even mental health professionals.

LEVEL 1 MEDICAL TRAUMA: PLANNED OR ROUTINE MEDICAL INTERVENTION

Of all forms of medical trauma, the Level 1 Medical Traumas are perhaps the least recognized by providers and patients alike. Why? One reason may be the ostensibly low lethality of many planned or routine medical interventions, prompting us to conclude that these episodes of care are without a propensity to cause a traumatic stress response. Another may be that many of the medical events included in this category are elected by patients; whether they desire the intervention or not, they choose to receive care. While the element of shock can certainly be absent from Level 1 Medical Traumas, before, during, and following these interventions there is a possibility of strong psychological reactions—especially for those patients with risk factors stemming from previous medical traumas or traumas unrelated to a medical experience.

It should be noted that even without prior history of medical trauma, patients can experience powerful psychological reactions to planned or routine medical intervention, as well as a cascade of secondary crises in every life domain. You will recall from Chapter 2 the numerous patient risk factors that can contribute to medical trauma, and just as such factors can influence a patient's response to a life-threatening medical event or disorder, so too can they color a patient's experience of routine medical care. We begin our discussion of the psychological impacts of Level 1 Medical Traumas by exploring outpatient surgery, and then we examine the prevalence of PTSD and anxiety related to primary medical and dental care.

Outpatient Surgery

Patients schedule surgeries and procedures in hospitals and ambulatory surgery centers for a wide variety of medical issues, including cataracts, lower intestinal problems, benign and malignant tumor removal, orthopedic injuries, and other medically necessary concerns. The CDC estimated that in 2006, there were 57.1 million surgical and nonsurgical interventions performed in outpatient settings of hospitals and free-standing clinics. While many of these surgeries do not have the acute feel or emergent qualities of Level 3 Medical Traumas, their medical necessity implores patients to submit to the procedures. What we have found from the research is a clear indication that for some patients, even scheduled procedures for relatively minor health concerns can incite strong emotional responses leading to anxiety, depression, and diminished quality of life. Beyond the surgery itself, what is perhaps more influential for quality of life is the outcome of a surgery and how a patient assimilates physical changes into his or her current lifestyle. Further, when patients have risk factors that increase their vulnerability to anxiety, depression, and diminished quality of life, they are more likely to experience detrimental effects from medical procedures, including those that are considered noncritical.

Outpatient surgeries are diverse with regard to settings, circumstances, and targets of medical intervention; however, there is one factor common to all procedures, and that is the awareness, anticipation, and experience of at least some level of pain or discomfort. The comorbidity of pain and PTSD should not be ignored in our discussion of outpatient surgery, for pain is a predictor of chronic PTSD *and* PTSD is a predictor of chronic pain (Beck & Clapp, 2011). Moeller-Bertram, Keltner, and Strigo (2012) explored how PTSD and pain each exacerbate the other, fueling a cycle of misery for patients. While research examining the prevalence of PTSD stemming from acute surgeries such as cardiac, vascular, and critical injuries is more plentiful, there is less research evidence for PTSD related to outpatient surgery; therefore, we focus on depression and anxiety as it relates to these types of procedures, beginning with surgery to remove cataracts.

Cataract Surgery

Cataract surgery is a common procedure that involves removing a cloudy lens from the eye and replacing it with an artificial lens. Performed by an ophthalmologist in an outpatient surgical clinic, the procedure often lasts less than 1 hour and typically requires only local anesthesia. Research in the area of cataract surgery and psychological distress focuses primarily on the effects of visual disturbances on overall quality of life and depression. Studies examining the effects of visual disability related to cataracts and other ocular disorders have shown an increase in depression, which is often tied to a decrease in ability to engage in valued activities such as recreation, driving, activities requiring fine motor skills, and other lifestyle factors (Rovner & Casten, 2002; Walker, Anstey, & Lord, 2006).

Orthopedic Surgery

Also very common in the United States are orthopedic surgeries, which aim to treat injuries, restore mobility, and reduce pain for people with degenerative disorders and other ailments of the musculoskeletal system. Regardless of the area of the body targeted, the overall goal of a procedure is to restore or even improve quality of life. Regardless of the site of injury or degeneration, one significant factor that affects all orthopedic patients is the experience of pain. Often, patients experience substantial preoperative pain, which can become unbearable leading up to a scheduled surgery and can have dramatic impacts on nearly all areas of life. Patients who experience significant pain also report sleep disturbances, disruptions in daily routines, inability to engage in hobbies and recreational activities, irritability that can impact relationships and job performance, and a wide variety of other factors. Further, patients who continue to have pain postoperatively can struggle to reengage in their lives in meaningful ways, which can lead to or exacerbate depression and have other emotional effects. Goebel, Steinert, Vierheilig, and Faller (2013) found a link between pain and depression in orthopedic surgery patients, noting that preoperative pain predicted postoperative depression in their sample of 200 orthopedic surgery patients. The authors advocate that treatment of orthopedic surgery patients should include components that address both pain and depression, as depression has been shown to exacerbate chronic pain as well.

In a study investigating incidence of depression and anxiety following lower limb arthroplasty (to restore or modify a joint), Nickinson, Board, and Kay (2009) found that half of their sample ($n = 56$) developed depression postoperatively, while 17 patients developed clinical or subclinical anxiety following their procedures. The authors also reported an increased length of stay in the hospital for patients who reported anxiety and depression, and underscored the importance of assessing psychological factors following surgery to screen for postoperative depression and anxiety.

As we see in the case of Keith in Chapter 6, orthopedic surgery and its after-effects can be life-altering for those who face the prospect of living with chronic pain and decreased ability to function at preinjury levels.

Primary/Preventive Care

Perhaps considered the least likely to trigger a traumatic stress response given their association with prevention, minor procedures, and higher likelihood of developed doctor–patient relationships, primary medical care and dental care are critical to examine in the context of medical trauma because of the potential of the trauma to influence nonadherence to medication and disease-management regimens and even avoidance of the health care system altogether. Edmondson's (2014) EST model of medical trauma is again significant here. Given what we know about PTSD, its symptoms, and various methods for coping, we know that experiential avoidance is central to people's management of distressing symptoms; in the case of medical trauma, experiential avoidance means avoidance of the medical setting and worrying about receiving medical care.

Medical Avoidance and Nonadherence

Medical trauma in the primary care setting can manifest differently depending on patients' risk factors, past and current physical and mental health diagnoses, and prior history of medical trauma. Patients who have experienced a Level 3 or Level 2 Medical Trauma and who have developed significant anxiety about facing reminders of their health, mortality, or past illnesses may avoid visiting doctors in the primary care setting. In an analysis of the 2007 Health Information National Trends Survey, Ye, Shim, and Rust (2012) found that people who have experienced what they call *serious psychological distress* are more likely to avoid visiting the doctor because of fear of illness or mortality, or to avoid thinking about being sick or dying. In another study validating this phenomenon, researchers found that people over 50 who worried about receiving a positive cancer diagnosis were more likely to avoid seeing the doctor, a decision with possibly deadly implications (Persoskie, Ferrer, & Klein, 2014). Isolating fear and worry as factors that contribute to medical avoidance further underscores the importance of integrating mental health treatment seamlessly into primary care.

Another way in which medical trauma can affect patient engagement in primary care is through nonadherence to medication regimens and medical advice—which can be detrimental to patients living with serious and life-threatening illnesses. In one study examining the relationship between medication nonadherence and PTSD, a strong and significant association was found between forgetting or skipping doses of medication and the disorder (Kronish, Edmondson, Yongmei, & Cohen, 2012). Studies examining medication nonadherence and PTSD in specific medical populations have yielded similar results, whether for stroke (Edmondson, Horowitz, Goldfinger, Fei, & Kronish, 2013), for patients who have experienced a myocardial infarction (Shemesh et al., 2001), and for patients living with HIV (Ricart et al., 2002). Clearly the issue of noncompliance in following medication regimens is an important one, especially for patients living with serious diseases that require consistent medical intervention; failing to adhere to such regimens can have disastrous consequences for patients, leading to acute, life-threatening medical events (and more Level 3 Trauma).

Gynecological Interventions

In our previous discussion of birth trauma, we highlighted the vulnerability inherent in the childbirth experience vis-à-vis the broad range of emotions felt and heightened concerns for the well-being of the baby, in addition to the physical state of the mother. In nonbirth gynecological traumas, risk factors play an important role in understanding women's traumatic responses to in-office gynecological procedures, such as pelvic exams and Pap smears, internal ultrasounds, and also abortion procedures, especially those involving prior history of sexual trauma and preexisting mental health diagnoses. Recall the Menage (1993) study discussed earlier, in which one fifth of the 500 women studied described gynecological interventions as terrifying and distressing. Beyond the possible emotional effects from preventive gynecological procedures, abortions have also been the focus of study in recent years. One study found that women who undergo medical abortions (i.e., being prescribed medication to end a pregnancy) as opposed to surgical abortions were at greater risk for experiencing PTSD, a potentially surprising finding given the absence of invasive procedures (Rousset, Brulfert, Séjourné, Goutaudier, & Chabrol, 2011).

In addition to the unique and complex emotional responses some women experience before, during, and after gynecological procedures, we should also note that for some, the prospect of the gynecological exam is so traumatic that women avoid them altogether, as evidenced by Akerson's (2012) qualitative study of African American women with a history of interpersonal (sexual) trauma. More research examining the prevalence of Level 1 Medical Traumas following Level 3 birth traumas is needed, especially regarding avoidance of seeking preventive gynecological care.

Dental Care

The experience of strong emotions, especially anxiety, in response to dental care is a phenomenon that is unlikely to surprise most readers, for the dental profession is highly aware of the fear prevalent among some patients. In fact, if you examined advertisements for dental practices around the country, you will see some touting services as being *pain-free, gentle,* and *kind*—thanks in large part to sedation dentistry. For some patients who experience dental care as traumatic, the usual personal risk factors are present, including preexisting anxiety; for others, the primary risk factor is a past dental experience that triggered a strong psychological response (medical trauma). In one study of 56 patients with a high level of dental anxiety, 59% reported past adverse experiences at the dentist as being the primary cause of their current anxiety (De Jongh, van der Burg, van Overmeir, Aartman, & van Zuuren, 2001); further, 10% met the full criteria for PTSD directly tied to the adverse dental experience. In a subsequent study of 34 patients who underwent wisdom tooth removal, those with a high level of anxiety 4 weeks after the procedure possessed two important risk factors that accounted for 71% of the variance: previous exposure to adverse dental events and preexisting anxiety (De Jongh et al., 2008).

For a significant percentage of patients who experience dental anxiety, the method of coping becomes avoidance. Liddell and Locker (2000) examined survey responses from a heterogeneous sample of 2,609 participants and found that 652 individuals had avoided dental visits because of fear, with 27% of "anxious avoiders" admitting they did not have a regular dentist. This pattern of avoidance due to medical trauma is troubling, and just as we see in medical primary care, there can be detrimental health consequences in dental primary care as well.

SUMMARY

This chapter provides just a snapshot of the numerous and complex psychological impacts of medical crises, chronic illnesses, and planned procedures, as well as the effects of trauma, be it medical or otherwise, on patient engagement in primary care. While the psychological sequelae of the various physical conditions presented here vary according to each individual patient's unique context, one theme is consistent: Medical experiences affect far more than the physical body, impacting one's emotional health, psychological functioning, relationships, lifestyle, spirituality, and sense of self. Further, such implications have a reciprocal effect on the body, often leading to a worsening of the condition that triggered the trauma in the first place.

REFERENCES

Akerson, K. (2012). A history of interpersonal trauma and the gynecological exam. *Qualitative Health Research, 22*(5), 679–688.

American Diabetes Association. (2016). *Statistics about diabetes*. Retrieved from http://www.diabetes.org/diabetes-basics/statistics/?loc=db-slabnav

American Psychological Association. (2015). *Postpartum depression*. Retrieved from http://www.apa.org/pi/women/programs/depression/postpartum.aspx

Asthma and Allergy Foundation of America. (2015). *Asthma facts and figures*. Retrieved from http://www.aafa.org/page/asthma-facts.aspx

Ayers, S., Joseph, S., McKenzie-McHarg, K., Slade, P., & Wijma, K. (2008). Post-traumatic stress disorder following childbirth: Current issues and recommendations for future research. *Journal of Psychosomatic Obstetrics and Gynecology, 29*(4), 240–250.

Baranyi, A., Leithgo, O., Kreiner, B., Tanzer, K., Ehrlich, G., Hofer, H., & Rothenhausler, H. (2010). Relationship between posttraumatic stress disorder, quality of life, social support, and affective and dissociative status in severely injured accident victims 12 months after trauma. *Psychosomatics, 15*(3), 237–247.

Barnes, S., Walter, K., & Chard, K. (2012). Does a history of mild traumatic brain injury increase suicide risk in veterans with PTSD? *Rehabilitation Psychology, 57*(1), 18–26.

Beck, C. T. (2004). Post-traumatic stress disorder due to childbirth. *Nursing Research, 53*(4), 216–224.

Beck, C. T., Gable, R. K., Sakala, C., & Declercq, E. R. (2011). Posttraumatic stress disorder in new mothers: Results from a two-stage U.S. national survey. *Birth, 38*(3), 216–227.

Beck, G., & Clapp, J. (2011). A different kind of comorbidity: Posttraumatic stress disorder and chronic pain. *Psychological Trauma Theory, Research, Practice, and Policy, 3*(2), 101–108.

Braden, A., Cuthbert, J., Brenner, L., Hawley, L., Morey, C., Newman, J., Staniszewski, K., & Harrison-Felix, C. (2012). Health and wellness characteristics of people with traumatic brain injury. *Brain Injury, 26*(11), 1315–1327.

Brain Trauma Foundation. (2015). *TBI statistics.* Retrieved from https://www.braintrauma.org/uploads/12/12/prognosis_guidelines.pdf

Brenner, L., Betthauser, L., Homaifar, B., Villarreal, E., Harwood, J., Jeri, E., Staves, P., & Huggins, J. (2011). Posttraumatic stress disorder, traumatic brain injury, and suicide attempt history among veterans receiving mental health services. *Suicide and Life-Threatening Behavior, 41,* 416–23.

Brown, L. F., Kroenke, K., Theobald, D. E., Wu, J., & Tu, W. (2010). The association of depression and anxiety with health-related quality of life in cancer patients with depression and/or pain. *Psycho-Oncology, 19,* 734–741.

Centers for Disease Control and Prevention. (2015a). *Injury prevention & control.* Retrieved from http://www.cdc.gov/injury/overview/index.html

Centers for Disease Control and Prevention. (2015b). *Severe maternal morbidity in the United States.* Retrieved from http://www.cdc.gov/reproductivehealth/MaternalInfantHealth/SevereMaternalMorbidity.html

Centers for Disease Control and Prevention. (2016a). *FastStats: Asthma.* Retrieved from http://www.cdc.gov/nchs/fastats/asthma.htm

Centers for Disease Control and Prevention. (2016b). *FastStats: Emergency department visits.* Retrieved from http://www.cdc.gov/nchs/fastats/emergency-department.htm

Chung, M., Allen, R., & Dennis, I. (2013). The impact of self-efficacy, alexithymia and multiple traumas on posttraumatic stress disorder and psychiatric co-morbidity following epileptic seizures: A moderated mediation analysis. *Psychiatry Research, 210,* 1033–1041.

Chung, M., Rudd, H., & Wall, N. (2012). Posttraumatic stress disorder following asthma attack (post-asthma attack PTSD) and psychiatric co-morbidity: The impact of alexithymia and coping. *Psychiatry Research, 197,* 246–252.

Chung, M., & Wall, N. (2012). Alexithymia and posttraumatic stress disorder following asthma attack. *Psychiatric Quarterly, 84,* 287–302.

Ciesla, J., & Roberts, J. (2001). Meta-analysis of the relationship between HIV infection and risk for depressive disorders. *American Journal of Psychiatry*, *158*(5), 725–730.

Clark, K., Loscalzo, M., Trask, P., Zabora, J., & Philip, E. (2010). Psychological distress in patients with pancreatic cancer—an understudied group. *Psycho-Oncology*, *19*, 1313–1320.

Claude, J., Hadjistavropoulos, H., & Friesen, L. (2014). Exploration of health anxiety among individuals with diabetes: Prevalence and implications. *Journal of Health Psychology*, *19*(2), 312–322.

Council on Patient Safety in Women's Health Care. (2015). *National Partnership for Maternal Safety.* Retrieved from http://www.safehealthcareforeverywoman .org/national-partnership.php

Czarnocka, J., & Slade, P. (2000). Prevalence and predictors of post-traumatic stress symptoms following childbirth. *British Journal of Clinical Psychology*, *39*(1), 35–51.

De Jongh, A., Olff, M., van Hoolwerff, H., Aartman, I., Broekman, B., Lindauer, R., & Boer, F. (2008). Anxiety and post-traumatic stress symptoms following wisdom tooth removal. *Behaviour Research and Therapy*, *46*, 1305–1310.

De Jongh, A., van der Burg, J., van Overmeir, M., Aartman, I., & van Zuuren, F. J. (2001). Trauma-related sequelae in individuals with a high level of dental anxiety. Does this interfere with treatment outcome? *Behaviour Research and Therapy*, *40*, 1017–1029.

Dirika, G., & Karancib, A. (2010). Psychological distress in rheumatoid arthritis patients: An evaluation within the conservation of resources theory. *Psychology and Health*, *25*(5), 617–632.

Edmondson, D. (2014). An enduring somatic threat model of posttraumatic stress disorder due to acute life-threatening medical events. *Social and Personality Psychology Compass*, *8*(3), 118–134.

Edmondson, D., Green, P., Ye, S., Halazun, H., & Davidson, K. (2014). Psychological stress and 30-day all-cause hospital readmission in acute coronary syndrome patients: An observational cohort study. *PLoS One*, *9*(3), e91477.

Edmondson, D., Horowitz, C., Goldfinger, J., Fei, K., & Kronish, I. (2013). Concerns about medications mediate the association of posttraumatic stress disorder with adherence to medication in stroke survivors. *British Journal of Health Psychology*, *18*, 799–813.

Edmondson, D., Richardson, S., Falzon, L., Davidson, K., Mills, M., & Neria, Y. (2012). Posttraumatic stress disorder prevalence and risk of recurrence in acute coronary syndrome patients: A meta-analytic review. *PLoS One*, *7*, e38915.

Edmondson, D., Richardson, S., Fausett, J., Falzon, L., Howard, V., & Kronish, I. (2013). Prevalence of PTSD in survivors of stroke and transient ischemic attack: A meta-analytic review. *PLoS One*, *8*(6), e66435. doi:10.1371/journal.pone.0066435

Ehlers, A., Mayou, R., & Bryant, B. (1998). Psychological predictors of chronic post-traumatic stress disorder after motor vehicle accidents. *Journal of Abnormal Psychology*, *107*(3), 508–519.

Elmir, R., Schmied, V., Jackson, D., & Wilkes, L. (2012). Between life and death: Women's experiences of coming close to death, and surviving a severe postpartum haemorrhage and emergency hysterectomy. *Midwifery*, *28*, 228–235.

Engelhard, I. M., van den Hout, M. A., & Arntz, A. (2001). Posttraumatic stress disorder after pregnancy loss. *General Hospital Psychiatry*, *23*(2), 62–66.

Evans, D., Charney, D., Lewis, L., Golden, R., Gorman, J., Krishnan, K., & Valvo, W. (2005). Mood disorders in the medically ill: Scientific review and recommendations. *Biological Psychiatry, 58*, 175–189.

Gavard, J., Lustman, P., & Clouse, R. (1993). Prevalence of depression in adults with diabetes. An epidemiological evaluation. *Diabetes Care, 16*, 1167–1178.

Goebel, S., Steinert, A., Vierheilig, C., & Faller, H. (2013). Correlation between depressive symptoms and perioperative pain: A prospective cohort study of patients undergoing orthopedic surgeries. *Clinical Journal of Pain, 29*(5), 392–399.

Hasan, S., Mamun, A., Clavarino, A., & Kairuz, T. (2015). Incidence and risk of depression associated with diabetes in adults: Evidence from longitudinal studies. *Community Mental Health Journal, 51*, 204–210.

Howsepian, A. A. (1998). Post-traumatic stress disorder following needle-stick contaminated with suspected HIV positive blood. *General Hospital Psychiatry, 20*(2), 123–124.

Hyphantis, T., Kotsis, K., Tsifetaki, N., Creed, F., Drosos, A., Carvalho, A., & Voulgari, P. (2013). Depressive and anxiety symptoms and illness perceptions associated with physical health-related quality of life in rheumatologic disorders. *Journal of Psychosomatic Research, 74*, 548.

Irish, L., Gabert-Quillen, C., Ciesla, J., Pacella, M., Sledjeski, E., & Delahanty, D. (2013). An examination of PTSD symptoms as a mediator of the relationship between trauma history characteristics and physical health following a motor vehicle accident. *Depression and Anxiety, 30*, 475–482.

Iseri, P., Ozten, E., & Aker, A. (2006). Posttraumatic stress disorder and major depressive disorder is common in parents of children with epilepsy. *Epilepsy and Behavior, 8*(1), 250–255.

Kean, E., Kelsay, K., Wamboldt, F., & Wamboldt, M. (2006). Posttraumatic stress in adolescents with asthma and their parents. *Journal of the American Academy of Child and Adolescent Psychiatry, 45*, 78–86.

Kelly, B., Raphael, B., Judd, F., Perdices, M., Kernutt, G., Burnett, P., … Burrows, G. (1998). Posttraumatic stress disorder in response to HIV infection. *General Hospital Psychiatry, 20*(6), 345–352.

Kronish, I., Edmondson, D., Yongmei, L., & Cohen, B. (2012). Post-traumatic stress disorder and medication adherence: Results from the Mind Your Heart Study. *Journal of Psychiatric Research, 46*, 1595–1599.

Leal, I., Engebretson, J., Cohen, L., Rodriguez, A., Wangyal, T., Lopez, G., & Chaoul, A. (2015). Experiences of paradox: A qualitative analysis of living with cancer using a framework approach. *Psycho-Oncology, 24*, 138–146.

Liddell, A., & Locker, D. (2000). Changes in levels of dental anxiety as a function of dental experience. *Behavior Modification, 24*(1), 57–68.

Martin, L., & Kagee, A. (2011). Lifetime and HIV-related PTSD among persons recently diagnosed with HIV. *AIDS Behavior, 15*, 125–131.

Mazurek, J., Knoeller, G., & Moorman, J. (2012). Effect of current depression on the association of work-related asthma with adverse asthma outcomes: A cross-sectional study using the Behavioral Risk Factor Surveillance System. *Journal of Affective Disorders, 136*, 1135–1142.

Menage, J. (1993). Post-traumatic stress disorder in women who have undergone obstetric and/or gynaecological procedures: A consecutive series of 30 cases of post-traumatic stress disorder. *Journal of Reproductive and Infant Psychology*, 11, 221–228.

Moeller-Bertram, T., Keltner, J., & Strigo, I. A. (2012). Pain and posttraumatic stress disorder—Review of clinical and experimental evidence. *Neuropharmacology*, 62, 586–597.

Morris, A., Yelin, E., Panopalis, P., Julian, L., & Katz, P. (2011). Long-term patterns of depression and associations with health and function in a panel study of rheumatoid arthritis. *Journal of Health Psychology*, 16(4), 667–677. doi:10.1177/1359105310386635

Myers, V., Boyer, B., Herbert, J., Barakat, L., & Scheiner, G. (2007). Fear of hypoglycemia and self-reported posttraumatic stress in adults with type I diabetes treated by intensive regimens. *Journal of Clinical Psychology in Medical Settings*, 14, 11–21. doi:10.1007/s10880-007-9051-1

Newman, J., Muntner, P., Shimbo, D., Davidson, K., Shaffer, J., & Edmondson, D. (2011). Post-traumatic stress disorder (PTSD) symptoms predict delay to hospital in patients with acute coronary syndrome. *PLoS One, 6*(11), e27640.

Nickinson, R., Board, T., & Kay, P. (2009). Post-operative anxiety and depression levels in orthopaedic surgery: A study of 56 patients undergoing hip or knee arthroplasty. *Journal of Evaluation in Clinical Practice*, 15, 307–310.

Norup, D., & Elklit, A. (2013). Post-traumatic stress disorder in partners of people with epilepsy. *Epilepsy & Behavior*, 27, 225–232.

Persoskie, A., Ferrer, R., & Klein, W. (2014). Association of cancer worry and perceived risk with doctor avoidance: An analysis of information avoidance in a nationally representative US sample. *Journal of Behavioral Medicine*, 37, 977–987.

Ricart, F., Cohen, M., Alfonso, C., Hoffman, R., Quiñones, N., Cohen, A., & Indyk, D. (2002). Understanding the psychodynamics of non-adherence to medical treatment in persons with HIV infection. *General Hospital Psychiatry*, 24, 176–180.

Rousset, C., Brulfert, C., Séjourné, N., Goutaudier, N., & Chabrol, H. (2011). Posttraumatic stress disorder and psychological distress following medical and surgical abortion. *Journal of Reproductive and Infant Psychology*, 29(5), 506–517.

Rovner, B. W., & Casten, R. J. (2002). Activity loss and depression in age-related macular degeneration. *American Journal of Geriatric Psychiatry*, 10(3), 305–310.

Schleifer, S. J., Macari-Hinson, M. M., Coyle, D. A., Slater, W. R., Kahn, M., Gorlin, R., & Zucker, H. D. (1989). The nature and course of depression following myocardial infarction. *Archives of Internal Medicine*, 149(8), 1785–1789.

Shelby, R., Golden-Kreutz, D., & Andersen, B. (2008). PTSD diagnoses, subsyndromal symptoms, and comorbidities contribute to impairments for breast cancer survivors. *Journal of Traumatic Stress*, 21(2), 165–172. doi:10.1002/jts.20316

Shemesh, E., Rudnick, A., Kaluski, E., Milovanov, O., Salah, A., Alon, D., … Cotter, G. (2001). A prospective study of posttraumatic stress symptoms and nonadherence in survivors of a myocardial infarction (MI). *General Hospital Psychiatry*, 23, 215–222.

Walker, J., Anstey, K., & Lord, S. (2006). Psychological distress and visual functioning in relation to vision-related disability in older individuals with cataracts. *British Journal of Health Psychology*, 11, 303–317.

Wijma, K., Soderquist, J., & Wijma, B. (1997). Posttraumatic stress disorder after childbirth: A cross sectional study. *Journal of Anxiety Disorders*, 11(6), 587–597.

World Health Organization. (2015). *Maternal mortality fact sheet*. Retrieved from http://www.who.int/mediacentre/factsheets/fs348/en

Ye, J., Shim, R., & Rust, G. (2012). Health care avoidance among people with serious psychological distress: Analyses of 2007 Health Information National Trends Survey. *Journal of Health Care for the Poor and Underserved, 23,* 1620–1629.

Yonas, M., Marsland, A., Emeremni, C., Moore, C., Holguin, F., & Wenzel, S. (2013). Depressive symptomatology, quality of life and disease control among individuals with well-characterized severe asthma. *Journal of Asthma, 50*(8), 884–890.

4 | MEDICAL TRAUMA FACTORS: MEDICAL STAFF

IN THIS CHAPTER, YOU WILL LEARN:

- *How characteristics of staff members' personalities, coping styles, and stress levels influence their ability to provide quality, patient-centered care and work effectively on interprofessional teams*

- *Beliefs about patient autonomy and patient-centered care that affect staff's approach to diagnosis and treatment in critical ways*

- *How emotional intelligence (EI) plays a role in staff members' willingness to address the psychological impacts of medical trauma and medical care, as well as their ability to use empathy effectively to preserve relationships with patients and staff*

- *That vicarious traumatization is an important phenomenon to consider within the landscape of medical trauma, and that some staff members are more vulnerable to experiencing traumatic stress as a result of patient crises*

- *How communication and staff members' behavior play a role in medical errors, and how valuing teamwork and integrating psychological health and patient context into the approach to conceptualization and treatment can help ensure patients get the highest quality care possible*

In Chapter 2, we began our exploration of the factors that contribute to medical trauma by examining risk factors that contribute to the development of serious psychological effects after a medical experience, including a history of trauma, history of current mental health issues, personality, coping strategies, lifestyle, support systems, existential issues, and resilience. Chapter 3 provides another piece of the medical trauma puzzle with its focus on many diagnoses and medical events that have a greater likelihood of being traumatic for patients. In Chapter 4, we revisit many of the personal factors we discussed in reference to the patient, yet now we focus on the medical staff and the role that their personal characteristics can play in the patient (and staff) experience of medical trauma. In addition to exploring characteristics of medical staff, we also examine significant staff behaviors that can lead to or exacerbate a medical trauma, namely, patient safety events and medical errors.

In order to simplify our discussion of medical staff characteristics, when we use the term "staff" we are referring to all health care professionals who work directly with patients to provide direct medical care (e.g., physicians, nurses, physician's assistants, nurse practitioners, medical assistants). We will indicate when we discuss research targeting a specific health care profession. Because our focus is on the interactions with health care professionals before, during, and after a medical trauma, we are not including mental health professionals at this point. We explore roles of mental health professionals in Part II of this book.

For now, let us begin with perhaps the most important aspect of the staff–patient relationship: communication, and how personal styles of interaction can affect the patient experience of receiving medical care.

STAFF COMMUNICATION STYLE

Communication styles are largely shaped by personality, the communication styles and interactions we observe, and the expectations and culture of the environments in which we interact. Perhaps just as important as these factors, though, are the needs of people with whom we communicate. In the medical setting, it is critical to consider the needs of our audience when communicating, and to be sensitive to the context of each interaction. This sensitivity is critical in cases of medical trauma, due in large part to the increased vulnerability of patients, family members, and other staff members. When you stop to think of the possible combinations of treatment scenarios, patient characteristics and responses, and staff communication styles, it is truly mind boggling. Just as it is important for staff to follow protocols in providing clinical care, it is also important to use sensitive, patient-centered communication *consistently*. This seems simple enough, although so many factors get in the way of staff members' ability to communicate in this manner. For example, think of the physician tasked with telling a patient of an unexpected cancer diagnosis. Certainly a brash, aloof, nonempathic way of doing so could have negative effects for the patient as he or she struggles to comprehend this new, potentially devastating information—yet a physician challenged daily by the expectation of using a sensitive communication style, or one who is temporarily impaired due to outside stressors, for example, may have difficulty adhering to this. In addition, many personal qualities, including EI, can affect the sensitivity of staff members' communication styles, and we explore these later in the chapter.

Earlier we explored how a person's coping style and life stressors can impact how they experience a medical trauma. These risk factors also apply to medical staff in their communication with one another and with patients. As much as we might try to compartmentalize daily stress (e.g., family relationships), it sometimes spills over into our work. Due to such stressors, we might find ourselves walking the hallways with a scowl, causing others to avoid us. We might lack awareness of how pressures from home are showing up at work, until we are prompted by colleagues' inquiries or feedback from patients or supervisors.

Beyond being affected by stress *outside* of the workplace, staff members are also vulnerable to the stress inherent in caring for patients. Vicarious traumatization is a common experience for providers and staff, and can have long-lasting emotional effects. Medical staff members often find themselves witness to the tragedies and crises of being human: After all, hospitals are ground zero for trauma care and for experiencing the most critical events of life and death. Additionally, sharing a life-changing diagnosis or participating in a critical intervention can also trigger strong feelings in staff and affect their ability to communicate sensitively as they strive to control their own emotions. These traumatic events can be damaging to staff in ways that negatively impact their relationships and ability to function to the best of their professional ability.

Within the medical setting, there are multiple pathways of communication: Interaction occurs between nurses, physicians, technicians, assistants, administrators, families, and patients. While all of these communication flows are important, we focus on staff–patient and team-based communication skills in our examination of communication relative to medical trauma. Research has shown that communication between the medical staff, namely physicians and nurses, and patients can have a direct effect on psychosocial outcome and symptom reduction (Neumann et al., 2011). This also holds true for other health care practitioners including mental health professionals. A positive therapeutic relationship must go beyond simply being outcome focused, such as reducing depression or increasing a patient's quality of life. The content (what is talked about) and the process (how the content is discussed) are critical in building the trust, safety, and empowerment patients find most helpful in their well-being (Duncan, Miller, Wampold, & Hubble, 2010). Let us take a closer look at the process of communication and how the quality of interactions affects the overall patient experience, especially in cases of medical trauma.

STAFF PERSONAL FACTORS

Personality

Personality and Career "Goodness of Fit"

The vast majority of those who enter the helping professions do so in part because of the compassion they feel toward their fellow human beings and because they are motivated by intrinsic values of care and concern. While these altruistic characteristics are part of the picture, financial gain and lifestyle factors are also motivating forces behind career choice, as well as personality characteristics of introversion/extraversion, interests, abilities, and experiences.

For example, consider Mariana, a high school student who did well in math and science, and who was caring and amiable in her interactions with others. For a class assignment she had to interview someone in the field of her interest, and she chose to interview her pediatrician because this physician was "always nice and patient and seemed to like her job." The high school student valued these characteristics and from the interview realized that she, too, might like to pursue a similar career path. She majored in pre-med in college, attended medical school, completed residency, and looked forward to a rewarding career in medicine. The "goodness of fit" described in this scenario is but one way a personality interacts with the environment. Sometimes, however, there might not be a best fit between a person and his or her chosen career: Too many times people choose careers because of the material wealth or status the job provides, only to discover that the best fit lies somewhere else.

Career satisfaction is influenced by the tasks a person performs, the people with whom the person interacts, and the settings in which the person works. Jane grew up in a small farming community and became a nurse initially because she enjoyed biology and chemistry. She also valued helping others, being part of a team, and having a career with job security, something her parents never had. Upon graduation from nursing school, Jane took a position as an RN in the emergency department at a large inner-city hospital. From the beginning, she felt differently about her job compared to how she felt during her internships in the small, rural town near her home. The hospital pace was overwhelming, as were the physical and intellectual demands that came with working with such critical cases. After a few months, Jane wanted out of nursing altogether. When asked if she liked the tasks nurses do, Jane quickly said she did. In fact, she considered nursing to be extremely meaningful work that she did well. Jane also liked her coworkers at the hospital. There was a shared interest in doing good work and friendships developed.

For Jane, the tasks and people were not the issue—it was the setting. The small, laid-back, isolated community from which she came contrasted sharply with the loud, frenetic atmosphere of the urban hospital environment. Back home, patients could talk with their nurses and doctors, developing relationships in ways that did not seem possible in her new environment. After much contemplation, Jane decided to leave the hospital, yet remain in nursing. She took a position in her hometown with an outpatient family doctor located in a small building with just three examination rooms. The new setting seemed to fit Jane's needs, and Jane was happy to have made the decision to change her work setting rather than leave the nursing profession. Finding the best fit between career choice and personal factors such as history, personality, and disposition certainly contributes to a meaningful existence. In Jane's case, she did not feel well suited to work in a setting and department that managed highly traumatic situations, perhaps several times during a single shift.

Optimism

In addition to goodness of fit between a staff member's personality and work setting, a person's level of optimism can significantly predict the sense of a meaningful life as found in a study of pediatric physicians and nurses (Taubman-Ben-Ari & Weintroub, 2008). Optimism might also be present among staff because of good coworker relationships, low stress, meaningful work, and goodness of fit. In other words, these factors are not mutually exclusive, so if there are deficits in any one (e.g., negative outlook, poor relationships or communication, high stress) then the patient experience can be negatively affected.

Perfectionism

Being part of the medical staff community can be uplifting and a daily reminder of a culture of healing and hope. Understanding this, many professionals tie their self-esteem to the outcome of their efforts. There are personality characteristics common in the health care setting that can present as disrespectful behavior and that are partly shaped by insecurity and anxiety (Leape et al., 2012). Environmental pressure to "get it right" and remain in control of everything from emotions to interventions to outcome can be daunting to say the least. Wondering if we "have what it takes" to be the best physician, nurse, and so forth that we aspire to be simply adds to the strain of an already stressful environment. It is common knowledge that health care professionals have invested much time and effort in their education and training—a process that required a high degree of self-discipline, perseverance, and competitiveness. When things go wrong in patient care, or one's caregiving competence is challenged, frustration can turn inward as depression or turn outward by blaming or disrespecting others. Lashing out in an angry tone or avoiding interaction are signals that tension exists and behavior is disruptive. Any professional's behavior that inhibits good teamwork and obstructs the team's ability to achieve good outcomes can be considered disruptive and consequently have a negative effect on patient care (Hickson & Pichert, 2010).

Medical Narcissism

Even though the focus is on the "other" within the health care field, far too often staff protect themselves from feelings of incompetence or a lack of control with self-involvement, a sense of superiority, perfectionism, and a misuse of authority. Such characteristics are what Banja (2005) terms "medical narcissism," which is more about narcissistic tendencies versus true, pathological narcissism. It is not a stretch to consider how this "medical narcissism" can affect a professional's ability to work well within an interprofessional team environment, which is predicated on one's ability to demonstrate mutual respect and shared responsibility.

For example, Michael was a highly successful vascular surgeon who prided himself on being one of the best in the county. He would rarely refer to colleagues or take a vacation for concern that other "inferior" surgery would take place. Michael was also very direct and abrasive in his interaction with other staff, believing that their sole function was to ensure that his efforts were without fault. His task-oriented approach to patient care, coupled with a narcissistic attitude developed over many years to mask his inadequacies, made for a difficult personality and strained relationships at work and in life. Michael's coworkers viewed him as being arrogant instead of confident, due in part to his tendency to verbally rebuke others if there were any hint of disagreement with his medical decisions. Staff described working in a culture of "walking on eggshells" and shared a reluctance to work with him. Patients also felt that consultations were one-sided and more about listening and accepting whatever Michael said than about being heard and understood: There was no discussion, no empathic reflection, and no interest in anything other than Michael's medical opinion. Patients reported feeling objectified and disrespected instead of cared for—the complete opposite of a patient-centered experience.

While it is normal to experience some self-doubt about the work that we do, it is how we handle these thoughts that matters, especially with regard to the quality of care we provide. When beginning a career in the helping professions (e.g., medicine, counseling, nursing, dentistry), new professionals can have a sense of doing meaningful work mixed with the stress of not feeling totally competent in their ability to be helpful (Beca, Browne, Repetto, Oritz, & Salas, 2007). Students who feel inadequate, whether justified or not, can quickly project their own insecurities onto patients in ways that present as indifference or frustration. It is interesting to note how the rationale for slow progress is oftentimes framed as "the patient is not amenable to treatment." When medical professionals can put ego aside in order to do what is best for patients, everyone wins.

Stress

Each person experiences life in a constant ebb and flow of stress. As we have noted before, stress, as with so many other human experiences, is subjective and interpreted differently by all. A busy emergency department or a chaotic life-or-death intervention in the ICU might energize you and be confirmation that you made the right career decision, or it could overwhelm you to the point of questioning your career choice and professional competence. How we manage stress can affect not only us, but also our environment, our working relationships, and our patients. Chang, Handcock, Johnson, Daly, and Jackson (2005) found that nurses exposed to high levels of occupational stress can develop self-doubt, irritability, depression, feelings of inadequacy, lowered self-esteem, sleep disorders, somatic disturbance, and burnout. In fact, stress has been identified as a significant risk factor for attrition (Evans & Kelly, 2004).

Stress is omnipresent in most health care settings, beginning with the process of becoming a health care professional. Attending medical or nursing school can be stressful with high expectations and the requirement to "keep it all together." One way such control is measured is through observation of student behaviors in the face of trauma, uncertainty, and challenge. In health care professions, students who can stay on task and remain clear thinking while working through the most difficult scenarios are considered competent and valued for their dependability, level headedness, and competence. In the professional setting, another mark of personal control is the extent to which one can manage emotions and cope with internal thoughts and reactions. Although some might view this as being professionally efficient or emotionally centered, there is the risk of disregarding and compartmentalizing emotions to the point of seeming aloof or insensitive with patients. In avoiding feelings such as fear, sadness, worry, or frustration within ourselves, we are less likely to address the same feelings within our patients. The consequence of this, unfortunately, is that an incomplete conversation occurs with patients who need health care professionals to fully embrace humanity—their own and their patients'.

Coping Style

The way in which medical staff members cope with medical traumas, everyday patient encounters, and conflict with other staff members can play a significant role in competence and quality of care. For some, these kinds of experiences lead to substantial stress and anxiety. In a study of student nurses, Humpel and Caputi (2001) noted how stress and anxiety can increase for those who cannot self-regulate emotions. However, those who learn to channel moods constructively and control emotions will in turn have a better chance of lowering the stress and anxiety related to their occupation. This could be said for most of us. What become important questions are: What is meant by *controlling* emotions, and how can professionals walk the important line of being able to maintain empathy and compassion while not becoming hijacked by their emotions?

Coping With Medical Errors

Stress and anxiety can become a vicious cycle within the health care setting. Professionals suffering from excessive stress can become impaired, leading to medical errors. As much as nurses and other health care practitioners try to ensure efficiency and successful outcomes, medical errors are numerous and contribute to more stress for staff and to medical trauma for the patient. Grober and Bohnen (2005) defined a medical error as "an act of omission or commission in planning or execution that contributes or could contribute to an unintended result" (p. 42). When medical errors occur they can take a high emotional toll on everyone involved. In a review of research related to this experience, Sirriyeh, Lawton, Gardner, and Armitage (2010) found that medical staff experienced major psychological and emotional distress immediately following a medical error. Guilt, shame, fear, shock, panic, and humiliation were common. A decrease in confidence was also prevalent in addition to changes in how the staff member viewed colleagues and patients. Because of this shift in perception, it was not uncommon for staff to lose positive feelings toward patients and withdraw from interaction. Depression and anxiety can quickly set in and carry over into life outside of the workplace. Consider Lydia, a community nurse practitioner in a third-generation family practice. A misdiagnosis several years earlier left a long-standing patient with advanced-stage cancer, which caused Lydia embarrassment and led to doubts about Lydia'a competence among her colleagues. Lydia could not seem to shake her constant thoughts of the misdiagnosis and questioned her own competence in not only her professional life, but with her family as well. She began shifting between lashing out in anger and withdrawing inward. Lydia's experience is not unlike most in that our life domains of career, relationships, leisure, and civic involvement are intertwined even though we sometimes try to keep them separate.

When we consider not only the medical error, but what a medical error represents, we can understand how it creates a major blow to one's identity as a competent health care provider. Good outcomes and medical errors give ongoing evidence that answer that constant question, "Do I have what it takes?" If the answer is "no" then our worth as a person, or in this case a health care provider, is at stake and we may feel shame, which can fuel our depression and isolation from others. This deep well of uneasy thoughts and feelings follows us home and can carry over into our relationships with others outside of work. Guilt, too, which is about what we have done or have not done, easily finds its place in our swirling emotions following a medical error. The ideology of infallibility and personal accountability, so prevalent in medical trainees, is the perfect foundation to keep guilt, shame, and self-doubt alive (Martinez & Lo, 2008; Mizrahi, 1984).

When we encounter conflict, most of us have a natural tendency to try to avoid it. A medical error creates conflict on an intra- and interpersonal level. How an error is handled can influence one's ability to cope and move forward in positive ways. While there are many reasons health care professionals may have concerns about reporting and discussing medical errors, two prominent fears include being sued and damaging relationships. In fact, Waterman et al. (2007) stated that 90% of physicians experienced insufficient support from colleagues following a medical error and that most colleagues seemed to not want to deal with it.

In an effort to better understand the views on medical errors, Blendon et al. (2002) conducted an extensive survey mailed to 1,332 physicians (831 respondents) and conducted telephone interviews with 1,207 adults deemed eligible to participate (from a pool of 1,803). The response rate for the physicians was 62% while the general public was 67% It is interesting to note that a $100 check was sent along with each survey to physicians as an incentive to participate and share their perceptions. No incentive, however, was given to the general public to participate, yet there was a higher response rate. This might be reflective of the medical community's expectations for incentives, the limited time available to complete a survey, or the speculated reluctance of physicians to share perspectives on such a delicate topic *without* such an incentive. The general public may have seen this as an opportunity to voice their opinion in ways that might have previously gone unnoticed.

Overall, however, the study found some interesting results. Physicians thought two very important causes for medical errors were understaffing of nurses in hospitals, and overwork, stress, and fatigue of health care professionals. The public's view was similar, yet they also considered limited time spent with patients, along with the staff members' failure to communicate as a team to be just as important. Regarding the reporting of medical errors, 86% of physicians surveyed thought that hospital reports of errors should remain confidential. Sixty-two percent of the public surveyed, however, said that error reports should be made public. This candid response of a need for error secrecy further underscores the general feeling by physicians that any error, whether accidental or avoidable, be kept quiet. In a separate study, nurses also reported how medical errors influenced what they thought about themselves, how they worked, and how they assumed a degree of personal responsibility in every episode of care. Nurses differed from physicians in their commitment to report medical errors regardless of an increased chance of being blamed (Crigger & Meek, 2007). Much of staff concern about medical errors is shaped by the culture in which care is provided.

Lack of institutional support and negative attitudes toward errors have long been the practice of the medical community (Sirriyeh et al., 2009), although in leading health care organizations this is beginning to change. When staff members receive support, however, they are better equipped to recognize, disclose, and resolve errors. According to Crigger and Meek (2007), when staff members discuss errors openly, they have better coping ability moving forward and they improve relationships with colleagues and patients. (We discuss strategies some health care organizations use to empower staff to better handle medical errors in Chapter 9.)

Beliefs About Patient Autonomy and Competence (Patient-Centeredness)

Patient-centeredness is considered one of the six main goals of a 21st-century health system as identified by the Institute of Medicine (IOM, 2010). To be patient-centered is to be empathic, compassionate, and responsive to each patient's unique needs, values, and preferences. This could be considered part of the *exposed* curriculum in medical training and should continue throughout one's career. The reality, however, is that an empathic approach to patients seems to decline in clinical practice when actual patients are being seen (Bellini & Shea, 2005). Stress, as we have noted, is a consistent part of medical training and often develops into distress, which is a main reason for a drop in empathy (Neumann et al., 2011). It also can contribute to increases in cynicism among medical students (Newton, Barber, Clardy, Cleveland, & O'Sullivan, 2008).

Because distress comes often and has a trigger or origin, we should pay attention to not only how it is managed, but also where it begins. West and Shanafelt (2007) reviewed parts of what might be considered the *hidden curriculum* in medical training. A tremendous work load requiring many hours with little time for sleep and relaxation, minimal social support from peers and infrequent contact with family, idealism about the profession challenged by the reality of patient suffering, and various forms of harassment and poor mentoring are some of health care professionals' experiences and somewhat expected in a medical (physician) training culture. One can readily see and understand how stress and anxiety are by-products of this hidden curriculum. When stress increases, the signal rate of mirror neurons drops significantly, reducing our ability to be compassionate toward others. You will recall that mirror neurons help us be empathic and "tune in" to the subtleties of communication with others (Bauer, 2005).

Empathy was also found to be a contributor to the specialty choice made by medical students as they neared the end of their medical school experience. In fact, students who chose patient-oriented specialties, such as primary care medicine, scored higher in empathy than students who selected patient-remote specialties such as surgery (Newton et al., 2000). Empathy levels, however, can diminish throughout one's medical or dental education because of the ongoing stress and challenges (Yarascavitch, Regehr, Hodges, & Haas, 2009).

Vicarious Traumatization

The helping professions, by design, are geared toward assisting persons in need. Sometimes the need is such that a patient's emotional experience is traumatic. Medical staff, mental health professionals, and others who witness either psychological or physical trauma can be affected in similarly challenging ways (Nimmo & Huggard, 2013). Boscarino, Figley, and Adams (2004) highlighted the term *vicarious trauma* as the undesirable outcomes experienced by health professionals resulting from direct work with traumatized patients. Secondary traumatic stress is a related concept and brings about a stress response that Huggard, Stamm, and Pearlman (2013) found to be motivated by fear for one's personal safety. Symptoms of vicarious trauma and secondary stress might present as absenteeism, poor efficiency in work activities, and even quitting the job (Darr & Johns, 2008). Continual exposure to difficult life stories can also tap the compassion reservoir of those who help. Clinically known as compassion fatigue (Figley, 1995), practitioners who experience it find that their ability to help and show compassion and empathy is diminished. They simply become tapped out. It is not difficult to imagine how secondary traumatic stress can impact health care providers, especially in cases of medical trauma when staff members are expected to be at their best in order to help patients. We take a closer look at programs to address vicarious trauma and compassion fatigue in Part II of this book.

There are many types of experiences that can contribute to the rise of compassion fatigue and burnout. Woolhouse, Brown, and Thind (2012) reported that witnessing and hearing about tragedy and death along with difficult patient behaviors (e.g., anger, threats, manipulation) can be especially burdensome for health care professionals. When you consider the goings-on in an average hospital or health care facility serving the needs of the community, there are ample opportunities for professionals to become traumatized or fatigued—leading to errors, depression, stress, and isolation. Furthermore, physicians who feel isolated from the mainstream medical community are at risk, especially if colleagues do not agree with or understand their specialization.

Unfortunately, many health care workers are not trained in trauma-informed care—either how to assess trauma or what to do about it (Kroenke, Spitzer, Williams, Monahan, & Lowe, 2007). In fact, primary care physicians have reported feeling unprepared and uneasy about discussing traumatic experiences with their patients (Green et al., 2015) despite trauma exposure and mental disorders being very common (Kroenke et al., 2007). Medical personnel who avoid addressing trauma, or using what we call "trauma talk," can inadvertently give the impression that an emotional response is unimportant or unrelated to the overall wellness of the patient. This in turn can influence a client's willingness to participate in their own preventive care, especially regarding mental health. Such was the case with Patrick, a patient who spent 6 weeks of painful recovery following neck vertebrae surgery. In the follow-up consultations with his physician, the focus seemed to always be about the physical healing and the associated pain. As important as this was for Patrick to know and understand, he also experienced multiple changes in his general abilities, which caused great distress. Left alone to self-manage what Patrick described as his "new normal" proved immensely more challenging than his physical recovery had been.

STAFF EMOTIONAL INTELLIGENCE

EI is an important psychological concept that is considered to be an asset in relationship building and in therapeutic outcomes. When people have high EI, they are aware of the various emotional states within themselves and others and understand emotions in context, being able to differentiate between emotional states in order to manage their emotions in useful ways (Salovey & Meyer, 1990). Suppose, for instance, you find yourself in a tension-filled conversation with a coworker about a disagreement regarding a patient plan of care. Awareness of your peer's frustration as well as your own prompts you to lower your voice, slow your pace, and reflect back to them what you are hearing from them. This interaction and self-awareness helps you and your colleague come to a mutually agreed upon course of action for the patient while preserving your working relationship.

In this example, you are using emotional skills that can be learned and fine-tuned with practice. McNaughton (2013) considers this to be one of the three discourses of emotions. Emotions are also universal in that everyone experiences them albeit in different ways. Likewise emotions are part of our biological makeup, which can affect certain pathological expressions for some people. We also cannot overlook the sociocultural influence of emotional experience and expression, and how our environment plays a role in our emotional communication. A home filled with high drama and passionate debate on things big and small will undoubtedly shape how family members learn (through observation and participation) ways to communicate in relationships. They may come to learn that the only way to be heard is through an emotional channel; anger, sadness, elation, or any other emotions are readily expressed. On the other hand, other family members may view this willing expression of emotion as too vulnerable and exhausting. They might learn to shut down and present a more flat affect while keeping their emotions and thoughts to themselves. Years later, we tend to draw on these same patterns when communicating in our personal and professional relationships.

Empathy

Embedded within the realm of EI is the feeling and expression of empathy. Being empathic is the hallmark of building relational trust and validation, and it demonstrates a cognitive awareness of and an emotional connection to another person (Chen & Giblin, 2014). It requires active listening and entails not only hearing or observing the patient's emotional state, but also reflecting that understanding back to the patient in ways that help the patient feel understood (Hojat, Vergare, Isenberg, Cohen, & Spanddorfer, 2015). Being empathic requires that we reflect the content of a patient's experience and, at a deeper level, the meaning of their experience. Consider the following interaction:

> Patient: "I hate not being able to go on long walks with my granddaughter anymore. It's been so difficult dealing with my hip injury."

> Medical Staff: "It sounds like spending time with your granddaughter is important to you and it's been disappointing that you've not been able to do activities you once loved. I can see how that would be difficult."

In this case, the medical staff member simply addressed the patient's statement using empathy, rather than attempting to minimize, fix, or provide false reassurance. Even though it might seem helpful to say something like, "Oh, you'll be back to those walks in no time!" or "Well, why don't you find something else to do with your granddaughter?"—these responses completely disregard the emotions being expressed by the patient. Sometimes, especially in cases of medical trauma, it is more important to validate and understand than to reassure, minimize, or solve. A conversation without empathy might be experienced by the patient as a devaluing of their thoughts and feelings.

Neumann et al. (2011) reported that being empathic had an influence on patients *and* physicians. When physicians used more empathy, patients were more willing to receive information about their diagnosis and reported more about their symptoms. In addition, patients were more satisfied with treatment and experienced a reduction of emotional stress and increase in quality of life. Physicians, in turn, increased their accuracy in diagnosing.

There are many concepts that relate to EI and empathy, such as clinical empathy (Halpern, 2001), relationship-centered care (Beach & Inui, 2006), emotional self-awareness (Decety & Lamm, 2006), emotional resilience (Wald, Davis, Reis, Monroe, & Borkan, 2009), and emotional equilibrium (Coulehan, 1995). Overall, however, they represent a common theme; that is, emotion represents a valuable part of individual and interpersonal well-being.

Unfortunately, the medical community, typically beginning with medical (physician) education, has historically been reluctant to delve too deeply into the realm of emotion. This has been the case for medical staff's own emotional experiences and for those of their patients (Shapiro, 2011). It is not that emotions are off the radar of the medical community; in fact, the Accreditation Council for Graduate Medical Education and the Association of American Medical Colleges highlight empathy as a valuable skill, a mark of professionalism, and something to be developed. This is also true of medical education in other countries such as Canada and Switzerland (Frank, 2005; Joint Commission of the Swiss Medical Schools, 2008).

Simply acknowledging the need, however, does not easily change the culture. Because medical caregivers are task oriented with a focus on the physical self, there is more of a cognitive and behavioral orientation to interventions and interactions with patients. Asking a patient about symptoms and then following up with recommendations, prescriptions, or procedures might seem to be the best way to "fix the problem." Unfortunately, this approach alone can often leave the patients' humanness behind with them feeling like they were "talked at" or "worked on." This runs counter to the kind of collaboration we advocate in patient-centered care.

Empathy is connecting with another person on a basic human level. It requires that the listener, in this case the medical professional, be aware of his or her own emotions and be comfortable in experiencing the emotions of others. If either part of the equation is missing, empathy is difficult to maintain. Physicians, for example, develop in a culture that can sometimes encourage emotional detachment. Studies have shown that physicians acknowledge emotions in their patients very minimally, if at all, and will often employ blocking behaviors such as changing the topic or breaking eye contact (Levinson, Gorawara-Bhat, & Lamb, 2000; Maguire, 1999). These "empathy escape" methods are designed to reduce the anxiety of the medical professional more so than to benefit the patient. Further, having positive feelings toward the patient is sometimes viewed as detrimental to the physician's ability to give difficult diagnoses or handle other difficult situations concerning the patient. In cases of medical trauma, this inability to get close to the patient can negatively impact physicians' or other health care professionals' ability to adequately assess the emotional reaction of patients and intervene accordingly. In essence, we do not see what we do not *want* to see.

Minimizing Emotion

Beyond a physician's unwillingness to connect with emotion, showing negative emotions (e.g., frustration and blame) can also be viewed as deeply unhelpful to the patient. As a result, physicians may draw back from time spent with the patient or spend less energy attempting to understand the patient's problems (Ahluwalia, Murray, Stevenson, Kerr, & Burns, 2010). If physicians and other health care professionals avoid both positive and negative emotions, then the only comfortable interaction is one with a cognitive and behavioral focus; this certainly can make for less complication in the short term for staff, but can have devastating consequences for patients in the long run.

In most medical training programs, students are indirectly encouraged to tolerate stress and minimize showing emotions (Angoff, 2001). It is much easier to focus on the task at hand when emotions are minimized. Seasoned medical professionals will often employ this approach as a way of dealing with the most difficult crises, becoming skilled at compartmentalizing their own emotions into a place just outside of awareness. In viewing this method of self-regulation, medical students learn to do the same, and can end up struggling with emotional distress and how to deal with it.

In the helping professions, power differentials can sometimes render collaborative, patient-centered care difficult to achieve. All too often, patients' reliance on medical professionals and the vulnerability within the treatment context can reinforce a superior–subordinate relationship despite efforts to maintain an egalitarian interaction. Seeing the patient as a problem to fix aligns with a "task oriented" approach to health care. A successful outcome in the operating room might be that the patient lived or that the source of cancer is removed, for example. These are but two criteria for success and reflect only the needs of the physical body; mental and emotional challenges, which may have been present prior to the surgery and/or develop in response to the medical experience, can have dramatic impacts on the patient's life for a long time to come. If professionals do not expand their lens to see and care for the whole patient, meaning to acknowledge the emotional experience as well as the physical illness or injury, the patient may suffer as a result.

TEAMWORK, PATIENT SAFETY, AND TRAINING

Health care professional training is a challenging mix of individual effort and teamwork. Having the ability to think critically, act independently when needed, and collaborate professionally are fundamental to good patient care. Working together requires skills in communication and a willingness to understand how each professional plays a vital role managing the physical, emotional/psychological, and environmental experiences of patients. Communication, as we have noted, is the key component of effective teamwork. When communication breaks down, the quality and safety of patient care suffers. According to the Joint Commission on Accreditation of Healthcare Organizations, communication error is the cause of 60% to 70% of preventable hospital errors (Murphy & Dunn, 2010). When stress and pressure rise, tempers shorten and disrespect appears (Leape et al., 2012). This is as true for the medical community as for the general population. *How* information is transmitted between practitioners is just as important as *what* information is shared. Leonard, Graham, and Bonacum (2004) noted how nurses are trained to describe clinical situations in very general and narrative ways, which sometimes makes the key points hard to determine. Physicians, however, learn to be very specific in their questions and value hearing key points rather than longer narrative. Without the freedom to make diagnoses themselves, nurses are often tasked with relaying information to the physician for final decisions on care. This dynamic creates a hierarchy within each physician–nurse interaction, creating the culture in which teams operate.

When deciding on a relationship style with patients, health care professionals have several options (Mosser & Begun, 2014). The *paternalistic* style is an assumed role of superiority or control over a patient's well-being without the patient necessarily being amenable. Using this more traditional style, health care professionals dispense advice and treatment interventions based on their interpretation of need with little collaboration or input from the patient. Sometimes, however, a patient is willing to relinquish all health care decisions to their providers, which would be considered *paternalism-by-permission*. Either style could be effective if all parties are in agreement as to the roles they play. If patients are not accepting of this style, then they may have unspoken and unmet expectations of their providers, as well as withhold important information that could be helpful for their care.

The *partnership* style seems closer to the ideal, as the patient and his or her health care provider both assume an active, transparent role in gathering and sharing information. Although there are variations to this kind of partnership, collaboration is paramount and is fostered as the provider learns about the patient's values and goals, and the patient approaches the relationship willing to share this information. Together they form a treatment plan, based on more than the diagnosed problem and direct intervention. Patients participate in their own well-being, which further supports their accountability and responsibility (Mosser & Begun, 2014). The partnership style is much more common in the health care system today, and is valued by both professionals and patients alike. This approach to patient-centered care is the backdrop to another important goal of every health care interaction: patient safety.

Patient Safety

Patient safety has long been a concern of the medical community, with massive national efforts by every major medical association, and is a primary goal of health care organizations. Patient safety events are considered to be harmful or potentially harmful to patients when the health care system either fails to follow accepted standards of care or because of the intrinsic risks of the health care interventions (Ricci-Cabello, Goncalves, Rojas-Garcia, & Valeras, 2015). Even though the quality of patient care has been a concern of many within health care, patient safety has been a bit more challenging to define and measure. In fact, the American Medical Association reported that in the ambulatory setting, there are still major gaps in not only our understanding of patient safety, but also in how to improve it (Lorincz et al., 2011). How to best gather reliable information from primary care physicians has been a problem, due in part to the underreporting of errors and patient consequences (Elder, Graham, Brandt, & Hickner, 2007). Gathering information from a patient's perspective regarding adverse events has been deemed as trustworthy, yet there remains a need to develop more comprehensive methods of assessment (Ricci-Cabello et al., 2015).

Preventable Adverse Events

A *preventable adverse event* (PAE) is a term that reflects the harmful and unexpected events experienced by a patient when in the care of a medical professional or health care system (James, 2013). Happenings that contribute to such events include methods of patient information collection and sharing among team members, high workload, and staffing shortages (Reid, Friedberg, Adams, McGlynn, & Mehrotra, 2010). There are several errors that are included in the definition of PAEs, with implications for the patients and the medical staff. *Errors of commission* result in patient harm because the wrong intervention was completed, or the right intervention was used but performed incorrectly (James, 2013). *Errors of omission* occur when an obvious intervention or action is necessary yet is not carried out for whatever reason. An example could be if a physician does not prescribe necessary medications or does not order required testing, resulting in a worsening of symptoms or delayed diagnosis (Weissman et al., 2008). Likewise, *diagnostic errors* can have a ripple effect in the type of treatment given, which might lead to errors of omission or commission (Welch, Schwartz, & Woloshin, 2011).

Another type of PAE involves *communication* between two or more professionals. The way information is passed between health care staff can either help the efficiency and timeliness of a coordinated treatment plan or create a fragmented approach wherein services overlap or gaps occur. Cook, Render, and Woods (2000) noted how care transitions (handoffs) can result in errors if there is a breakdown in communication. Errors during handoff have been well documented (Raduma-Tomas, Flin, Yule, & Williams, 2011) and as a result, standardized patient handoff procedures in hospitals exist and are part of the National Patient Safety Goals. Additionally, Gittell (2009) noted that communication between the medical professional and patient is especially critical in quality health care. Communication failures also directly affect surgical errors, which represent 40% to 45% of all in-hospital adverse events (deVries, Ramrattan, Smorenburg, Gouma, & Boermeester, 2008). Accidently leaving a sponge or gauze in a patient because of a miscommunicated count check is one such error. Another well-documented mishap occurs when surgery is performed on the wrong site of the patient because of miscommunication in how the site was recorded and then marked for surgery (Clarke, Johnston, & Finley, 2007). Communication is critical to providing quality health care, yet becomes a double-edged sword when information gets lost in translation.

Contextual errors constitute yet another type of PAE. Part of being a quality health care provider is to consider the patient in the context of his or her environment. For example, I (Scott) might see a patient who indicates experiencing depression. That diagnosis, and its symptoms, is only a small piece of the puzzle I need to explore for effective therapy. I need to know much more about that patient as a person and qualities of his or her life domains in order to be an effective helper. If you will recall, the word *diagnosis* means to know a patient through and through (*dia* is Greek for *passing through* and g*nosis* means *to know*; Merriam-Webster, 2015). The only way for me to achieve this "knowing through and through" is to explore beyond the patient's symptoms and diagnosis—so in effect, the term is a bit of a misnomer.

Suppose, for example, a new patient reports feeling "depressed" and is often sad, has low energy, little appetite, and is apathetic about most things. If I stop there and recommend the patient talk with her primary care physician for potential medication management I would most certainly be doing a disservice. Instead, I seek to know the context of the patient's symptoms. I quickly learn that my patient's best and only friend took a job in a city 5 hours away and that her own job was not going as expected, leaving little meaning and chance for advancement. The long hours she had to work left limited time for exercise or to prepare well-balanced meals. On top of that, the patient states that she has a strong aversion to taking depression medication. Knowing the context of my patient's depression gives me insight to connect the dots and better understand the relationship of her life domains and current state of despair. The symptoms of depression are there, true, yet by knowing the patient's context I am better able to intervene in ways that counterbalance the deficits in her life (e.g., diet, exercise, relationship development, meaningful work, and cognitive processing). If, however, I bypass the context I would potentially miss the most important interventions and at the same time reduce my patient to just symptoms versus her uniqueness as an individual.

The latter approach to diagnosis is what Norman (2009) refers to as pattern recognition without thoroughly gathering additional information. Likewise, Croskerry (2009) identifies this method of cognitive processing as System 1 (fast and intuitive) and System 2 (slow and analytical) with clinicians using one or the other or a combination when diagnosing. Diagnostic errors alone account for over 160,000 deaths in the United States each year (Sabertehrani et al., 2013) and are the largest type of medical error for emergency departments (Brown, McCarthy, Kelen, & Levy, 2010). Think for a moment about the various aspects of personality we discussed earlier and how they can influence how a clinician approaches the diagnostic process, communication with other staff, and willingness to consider a patient's unique context.

A last type of preventable medical error relates to medication intervention and is aptly named *adverse drug events* (ADEs). The IOM submits that there are approximately 1.5 million ADEs each year in the United States (Aspden, Wolcott, Bootman, & Cronenwett, 2006). Dosing errors are considered the most common resulting from mistakes in transcription, limited information about the patient or about the drug itself, and gaps in performance and judgment (Pham et al., 2012). In an effort to address medication safety, the IOM recommended prescriber actions and specific responsibilities to help avoid mistakes (Aspden et al., 2006). The prescribers identified were inpatient (nursing home/assisted living), outpatient (ambulatory care pharmacist), and hospital (hospital pharmacist). The recommendations appear to be comprehensive and relevant to the known gaps in medication safety issues.

There is a common thread connecting all of the medical errors discussed previously: They occur because of human error, and at some level suggest a breakdown of effective teamwork. As we have already suggested, a team is only as good as its members, and by extension, only as good as its members' willingness to collaborate and their skill in working effectively with others. Along with the problem of medical errors, there are shortfalls in comprehensive and integrated continuing education for both individuals and entire systems, which have greatly influenced the knowledge and performance deficits at both levels (IOM, 2010). Integrative health care is a popular buzzword that has yet to be *consistently* defined and systematically implemented. Too many patients are left to navigate a health care system that is often viewed as fragmented and disconnected. Some practitioners stay on top of best practices in their field and embrace the notion of being a lifelong learner while others may become complacent and comfortable with what they know and simply go through the motions of continuing education requirements just to stay licensed. A few years ago I (Scott) was impressed with the amount of years that a colleague in health care had been practicing. When I mentioned that over a 40-year career he must have seen thousands of patients, he replied, "There are some who treat thousands of patients and others who treat one patient thousands of times . . . treating everyone the same way simply because their diagnoses and symptoms might be similar." Getting to know patients beyond their diagnosis takes effort yet can go a long way in building the trust and understanding that good health care requires.

In an effort to understand how medical errors have a cascading effect and subsequently impact patient outcomes, Woolf, Kuzel, Dovey, and Phillips (2004) conducted a study of 75 anonymous error reports filed by 18 U.S. family physicians, which was part of a larger six-country study. Incidents were noted along with individual mistakes (errors) and how those errors caused additional errors (cascade). Personal or informational communication represented 80% of the errors that began the cascade effect. Consequences of these errors were then classified into physical injuries such as health complications during the reporting period, complication risks after the reporting period, and psychological or emotional injuries. The anonymous reports were evaluated for potential harm to the patient (harm that was not specified in the physicians' narratives). *Of particular interest to our discussion was that only 17% of the health consequences reported by physicians were related to psychological and emotional effects; however, in their own analysis investigators found that 69% of health consequences reported were related to emotional–psychological harm.* Physicians tended to report incidents and immediate physical consequences rather than speculate or even acknowledge the psychological impact of errors. The medical errors most readily identified, unfortunately, are surgical mistakes or medication/prescription blunders (Kohn, Corrigan, & Donaldson, 2000). This view is typically out of sync with how patients view errors. In fact, Kuzel et al. (2004) found that primary care patients overwhelmingly identified with psychological and emotional consequences of medical errors. Given the estimated 400,000 premature and preventable deaths that occur each year in the United States and that serious harm appears to occur 10 to 20 times more frequently than does harm leading to death (James, 2013), it makes sense that patient safety is a priority; however, given the many psychological impacts that can come with serious harm, it also makes sense that we put equal effort into developing and providing resources to help patients with the emotional effects as well. This can happen when health care and mental health professionals work together.

SUMMARY

In this chapter, we explored numerous factors that challenge the quality of care patients receive. Communication style is understood to be the pivotal bridge between staff members and with patients. *How* and *when* staff members communicate must be considered and practiced in ways that avoid the interpersonal pitfalls leading to medical errors, stressful environments, or patients feeling "worked on" instead of "worked with." Personal factors also play a unique role in staff–patient relationships and teamwork, and include personality, coping styles, EI, and styles of collaboration and teamwork. Regarding staff members' styles of managing stress, we learned about how external and work-related stress can influence professionals' thoughts, feelings, and behavior at work, and how vulnerabilities can lead to vicarious traumatization, an important problem we need to address. Lastly, we explored how breakdowns in communication, teamwork, and ongoing education and training influence medical errors and the overall quality of the patient experience.

REFERENCES

Ahluwalia, S., Murray, E., Stevenson, F., Kerr, C., & Burns, J. (2010). 'A heartbeat moment': Qualitative study of GP views of patients bringing health information from the internet to a consultation. *British Journal of General Practice, 60*, 88–94.

Angoff, N. R. (2001). A piece of my mind: Crying in the curriculum. *JAMA, 286*(9), 1017–1018.

Aspden, P., Wolcott, J., Bootman, J. L., & Cronenwett, L. R. (Eds.). (2006). *Preventing medication errors: Quality Chasm Series*. Institute of Medicine of the National Academies. Washington, DC: National Academies Press.

Banja, J. D. (2005). *Medical errors and medical narcissism*. Boston, MA: Jones & Bartlett.

Bauer, J. (2005). *Why I feel what you feel: Communication and the mystery of mirror neurons* [in German]. Hamburg, Germany: Hoffman und Campe.

Beach, M. C., & Inui, T. (2006). Relationship-centered care: A constructive reframing. *Journal of Internal Medicine, 21*(S1), S3–S8. doi:10.1111/j.1525-1497.2006.00302.x

Beca, I. J. P., Browne, L. F., Repetto, L. P., Ortiz, P. A., & Salas, A. C. (2007). Medical student–patient relationship: The students' perspective [in Spanish]. *Revista Médica de Chile, 135*(12), 1503–1509.

Bellini, L. M., & Shea, J. A. (2005). Mood change and empathy decline persist during three years of internal medicine training. *Academic Medicine, 80*, 164–167. Retrieved from http://journals.lww.com/academicmedicine/Fulltext/2005/02000/Mood_Change_and_Empathy_Decline_Persist_during.13.aspx

Blendon, R., DesRoches, C., Brodie, M., Benson, J., Rosen, A., Schneider, E., . . . Steffenson, A. (2002). Views of practicing physicians and the public on medical errors. *New England Journal of Medicine, 347*(24), 1933–1940. doi:10.1056/NEJMsa022151x

Boscarino, J. A., Figley, C. R., & Adams, R. E. (2004). Compassion fatigue following the September 11 terrorist attacks: A study of secondary trauma among New York City social workers. *International Journal of Emergency Mental Health, 6*(2), 57–66.

Brown, T. W., McCarthy, M. L., Kelen, G. D., & Levy, F. (2010). An epidemiologic study of closed emergency department malpractice claims in a national database of physician malpractice insurers. *Academic Emergency Medicine, 17*(5), 553–560. doi:10.1111/j.1553-2712.2010.00729

Chang, E. M., Hancock, K. M., Johnson, A., Daly, J., & Jackson, D. (2005). Role stress in nurses: Review of related factors and strategies for moving forward. *Nursing & Health Sciences*, 7(1), 57–65.

Chen, M., & Giblin, N. J. (2014). *Individual counseling skills and techniques* (2nd ed.). Denver, CO: Love Publishing Company.

Clarke, J. R., Johnston, J., & Finley, E. D. (2007). Getting surgery right. *Annals of Surgery*, 246(3), 395–403.

Crigger, N. J., & Meek, V. L. (2007). Toward a theory of self-reconciliation following mistakes in nursing practice. *Journal of Nursing Scholarship*, 39(2), 177–183.

Croskerry, P. (2009). A universal model of diagnostic reasoning. *Academic Medicine*, 84(8), 1022–1028.

Cook, R. I., Render, M., & Woods, D. D. (2000). Gaps in the continuity of care and progress on patient safety. *BMJ*, 320(7237), 791–794.

Coulehan, J. L. (1995). Tenderness and steadiness: Emotions in medical practice. *Literature and Medicine*, 14(2), 222–236.

Darr, W., & Johns, G. (2008). Work strain, health, and absenteeism: A meta-analysis. *Journal of Occupational Health Psychology*, 13(4), 293–318.

Decety, J., & Lamm, C. (2006). Human empathy through the lens of social neuroscience. *The Scientific World Journal*, 6, 1146–1163. doi:10.1100/tsw.2006.221

deVries, E. N., Ramrattan, M. A., Smorenburg, S. M., Gouma, D. J., & Boermeester, M. A. (2008). The incidence and nature of in-hospital adverse events: A systematic review. *Quality and Safety in Health Care*, 17(3), 216–223. doi:10.1136/qshc.2007.023622

Diagnosis. (2015). In *Merriam-Webster.com*. Retrieved from http://merriam-webster.com/dictionary/diagnosis

Doerty, E., Cronin, P., & Offiah, G. (2013). Emotional intelligence assessment in a graduate entry medical school curriculum. *BMC Medical Education*, 13, 38. Retrieved from http://www.biomedcentral.com/1472-6920/13/38

Duncan, B., Miller, S., Wampold, B., & Hubble, M. (2010). *The heart and soul of change: Delivering what works in therapy* (2nd ed.). Washington, DC: American Psychological Association.

Elder, N. C., Graham, D., Brandt, E., & Hickner, J. (2007). Barriers and motivators for making error reports from family medicine offices: A report from the American Academy of Family Physicians National Research Network (AAFPNRN). *Journal of the American Board of Family Medicine*, 20(2), 115–123.

Evans, W., & Kelly, B. (2004). Pre-registration diploma student nurse stress and coping measures. *Nurse Education Today*, 24(6), 473–482.

Figley, C. R. (1995). Compassion fatigue as secondary traumatic stress disorder: An overview. In C. R. Figley (Ed.). *Compassion fatigue: Coping with secondary traumatic stress disorder in those who treat the traumatized* (pp. 1–20). New York, NY: Brunner/Mazel.

Frank, J. R. (Ed.). (2005). *The CanMEDS Physician Competency Framework. Better standards. Better physicians. Better care*. Ottawa, ON: Royal College of Physicians and Surgeons of Canada.

Green, B., Saunders, P., Power, E., Dass-Brailsford, P., Schelbert, K., Giller, E., . . . Mete, M. (2015). Trauma-informed medical care: A CME communication training for primary care providers. *Family Medicine*, 47(1), 7–14.

Grober, E. D., & Bohnen, J. M. A. (2005). Defining medical error. *Canadian Journal of Surgery*, 48(1), 39–44.

Halpern, J. (2001). *From detached concern to empathy: Humanizing medical practice.* Oxford, UK: Oxford University Press.

Hickson, G., & Pichert, J. (2010). One step in promoting patient safety: Addressing disruptive behavior. *Physician Insurer, Fourth Quarter,* 40–43.

Hojat, M., Vergare, M., Isenberg, G., Cohen, M., & Spandorfer, J. (2015). Underlying construct of empathy, optimism, and burnout in medical students. *International Journal of Medical Education, 6,* 12–16. doi:10.5116/ijme.54c3.60cd

Huggard, P. K., Stamm, B. H., & Pearlman, L. A. (2013). Physician stress: Compassion satisfaction, compassion fatigue and vicarious traumatization. In C. R. Figley, P. K. Huggard, & C. Rees (Eds.), *First do no self-harm* (pp. 127–145). New York, NY: Oxford University Press.

Humpel, N., & Caputi, P. (2001). Exploring the relationship between work stress, years of experience and emotional competency using a sample of Australian mental health nurses. *Journal of Psychiatric and Mental Health Nursing, 8,* 399–403.

Institute of Medicine. (2010). *Redesigning continuing education in the health professions.* Washington, DC: National Academies Press.

James, J. (2013). A new, evidence-based estimate of patient harms associated with hospital care. *Journal of Patient Safety, 9*(3), 122–128.

Joint Commission of the Swiss Medical Schools. (2008). *Swiss catalogue of learning objectives for undergraduate medical training.* Retrieved from http://sclo .smifk.ch

Kohn, L. T., Corrigan, J. M., & Donaldson, M. S. (Eds.). (2000). *To err is human: Building a safer health system.* Institute of Medicine Committee on Quality of Health Care in America. Washington, DC: National Academies Press.

Kroenke, K., Spitzer, R. L., Williams, J. B., Monahan, P. O., & Lowe, B. (2007). Anxiety disorders in primary care: Prevalence, impairment, comorbidity, and detection. *Annals of Internal Medicine, 146*(5), 317–325. [PubMed: 17503105].

Kuzel, A. J., Woolf, S. H., Gilchrist, V. J., Engel, J. D., LaVeist, T. A., Vincent, C., & Frankel, R. M. (2004). Patient reports of preventable problems and harms in primary health care. *Annals of Family Medicine, 2*(4), 333–340.

Leape, L., Shore, M., Dienstag, D., Mayer, R., Edgman-Levitan, S., Meyer, G., & Healy, G. (2012). A culture of respect, part 1: The nature and causes of disrespectful behavior by physicians. *Academic Medicine, 87*(7), 1–8.

Leonard, M., Graham, S., & Bonacum, D. (2004). The human factor: The critical importance of effective teamwork and communication in providing safe care. *Quality and Safety in Health Care, 13*(Suppl. 1), i85–i90. doi:10.1136/qshc.2004.010033

Levinson, W., Gorawara-Bhat, R., & Lamb, J. A. (2000). A study of patient clues and physician responses in primary care and surgical settings. *JAMA, 284*(8), 1021–1027.

Lorincz, C. Y., Drazen, E., Sokol, P. E., Neerukonda, K. V., Metzger, J., Toepp, M. C., . . . Wynia, M. K. (2011). *Research in ambulatory patient safety 2000–2010: A 10-year review.* Chicago, IL: American Medical Association. Retrieved from http://www .ama-assn.org/go/patientsafety

Maguire, G. P. (1999). Breaking bad news: Explaining cancer diagnosis and prognosis. *Medical Journal of Australia, 171,* 288–289. Retrieved from http://www.mja.com .au/public/issues/171_6_200999/maguire/maguire.html

Martinez, W., & Lo, B. (2008). Medical students' experiences with medical errors: An analysis of medical student essays. *Medical Education, 42,* 733–741.

McNaughton, N. (2013). Discourse(s) of emotion within medical education: The ever-present absence. *Medical Education*, *47*(1), 71–79. doi:10.1111/j.1365-2923 .2012.04329.x

Mizrahi, T. (1984). Managing medical mistakes: Ideology, insularity, and accountability among internists-in-training. *Social Science & Medicine*, *19*(2), 135–146.

Mosser, G., & Begun, J. W. (2014). *Understanding teamwork in health care*. New York, NY: McGraw-Hill Education.

Murphy, J., & Dunn, W. (2010). Medical errors and poor communication. *Chest*, *138*(6), 1292–1293. doi:10.1378/chest.10-2263

Neumann, M., Bensing, J., Mercer, S. W., Ernstmann, N., Ommen, O., & Pfaff, H. (2009). Analyzing the "nature" and "specific effectiveness" of clinician empathy: A theoretical overview and contribution towards a theory-based research agenda. *Patient Education and Counseling*, *74*(3), 339–346.

Neumann, M., Edelhauser, F., Tausschel, D., Fischer, M., Wirtz, M., Woopen, C., . . . Scheffer, C. (2011). Empathy decline and its reasons: A systematic review of studies with medical students and residents. *Academic Medicine*, *86*(8), 996–1009.

Newton, B. W., Barber, L., Clardy, J., Cleveland, E., & O'Sullivan, P. (2008). Is there hardening of the heart during medical school? *Academic Medicine*, *83*(3), 244–249. Retrieved from http://journals.lww.com/academicmedicine/ Fulltext/2008/03000/Is_There_Hardening_of_the_Heart_During_Medical.6.aspx

Newton, B. W., Savidge, M. A., Barber, L., Cleveland, E., Clardy, J., Beeman, G., & Hart, T. (2000). Differences in medical students' empathy. *Academic Medicine*, *75*(12), 1215. Retrieved from http://journals.lww.com/academicmedicine/ Fulltext/2000/12000/Differences_in_Medical_Students_Empathy.20.aspx

Nimmo, A., & Huggard, P. (2013). A systematic review of the measurement of compassion fatigue, vicarious trauma, and secondary traumatic stress in physicians. *Australasian Journal of Disaster and Trauma Studies*, *2013*(1), 37–44. Retrieved from http://trauma .massey.ac.nz/issues/2013-1/AJDTS_2013-1_Nimmo.pdf

Norman, G. (2009). Dual processing and diagnostic errors. *Advances in Health Sciences Education: Theory and Practice*, *14*(Suppl. 1), 37–49.

Pham, J. C., Aswani, M., Rosen, M., Lee, H., Huddle, M., Weeks, K., & Pronovost, P. (2012). Reducing medical errors and adverse events. *Annual Review of Medicine*, *63*, 447–463. doi:10.1146/annurev-med-061410-121352

Por, J., Barriball, L., Fitzpatrick, J., & Roberts, J. (2011). Emotional intelligence: Its relationship to stress, coping, well-being and professional performance in nursing students. *Nurse Education Today*, *31*(8), 855–860.

Raduma-Tomas, M. A., Flin, R., Yule, S., & Williams, D. (2011). Doctors' handovers in hospitals: A literature review. *BMJ Quality & Safety*, *20*(2), 128–133. doi:10.1136/ bmjqs.2009.034389

Reason, J. T. (1990). *Human error*. New York, NY: Cambridge University Press.

Reid, R. O., Friedberg, M. W., Adams, J. L., McGlynn, E. A., & Mehrotra, A. (2010). Associations between physician characteristics and quality of care. *Archives of Internal Medicine*, *170*(16), 1442–1449. doi:10.1001/archinternmed.2010.307

Ricci-Cabello, I., Goncalves, D., Rojas-Garcia, A., & Valderas, J. (2015). Measuring experiences and outcomes of patient safety in primary care: A systematic review of available instruments. *Family Practice*, *32*(1), 106–119. doi:10.1093/fampra/ cmu052

Sabertehrani, A. S., Lee, H. W., Matthews, S. C., Shore, A., Makary, M. A., Pronovost, P. J., & Newman-Toker, D. E. (2013). 25-year summary of US malpractice claims for diagnostic errors 1986-2010: An analysis from the National Practitioner Data Bank. *BMJ Quality & Safety, 22*(8), 672–680. doi:10.1136/bmjqs-2012-001550

Salovey, P., & Mayer, J. (1990). Emotional intelligence. *Imagination, Cognition, and Personality, 9*(3), 185–211.

Shapiro, J. (2011). Does medical education promote professional alexithymia? A call for attending to the emotions of patients and self in medical training. *Academic Medicine, 86*(3), 326–332. doi:10.1097/ACM.0b013e3182088833

Sirriyeh, R., Lawton, R., Gardner, P., & Armitage, G. (2009). Coping with medical error: A systematic review of papers to assess the effects of involvement in medical errors on health care professionals' psychological well-being. *Quality and Safety in Health Care, 19*(e43), 1–8. doi:10.1136/qshc.2009.035253

Taubman-Ben-Ari, O., & Weintroub, A. (2008). Meaning in life and personal growth among pediatric physicians and nurses. *Death Studies, 32*(7), 621–645.

Wald, H., Davis, S., Reis, S., Monroe, A., & Borkan, J. (2009). Reflecting on reflections: Enhancement of medical education curriculum with structured field notes and guided feedback. *Academic Medicine, 84*(7), 830–837. doi:10.1097/ACM.0b013e3181a8592f

Waterman, A. D., Garbutt, J., Hazel, E., Dunagan, W. C., Levinson, W., Fraser, V., & Gallagher, T. (2007). The emotional impact of medical errors on practicing physicians in the United States and Canada. *The Joint Commission Journal on Quality and Patient Safety, 33*(8), 467–476.

Weissman, J. S., Schneider, E. C., Weingart, S. N., Epstein, A. M., David-Kasdan, J., Feibelmann, S., . . . Gatsonis, C. (2008). Comparing patient-reported hospital adverse events with medical record review: Do patients know something that hospitals do not? *Annals of Internal Medicine, 149*(2), 100–108.

Welch, H. G., Schwartz, L. M., & Woloshin, S. (2011). *Over-diagnosed: Making people sick in the pursuit of health.* Boston, MA: Beacon Press.

West, C. P., & Shanafelt, T. D. (2007). The influence of personal and environmental factors on professionalism in medical education. *BMC Medical Education, 7*(1), 1–9.

Woolf, S., Kuzel, A., Dovey, S., & Phillips, R. (2004). A string of mistakes: The importance of cascade analysis in describing, counting, and preventing medical errors. *Annals of Family Medicine, 2*(4), 317–326.

Woolhouse, S., Brown, J., & Thind, A. (2012). "Building through the grief": Vicarious trauma in a group of inner-city family physicians. *Journal of the American Board of Family Medicine, 25*(6), 840–846. Retrieved from http://jabfm.org

Working Group under a Mandate of the Joint Commission of the Swiss Medical Schools. (2008). *Swiss catalogue of learning objectives for undergraduate medical training.* Retrieved from http://sclo.smifk.ch

Yarascavitch, C., Regehr, G., Hodges, B., & Haas, D. A. (2009). Changes in dental student empathy during training. *Journal of Dental Education, 73*(4), 509–517.

5 | MEDICAL TRAUMA FACTORS: THE ENVIRONMENT

IN THIS CHAPTER, YOU WILL LEARN:

- *How factors within the medical treatment setting influence the patient experience of medical trauma*

- *The relationship between sensory memory, the hospital environment, and the experience of medical trauma*

- *Unique environmental characteristics of the emergency department (ED) and intensive care unit (ICU)*

- *How hospital contextual factors such as privacy, light, sound, temperature, and odors can contribute to patient distress*

So far we have explored many of the elements that contribute to the experience of medical trauma, recognizing the powerful effects of preexisting risk factors and the unique response of the patient, the communication style and treatment approach of medical staff, and the psychophysiological experience of specific illnesses and medical procedures. What is missing—and integral to our understanding of the medical trauma experience—is the context in which medical events occur. The unique treatment environments of medical traumas, whether emergency departments (EDs), intensive care units (ICUs), ambulatory treatment centers, or primary care offices, are not simply the backdrop for events to unfold; environmental elements play a key role in patients' psychological responses to medical care, sometimes directly contributing to the traumatic stress response and subsequent anxiety about future medical treatment.

In this chapter, we explore the myriad environmental factors of medical trauma, highlighting elements within the contexts of specific treatment environments. We begin by examining the setting that is ubiquitous in the experience of Level 3 Medical Traumas: the hospital.

THE HOSPITAL ENVIRONMENT AND MEDICAL TRAUMA

For many patients and their families, hospitals and medical centers are places to avoid, save for the birth of a baby. For some, these buildings, inanimate though they are, become keen representations of death, pain, illness, or injury—all human experiences we often try desperately to evade. Conversely, for patients who suffer a serious medical emergency, the hospital is the most appropriate setting giving them the best chances for survival. This dichotomy plays out for patients time and time again as they are challenged to cope with managing their emotions in a foreign context in which they struggle to maintain their own identity and sense of control—both of which can be monumental challenges in a medical emergency requiring treatment in the hospital setting.

Before we explore specific departments within the hospital and contextual factors present within this environment, it may be helpful to review key aspects of the trauma process and how sensory stimuli play a unique role in the traumatic stress response. As we know, trauma is a psychophysiological process in that a traumatic event is experienced with both the mind and the body. Whereas our initial response to trauma is the lightning-fast appraisal of threat, the cascade of physiological responses following that appraisal is largely governed by the autonomic nervous system, which sends our bodies into fight, flight, or freeze. In an event of acute stress, our bodies move to the vulnerable state of high alert in which our sensory acuity becomes razor sharp while our rational thought can be compromised due to reduced activity in the executive functioning areas of the brain, namely the prefrontal cortex. In this state, the sensory context in which the trauma unfolds can quickly become imprinted in our implicit memory system, prompting future fear associations to elements within the trauma environment, leading the body to respond as if the threat remained (Schelling, 2002). This is a basic mechanism for the reexperiencing symptoms of posttraumatic stress disorder (PTSD).

To further elucidate this process, let us take a closer look at trauma and sensory memory. In *The Body Remembers: The Psychophysiology of Trauma and Trauma Treatment*, Rothschild (2000) examines the relationship between sensory perception and memory in the context of trauma. The author describes the two sensory systems within the body, the *exteroceptive* and *interoceptive* sensory systems. The exteroceptive system consists of nerves that respond to the external environment by taking in sensory information through the five senses, while the interoceptive system, which can be further delineated into proprioception and vestibular sense, responds to stimuli *within* the body. Of particular interest in examining medical trauma is the exteroceptive sensory system as well as the internal sense of proprioception, or the perception of the body's internal sensations (e.g., heart rate, pain, muscle tension) and emotion. Both systems encode sensory information into our memory and, when a trauma occurs, these memories—along with their corresponding sensations and emotions— can be recalled and lead to psychophysiological arousal. Understood through these systems, we can see how all aspects of a medical trauma experience, from the sensations within the body to every detail within the physical environment, have the potential to emerge as triggers for traumatic memories and the traumatic stress response. Indeed, the body does remember.

Many factors contribute to determining *what* the body remembers, as well as what triggers the traumatic stress response in patients. The constellations of risk factors combined with the innumerable variables present in medical events can make predicting "traumatic" stimuli difficult. As we have already established, what can be considered a traumatic experience to one person may be entirely innocuous to another; however, by applying what we know about the brain under acute stress, we can begin to paint a picture of how specific environmental factors or stimuli can play a role in subsequent traumatic stress responses. Perhaps more important, we can establish that for some patients who do experience trauma as a result of a medical event, they can continue to be triggered or traumatized while remaining in the hospital setting. The sights, smells, and sounds of the hospital—along with internal sensations of the body—become the brush strokes of a trauma picture burned into memory. In a state of acute stress, the trauma picture is painted with wide brush strokes to account for all possible threats, including nonthreatening stimuli that happen to be present during the crisis. The amygdala becomes increasingly more sensitive when activated, and at the same time becomes less discerning in an attempt to protect from harm (van Marle, Hermans, Qin, & Fernández, 2009). This is critical for medical staff to remember: The body's response to trauma is not a rational process. Sometimes, even a patient's understanding of a doctor's or nurse's beneficent intent is overwhelmed by the body's response to fear and perceived threat, and the environment in which the threat occurs is integral to that experience.

Let us now take a closer look at specific departments within the hospital setting and how their unique characteristics play a role in patients' experience of medical trauma, beginning with the ED.

Emergency Department

According to the Centers for Disease Control and Prevention (CDC), 136 million people visit EDs of hospitals each year for treatment of severe injuries, medical crises (such as heart attacks and strokes), and psychiatric crises. Hospital trauma centers and EDs are often the first level of care for acute situations requiring immediate treatment to ensure survival. Patients often arrive by ambulance to the busiest department in the hospital, where they can quickly become overwhelmed by stimuli unfamiliar and unwelcome to them at a time of great vulnerability, both physically and psychologically. Through the lens of the diathesis–stress model, we can understand how the ED environment can exacerbate adverse psychological reactions, given its rapid, even frenetic pace at times. The ED could be considered the epitome of stress.

As you saw in Chapter 3, much research has been conducted to increase our understanding of the psychological impacts of specific medical crises, such as cardiovascular emergencies, accidents, and birth trauma; however, less is known about the effects of various stimuli and elements of the ED environment on the traumatic stress response in patients, requiring us to piece together such effects to get a clearer picture of environmental influences. One study sought to examine the psychological sequelae of the ED experience by focusing on the effects of crowding (Edmondson et al., 2014). In this study, researchers found a significant interaction between a high level of crowdedness, preexisting depression, and subsequent PTSD in patients with acute coronary syndrome, with women being more affected due to higher prevalence of preexisting depression. In their discussion of these effects, the authors conclude that some patients, especially those with risk factors, are more vulnerable to medical trauma due to their perceptions of medical emergencies as being stressful or threatening. Patients' perceptions, as we know, are highly influenced by the environment around them; further, patients' cognitions about and appraisal of their medical experience have a direct effect on their physiological reactions to stress, which in turn affects their unfolding psychological response.

Tachycardia, or elevated heart rate, is an indicator of the traumatic stress response and a sign that patients may be in psychological as well as physical distress. Research has demonstrated strong correlations between elevated vital signs such as tachycardia and blood pressure while in the ED and subsequent development of PTSD. Shalev et al. (1998) found a link between elevated heart rate at 1 week posttrauma and PTSD at 4 months posttrauma, while Bryant, Harvey, Guthrie, and Moulds (2000) found the same to be true at 6 months. Studies examining other physiological risk factors for PTSD, such as levels of stress hormones such as cortisol and adrenaline while in the ED, are also useful in expanding our understanding of potential indicators or vulnerabilities to developing PTSD following medical trauma. While we can assume that one's physical condition is a major stressor leading to such elevated vital signs, we also understand that environmental cues can heighten such responses, potentially exacerbating an already challenging situation.

Intensive Care Unit

When patients remain in critical or unstable condition due to illness, injuries, or complications from surgery, they are often transferred to the ICU (synonymous terms include critical care unit [CCU] and intensive treatment unit [ITU]). In the ICU, patients receive intensive monitoring and specialized treatment to save their lives and bring them to a condition stable enough to transfer to a lower level of care, typically still within the hospital. The experience of patients in the ICU, as well as the psychological responses common for longer stays (over 4 days), have been the focus of research for the last few decades. Research has uncovered the occurrence of depression and anxiety following ICU treatment (Jones, Griffiths, Macmillan, & Palmer, 1994), as well as an alarming incidence of PTSD, ranging from 15% (Koshy, Wilkinson, Harmsworth, & Waldmann, 1997) to 27.5% (Schelling et al., 1998). For a healthy percentage of patients who experience such serious psychological and emotional consequences as a result of time spent in the ICU, effects linger long after discharge from the hospital with approximately 45% struggling with anxiety and depression 3 months postdischarge (Wade et al., 2012) and roughly 30% struggling at 9 months postdischarge (Sukantarat, Williamson, & Brett, 2007). The high percentage of patients experiencing such intense psychological distress has prompted many researchers to explore what exactly about treatment in the ICU leads to PTSD, as studies have emerged that demonstrate the occurrence of psychological distress from the ICU that is independent of the traumatic injuries that led patients to that level of care in the first place (Hatch, McKetchnie, & Griffith, 2011).

The context of intensive care gives us clues as to possible causes of extreme psychological reactions (Skirrow, Jones, Griffiths, & Kaney, 2001). For patients, this can be a time of great vulnerability, as uncertainty about one's health and mortality looms large. Patients who are conscious and lucid can experience discomfort, fear, and even terror as a result of this uncertainty and in response to the powerlessness inherent in this level of care. The lack of control over many basic aspects of life, such as routine, diet, mobility, and even elimination, coupled with being cut off from the roles and functions of patients' normal daily lives, can leave people feeling decontextualized, uprooted—lost. In addition, the effects of pain killers and other medications, along with sleep disturbance and other physiological disruptions, can contribute to disorientation and even psychosis for some patients in the ICU (Curtis, 1998). Research has demonstrated the strongest risk factor for developing PTSD in the ICU to be the duration of sedation (Wade et al., 2012). In addition, inotropes and vasopressors are known to enhance emotional memories (Brewin, Dalgleish, & Joseph, 1996), and studies have shown benzodiazepines to be linked with depression following an ICU stay (Wade et al., 2012).

As we know from research, perceived or actual powerlessness can lead to powerful psychological responses, including PTSD, depression, and anxiety (Jones et al., 2007), and heavy use of strong medications, such as those listed previously, can certainly contribute to a patient feeling out of control.

The uncertainty, proximity to death or long-term physical disability, and decontextualization are in and of themselves significant stressors for some patients receiving treatment in the ICU. Yet, to get a fuller picture of the environmental impacts of the ICU experience, we need to look beyond such existential concerns to the contextual factors that can exacerbate distress and have the potential to trigger a traumatic stress response in patients. Research in torture and in cruel, inhuman, and degrading treatments (CIDTs) expand our insight into the psychological sequelae of intensive medical treatment, despite the fact that the motivations and spirit behind each could not be more diametrically opposed. Whereas the intent behind every intervention and process within the health care system is to heal and save, CIDT or "captivity stressors" include some of the same contextual elements as in an intensive care environment, as unsettling as this may seem.

Dr. Metin Başoğlu has examined the experiences of torture and the context of captivity within several populations of detainees and political prisoners to better understand the complex psychological responses of victims, as well as the factors which seem to provide some protection against long-term psychological distress. Başoğlu (2009) suggests that an act or series of acts can be defined as torture if the following four criteria are met:

A. Intent

B. Purpose (e.g., to extract information/confession or as an act of punishment or vengeance)

C. Exposures to often multiple, unpredictable, uncontrollable, and potentially traumatic stressors likely to induce intense distress in most people

D. Deliberate and systematic attempts to remove all forms of control from the person to maximize stressor impact and induce a state of total helplessness (p. 136)

It is obvious from the aforementioned criteria that medical treatment is *not* torture, for the intent of treatment is to heal, save, and protect, with the overall purpose being to help patients return to a greater level of health and well-being; however, criteria (C) and (D) deserve closer examination, especially given the subjectivity inherent in the experience of medical trauma. First, a medical crisis *for a patient* is inherently unpredictable, often uncontrollable, and has the potential to be traumatic and to trigger a traumatic stress response (criteria C). Treatment can require ongoing exposure to traumatic stress, especially during long stays in the ICU. In the intensive care environment, the by-product of treatment is often the removal of much of the personal control that people normally have over their everyday lives. While the motives for removing control could not be more different between torture and medical treatment, the end result is the same: People no longer have the basic freedom, independence, and abilities they are accustomed to having, which in some can cause elevated distress.

You might be wondering, if the motives for torture and medical treatment are so very different, why even address the topic in our discussion of the environment of medical trauma? First, it is important to remember that medical trauma is subjective, and that what may be considered a difficult, yet necessary medical intervention to one patient could be considered torture to another. Second, the work of Başoğlu (2009) demonstrates that more influential on the development of PTSD than physical torture is the environment in which torture takes place—in other words, captivity stressors within the environment. In Table 5.1, we have listed examples of captivity stressors from Başoğlu's analysis alongside environmental elements common in the ED, ICU, or more generally in the hospital environment. When we strip away the differences in intentionality and motivations, the contextual elements in each experience show striking similarities. For example, sensory discomforts, disruptions in basic needs, movement restrictions, physical pain and discomfort, and possibly a fear of losing one's life or health are present in both contexts and can be significant factors in the mental health status of patients in the hospital setting.

The impact of environmental stressors on a person's mental health is widely understood, and in the context of torture it is startling to see just how influential these factors can be. In the general hospital setting, which for many is a stark contrast to their normal environment, contextual elements can play a significant role in patients' overall experience and can contribute to medical trauma. To see how, let us examine some of the factors within the hospital environment and how they can influence mental health and contribute to the traumatic stress response.

Hospital Contextual Factors

Before we examine specific environmental factors commonly present in the hospital setting, it might be helpful to frame the discussion using the ecological lens in order to understand the interactions between patients and the medical context. According to the ecological model, people's thoughts, feelings, and behavior can best be understood within the context of their environment; further, when dysregulation, dysfunction, or distress occurs, it sometimes is triggered by environmental change. We experience this all of the time in very simple ways. For example, think of last time you visited

TABLE 5.1: A COMPARISON OF CIDT/CAPTIVITY STRESSORS AND HOSPITAL STRESSORS

Torture and CIDT/Captivity Stressors (Başoğlu, 2009)	ED/ICU/Hospital Stressors
Sexual torture • Rape, fondling of genitals	Treatment interventions involving genitalia and private body parts • Childbirth • Cancer surgeries and testing (colon, breast, ovarian/cervical/uterine)
Physical torture • Inflicting of intense physical pain using multiple methods	Treatment interventions involving • Pain • Extreme discomfort
Psychological manipulations • Explicit threats of harm for the purpose of inciting psychological distress	Psychological sequelae of medical intervention • Explicit or implicit threats to life and well-being due to severity of illness/injuries
Humiliating treatment • Purposeful humiliation in order to dehumanize and shame • Stripping naked, verbal abuse, excrement in food, on body	Vulnerability due to decontextualization • Unintentional embarrassment due to removal of clothing • Required to wear hospital gown, to give unfamiliar people access to body • Requiring assistance with private bodily functions (elimination)

Forced stress positions • Bondage • Forced standing • Restriction of movement	Movement restrictions due to illness/injury/treatment • Inability to move from bed • For women: stirrups during gynecological/obstetrical intervention • Connections to monitors, IVs, ventilators, and so forth
Sensory discomfort • Exposure to extreme hot/cold • Exposure to bright light • Exposure to loud music	Sensory discomfort • Exposure to uncomfortable temperatures • Exposure to fluorescent lighting • Exposure to unwanted sounds: monitors, hospital staff, TV • Exposure to tactile discomforts: IVs, needles, gown/bedding
Deprivation of basic needs • Isolation • Sleep deprivation • Water deprivation • Food deprivation • Hygiene deprivation • Denial of privacy	Disruption in basic needs and routine • Lack of normal schedule • Irregular sleep • Monitored liquid intake • Restricted diet (or food deprivation with upcoming surgery) • Lack of normal hygiene routine (e.g., bathing, appearance regimen) • Denial of privacy

a restaurant. If you have never visited this restaurant before, you may have quickly scanned the room to get a sense of the layout, lighting, seating choices, noise, and crowding. You may have spotted a table or set of tables that seemed to fit your criteria for pleasant seating. Depending on your level of assertiveness, you may have asked the host if you could sit at one of those pleasant-looking tables, because it just seemed perfect for you. In ecological terms, this table had *ecological concordance*, or good person–environment fit (Cook, 2012). We seek ecological concordance all of the time; just like every other living species, we are drawn to environments that have the most potential for us to thrive. In the restaurant example, if we sit where we are most comfortable, then it is likely that we perceive the food as tasting better, ourselves as more relaxed, and our overall experience as being more pleasant, at least from an environmental perspective.

Now think of the same example, but this time you do not get to sit at your preferred table. This time, your only choice is the table where you would least like to sit. Let us say the lighting is harsh, the table is situated in a high-traffic, high-noise area, and the seats are uncomfortable. You may find it very difficult to settle into the experience, becoming more irritable, quicker to react to other discomforts or disappointments, and perhaps even struggle to maintain positive conversation because you feel uneasy at this table. This is a simple example of *ecological discordance* or person–environment ill fit, and we experience this in both big and small ways throughout our lives. When we are at our best and the ecological discordance is temporary (e.g., the restaurant example), most of us bounce back rather quickly and can access coping strategies while having the experience; however, when we are at our most vulnerable—perhaps dealing with pain, uncertainty, and threat to life—it can be more difficult to cope with environments in which we do not feel comfortable. For most of us, the hospital is such an environment.

Beyond the stress that can come with being in an unfamiliar and discordant environment, factors within the environment such as lighting, sounds, odors, and other stimuli can either trigger or prolong a traumatic stress response. We know from research about PTSD and other serious mental health consequences of trauma that the stress response to contextual threats is very high, prompting us to consider the impacts of environmental factors on the psyche of the patient who has experienced medical trauma and who remains in the same setting in which the trauma occurred, potentially prompting a more chronic stress response. (Think back to our preceding discussion of sensory memory, and how the context and environmental factors of a trauma can become encoded, creating fear associations, and potentially triggering a traumatic stress response).

Interestingly, the effects of environmental factors on the well-being of patients have been of interest to nurses for well over a century, as evidenced by the great detail in which famed Founder of Nursing Florence

Nightingale wrote about them. In her *Notes on Nursing: What It Is, and What It Is Not*, Nightingale (1898) expounds on psychological implications of numerous nursing activities, and pays particular attention to the effect of environmental influences on health and emotional wellness. While many of her examples may be greatly outdated, the overall spirit of her words rings true today as a testament to the importance of patient-centeredness and to creating a healing context in which to treat patients. Nightingale seemed to recognize the effects of being confined to a bed in the hospital, and advocated that nurses do their best to connect patients to the outdoors. Research on animal stress in captivity echoes much of Nightingale's findings, suggesting that living things in general thrive best when in their natural, concordant environment (Morgan & Tromborg, 2006). We also know that human beings do best when we have the ability to regulate the sensory input from our environments, and when environmental stressors outside of our control exceed our ability to cope (such as in cases of medical trauma), we can experience severe psychological consequences (Baker, 1984). To better understand the influences of environmental factors on the traumatic stress response and on general well-being in the acute care setting, we review current research on environmental factors that can be found in the hospital environment, namely privacy, lighting, sound, temperature, and odors. We begin our exploration of contextual factors with a look at privacy, for without it patients have less control over all other aspects of their environment.

Privacy

Privacy is a universal need of patients throughout every level of the health care system, and medical providers and staff strive to protect patient privacy whenever possible. Beyond what the Health Insurance Portability and Accountability Act (HIPAA) requires regarding protecting patient information, efforts to protect personal privacy within the acute care setting can reduce patient stress at a time of great vulnerability. While hospitals and other health care settings can vary significantly with respect to environmental factors, such as design elements, lighting, and acoustics, the very nature of most medical experiences requires that patients compromise their privacy in order receive care. Despite staff's efforts to protect patient privacy, patients potentially compromise their privacy regarding the sharing of health care information, exposing their bodies to staff, being minimally covered in front of other patients or visitors, and possibly having limited control over the frequency and duration of interactions with others. While in the hospital, patients can have interactions with perhaps several new staff during an episode of care, as well as with fellow patients and family members, and they receive many medical interventions that require they expose their bodies, either in part or in full, to staff at various times throughout their treatment.

Think of the patient in the ICU at an academic medical center, where a doctor may be accompanied by a large group of medical students as he or she makes rounds—this is one all-too-common example of strains on patients' privacy. Additionally, depending on the flow of pedestrian traffic throughout the hospital, patients may encounter other patients, visitors, and staff as they are transported for testing and other interventions. In sum, the hospital is a place where, despite efforts to protect privacy, the nature of the work requires a certain level of vulnerability from patients.

Vulnerability is an important factor to consider when examining the effects of limited privacy on the stress level of patients, especially for those who experience medical trauma; patients under acute stress due to their health circumstances may exhaust their ability to cope with the additional stress of feeling vulnerable. In a phenomenological study examining the experiences of hospitalized antepartum patients, participants labeled lack of privacy a "major stressor," especially for those staying in multioccupancy rooms (Richter, Parkes, & Chaw-Kant, 2007). The desire for the privacy afforded by single-occupancy rooms was echoed in an earlier study by Pease and Finley (2002), and this and other research has prompted a new industry standard in the construction of new hospitals: the single room. Single-occupancy rooms, in addition to being the preference of patients, are also lauded by nurses as being more conducive for patient examinations and communication, family and staff interaction, patient ambulation, medication management, and more patient control of environmental factors such as lighting, noise, and temperature (Chaudhury, Mahmood, & Valente, 2006). Another benefit of single-occupancy rooms, from the patients' perspective, is the ability to have agency over their surroundings and to minimize distractions (Persson, Anderberg, & Ekwall, 2014). This is an important point to consider as we explore additional sensory factors within the environment and their effects on patient stress, beginning with light.

Light

The effect of lighting on people's emotional states and stress levels has been the subject of much research, especially related to depression, seasonal affective disorder, stress, and concentration. From a design perspective, lighting is a critical element that adds or detracts from the functionality of a space. In the hospital and other health care settings, lighting can be tricky because it must be sufficient for medical staff to perform their duties effectively while at the same time it should not exacerbate patient stress or impair sleep. While it has been long established that natural sunlight is the most health promoting for all living things, we must adapt to artificial light while indoors; for those who spend a significant number of days confined to a hospital room, a lack of natural light can be a contributing factor in both physical and emotional well-being.

Just as light can promote health and well-being, it can contribute to increased stress, psychological arousal, and impaired sleep. Basso (2001) studied the differences in arousal levels under several lighting conditions (dim and bright levels for both cool-white fluorescent and full-spectrum lighting) and found that higher arousal levels were detected under the cool-white fluorescent conditions (both dim and bright), as well as the dim condition for full-spectrum lighting. The study validated earlier research that demonstrated fluorescent lighting to be more stressful than lighting that more closely approximates natural light. Beyond the type of lighting used, the maintenance of lights is also important in order to avoid the heightened arousal of the central nervous system caused by the flicker of fluorescent lighting (Küller & Laike, 1998). For patients who experience medical trauma in the hospital setting, the lighting environment can play a critical role in mediating stress and psychophysiological arousal.

Another important consideration regarding light, especially with respect to caring for critically ill patients, is how its use can affect sleep quality. Hu, Jiang, Zeng, Chen, and Zhang (2010) found healthy subjects to have poorer sleep in a simulated ICU environment, while studies examining the sleep quality of actual ICU patients found the same to be true (Le et al., 2012). One contributing factor of poor sleep quality in the ICU is the frequency of nocturnal nursing interactions, which are often necessary to administer care to the patient but require light in order to do so. Elevated light levels have also been found in the pediatric ICU (Linder & Christian, 2011), which can also lead to sleep disturbances and increased arousal levels, especially at night.

The frequency, duration, and strength of artificial light used in the hospital setting is a balancing act, for light is certainly needed for staff to perform their jobs effectively. In one study of nurses' perceptions of environmental factors that contribute to medication errors, poor lighting was cited as one cause (Mahmood, Chaudhury, & Valente, 2011).

The soundscape of the care environment is another important factor affecting patients' quality of sleep and arousal levels, in addition to how patients respond to the sounds and noises they encounter while hospitalized.

Sound

The relationship between sound and trauma has been well studied (Metzger, 1999). The exaggerated startle response, or heightened involuntary reactions to stimuli such as sound and sudden movements, is a hallmark symptom of PTSD. While this exaggerated response (hypervigilance) can be expected immediately following a trauma, research has also shown it to be a predictor of subsequent PTSD if it is present after a threat has passed (Pole et al., 2009). For many patients who experience medical trauma in the hospital setting, their continued stay in the hospital can prolong the fear response, creating vulnerability to stressors present within that environment. Imagine for a moment a patient who experiences a heart attack while in the ED. The flurry of activity occurring around him, the sounds emanating from equipment, conversations, doors, curtains, footsteps—these stimuli become the backdrop of an unfolding trauma occurring simultaneously with the patient's realization that his life could possibly end. If the patient survives, he will likely be transferred to another department within the hospital. While his condition may have stabilized, the environment that he continues to inhabit includes many of the same stimuli present when life seemed to dangle from a precipice.

There are many sources of sound within the hospital, with numerous variables to consider when assessing the overall influence of sound on the mental health status of patients who experience medical trauma. Considering the diathesis–stress model, we are reminded that some patients can be predisposed to having greater sensitivity to sounds and other stimuli, such as overcrowding. What some patients might perceive as grating noise, others might block completely from awareness. Additionally, environmental factors that some patients might experience as completely nonthreatening, others may process as signs of contextual threat, leading to a constant state of hypervigilance. Patients who experience medical trauma may have trouble filtering sensory stimuli given what we know about PTSD and the impaired ability to inhibit responses to stimuli in the environment (Stewart & White, 2008). Thus, the beeping from a bedside monitor might be easily tuned out by a nurse, but to a patient it might be a harsh and powerful reminder of a recent medical trauma.

Studies of sound within the hospital setting often focus more precisely on the presence and effects of a particular kind of sound—*noise*. Noise is considered any sound that is undesirable, or that interferes with chosen tasks or conversation. Ortiga et al. (2013) studied noise levels and sources within an ED in order to determine if and how often the levels exceeded guidelines from the World Health Organization (WHO; Berglund, Lindvall, & Schwela, 1999). The researchers found that most noise originated from conversations, administrative functions, medical equipment (such as beeping monitors and ventilators), and other sources (such as TVs and bathrooms), and that levels exceeded guidelines from the WHO, which stipulate that background noise in hospital rooms should not exceed 35 decibels during the day and 30 decibels at night, while hospital ward peak levels at night should not exceed 40 decibels. Similar studies of both adult and pediatric acute care settings have shown similar results (Linder & Christian, 2011). The fact that the WHO has guidelines for noise levels within the hospital setting suggests the importance of controlling this stimulus for the protection of patients. Florence Nightingale thought noise such a negative factor that she asserted it "will do a patient more harm than all the medicines in the world do him good" (1898).

Excessive noise can have many effects for patients and staff alike, leading to "alarm fatigue" (Appold, 2015). Baker (1984) studied several environmental factors within the ICU and how such factors influenced the psychological responses of patients. In her analysis of noise, she found four primary factors that influenced a patient's annoyance or arousal level in response to the stimulus: (a) whether the source of the noise directly impacted his or her care and well-being, (b) whether the people creating the noise seemed to care about the patient's well-being, (c) if the patient has a certain set of beliefs or expectations about how noisy or quiet hospitals *should* be, and (d) whether the person perceives himself or herself having any control over the noise. The author also found that annoyance or stress level tends to increase, rather than decrease, with prolonged exposure to noise, which in the case of medical trauma and lengthy hospital stays is a concern for the development of a more chronic traumatic stress response. Additional empirical research has demonstrated that excessive noise can exacerbate stress and anxiety and lengthen recovery time (Baker, Garvin, Kennedy, & Polivka, 1993).

Patients have demonstrated a clear preference for having the ability to manage as much of their environmental surroundings as possible while in the hospital and having control over noise level is no exception (Chaudhury et al., 2006). Nurses have reiterated a need for reduced noise as well, for noisy nursing stations have been cited as a distraction that has led to medication errors (Mahmood et al., 2011). The Joint Commission on Accreditation of Healthcare Organizations names noise as an important risk factor for medical and nursing errors, citing the stimulus as impeding effective communication. Hospitals continue to struggle with the issue and strive to find strategies to reduce noise given its direct ties to patient safety (Mazer, 2006). Considering what we know about the effects of noise on the stress level, sleep quality, and psychophysiology of patients—especially for those with heightened sensitivity due to medical trauma—we understand *patient safety* to include psychological well-being as well as survival and physical recovery.

Temperature

Even when we are at our best, extreme temperatures are a source of stress, and many people will go to great lengths and expense to maintain an indoor temperature that is comfortable to them, regardless of the air temperature outside. For patients in the hospital setting, there are a number of variables that impact body temperature and comfort level. Medical staff work to ensure that patients are as comfortable as possible with respect to temperature, for a patient who is too cold or too hot can experience physiological effects that can complicate recovery; further, thermal discomfort can lead to psychological distress, which can exacerbate a traumatic stress response. Still further, when a patient experiences trauma, the body's thermoregulatory system can become affected, which can lead to an inability to maintain core body temperature—an important consideration when attempting to regulate the ambient temperature in the room of a patient who has been traumatized.

As with light and sound, temperature becomes a balancing act, for hospitals must adhere to quality standards with regard to temperature in order to control infection—and these temperatures can be uncomfortable to some patients. The CDC recommend that areas of the hospital with the highest possibility of infection (and most severe consequences if infection occurs, such as operating rooms) be kept between 68°F and 73°F, while patient rooms can be kept slightly warmer at 75°F. Humidity can hover between 30% and 60%, which is considered a comfortable range for most.

While there have been numerous studies examining the effects of light and sound on the well-being of patients in the hospital setting, less is known about the impact of temperature; however, given that temperature is not directly tied to the variation in human activity as is light and sound, it is likely that temperature can be more easily regulated. One important effect of temperature is its influence on sleep quality. In their study of the nighttime bedside care environment in a pediatric ICU, Linder and Christian (2011) found the temperature in patients' rooms varied minimally, though the average temperature did reach near the upper limit of what is considered most conducive to sleep (i.e., 75°F).

Odors

Like all of the other sensory factors we have discussed, odors or scents can influence people's emotional states and overall experience. While little research exists examining these effects empirically, our understanding of human nature and personal experience gives us clues as to the influence of displeasing odors on patients' mood and level of stress. Beyond the effects of olfactory stimuli on present mood, odors can be a powerful trigger for traumatic memories if they become encoded into the trauma picture (Rothschild, 2000). For patients who experience medical trauma and remain in the hospital following the medical crisis, ambient scents that were present during the event and are part of the hospital environment can be a potent psychological trigger throughout the rest of their hospital stay. For example, when I (Michelle) entered the hospital to have my daughter, I brought with me some items I felt would help me relax: a plug-in citrus air freshener and a CD of one of my then-favorite musical artists, Enya. A few hours into my induced labor, my daughter's heart rate began to dangerously decelerate, and after that I experienced a placental abruption and profuse bleeding. After my emergency C-section, I was taken to recovery where I continued to hemorrhage for the next 6 hours, prompting painful interventions and significant psychological trauma. Throughout my labor, the smell of citrus wafted through the air as Enya played quietly in the background. After I had my daughter and experienced the hemorrhage, the nurses brought the air freshener to my new location thinking it would help me relax. To this day, the smell of citrus or beautiful sounds of Enya send my heart rate skyrocketing.

Regardless of whether a scent becomes part of a patient's sensory experience of trauma, the presence of offensive or harsh odors can be off-putting at best, and many hospitals explore ways of masking such odors (Dunn, Sleep, & Collett, 1995). Interventions involving aromatherapy show promising emotional effects, as evidenced by studies examining dental patient responses to orange and lavender scents in the waiting room (Lehrner, Eckersberger, Walla, Pötsch, & Deecke, 2000; Lehrner, Manwinski, Lehr, Johren, & Deecke, 2005). In both studies, patient anxiety levels decreased and mood improved as a result of the olfactory intervention. It makes sense that people respond positively to neutral, fresh, or pleasing scents they do not readily associate with anxiety-provoking places like hospitals. In a study of patient recommendations for designing an ideal ED, patients insisted that the space not smell like a typical hospital, which can smell of cleaners, antiseptics, food, and bodily fluids (see "Planning a Brand New ED?" 2012). Even Florence Nightingale spoke of the importance of ventilation to guard against foul air!

THE SENSORY EXPERIENCE AND LEVELS 1 AND 2 MEDICAL TRAUMAS

When patients experience a traumatic medical event such as a heart attack, stroke, or obstetrical trauma that requires a lengthy stay in the hospital, they are at risk of experiencing psychological distress that can lead to depression, anxiety, and even PTSD. As we have learned, any aspects of their trauma can become burned into memory as part of the trauma experience—and this includes aspects of the medical environment. Patients who survive Level 3 Medical Traumas and return back to their lives are sometimes permanently changed as a result of such a terrifying crisis. For some patients, coping with the trauma means avoiding any reminders (triggers) of the traumatic event, and sadly this can mean avoiding the medical setting altogether.

For those patients who do not avoid the medical setting and who continue to seek the treatment necessary to maintain their physical health, they may find it challenging to spend time in primary care offices, testing centers, and other health care facilities. An encounter with any of the contextual factors we discussed earlier could trigger the previous medical trauma, prompting a tidal wave of psychophysiological responses. In Part II of this book, we explore further how to better assess for these responses and how interprofessional teams of medical and mental health professionals can help patients at every level of the medical trauma continuum.

SUMMARY

In this chapter, we examined the environmental factors that can contribute to the experience of medical trauma by increasing patients' distress, impairing their sleep, and by becoming part of the trauma picture encoded in patient memory. We explored the areas of the hospital most associated with medical trauma—the ED and ICU—as well as the many factors that create the sensory experience of the hospital. Stimuli such as light, sound, and odors can be distressing to patients, and can become powerful reminders of a traumatic event. From research on trauma and torture, we know that stressors present in the physical environment can play a powerful role in experiences involving pain and fear, and in subsequent psychological distress that can develop as a result.

REFERENCES

Appold, K. (2015). Noise complaint: Hospitalists are in a key position to champion efforts to address alarm fatigue. *The Hospitalist, 16*(6), 1, 20–22.

Baker, C. (1984). Sensory overload in the ICU. *Critical Care Quarterly, 6*(4), 66–80.

Baker, C., Garvin, B., Kennedy, C., & Polivka, B. (1993). The effect of environmental sound and communication of CCU patients' heart rate and blood pressure. *Research in Nursing and Health, 26*, 415–421.

Başoğlu, M. (2009). A multivariate contextual analysis of torture and cruel, inhuman, and degrading treatments: Implications for an evidence-based definition of torture. *American Journal of Orthopsychiatry, 79*(2), 135–145.

Basso, M. R. (2001). Neurobiological relationships between ambient lighting and the startle response to acoustic stress in humans. *International Journal of Neuroscience, 110*, 147–157.

Berglund, B., Lindvall, T., & Schwela, D. (1999). *Guidelines for community noise* (pp. 55–65). Geneva, Switzerland: World Health Organization.

Brewin, C. R., Dalgleish, T., & Joseph, S. (1996). A dual representation theory of posttraumatic stress disorder. *Psychology Review, 103*, 670–686.

Bryant, R. A., Harvey, A. G., Guthrie, R. M., & Moulds, M. L. (2000). A prospective study of psychophysiological arousal, acute stress disorder, and posttraumatic stress disorder. *Journal of Abnormal Psychology, 109*, 341–344. doi:10.1037/0021-843X.109.2.341

Chaudhury, H., Mahmood, A., & Valente, M. (2006). Nurses' perception of single-occupancy versus multioccupancy rooms in acute care environments: An exploratory comparative assessment. *Applied Nursing Research, 19*, 118–125.

Cook, E. P. (2012). *Understanding people in context: The ecological perspective in counseling.* Alexandria, VA: American Counseling Association Press.

Curtis, T. (1998). Climbing the walls. ICU psychosis: Myth or reality? *Nursing in Critical Care, 4*(1), 18–21.

Dunn, C., Sleep, J., & Collett, D. (1995). Sensing an improvement: An experimental study to evaluate the use of aromatherapy, massage and periods of rest in an intensive care unit. *Journal of Advanced Nursing, 21*, 34–40.

Edmondson, D., Kronish, I., Taggart Wasson, L., Giglio, J., Davidson, K., & Whang, W. (2014). A test of the diathesis–stress model in the emergency department: Who develops PTSD after an acute coronary syndrome? *Journal of Psychiatric Research, 53*, 8–13.

Hatch, R., McKetchnie, S., & Griffith, J. (2011). Psychological intervention to prevent ICU-related PTSD: Who, when, and for how long? *Critical Care, 15*(141), 1–3.

Hu, R., Jiang, X., Zeng, Y., Chen, X., & Zhang, Y. (2010). Effects of earplugs and eye masks on nocturnal sleep, melatonin and cortisol in a simulated intensive care unit environment. *Critical Care, 14*, R66. doi:10.1186/cc8965

Jones, C., Bäckman, C., Capuzzo, M., Flaatten, H., Rylander, C., & Griffiths, R. D. (2007). Precipitants of post-traumatic stress disorder following intensive care: A hypothesis generating study of diversity in care. *Intensive Care Medicine, 33*, 978–985. doi:10.1007/s00134-007-0600-8

Jones, C., Griffiths, R. D., Macmillan, R. R., & Palmer, T. E. A. (1994). Psychological problems occurring after intensive care. *British Journal of Intensive Care, 2*, 46–53.

Koshy, G., Wilkinson, A., Harmsworth, A., & Waldmann, C. S. (1997). Intensive care unit follow-up program at a district general hospital. *Intensive Care Medicine, 23*, S160.

Küller, R., & Laike, T. (1998). The impact of flicker from fluorescent lighting on well-being, performance, and physiological arousal. *Ergonomics, 41*(4), 433–447.

Le, A., Friese, R., Hsu, C., Wynne, J., Rhee, P., & O'Keeffe, T. (2012). Sleep disruptions and nocturnal nursing interactions in the intensive care unit. *Journal of Surgical Research, 177*, 310–314.

Lehrner, J., Eckersberger, C., Walla, P., Pötsch, G., & Deecke, L. (2000). Ambient odor of orange in a dental office reduces anxiety and improves mood in female patients. *Physiology and Behavior, 71*(1–2), 83–86.

Lehrner, J., Manwinski, G., Lehr, S., Johren, P., & Deecke, L. (2005). Ambient odors of orange and lavender reduce anxiety and improve mood in a dental office. *Physiology and Behavior, 86*(1–2), 92–95.

Linder, L., & Christian, B. (2011). Characteristics of nighttime hospital bedside care environment (sound, light, and temperature) for children with cancer. *Cancer Nursing, 34*(3), 177–184.

Mahmood, A., Chaudhury, H., & Valente, M. (2011). Nurses' perceptions of how physical environment affects medication errors in acute care settings. *Applied Nursing Research, 24*, 229–237.

Mazer, S. (2006). Increase patient safety by creating a quieter hospital environment. *Biomedical Instrumentation and Technology, 40*(2), 145–146.

Metzger, L., Orr, S., Berry, N., Ahern, C., Lasko, N., & Pitman, R. (1999). Physiological reactivity to startling tones in women with posttraumatic stress disorder. *Journal of Abnormal Psychology, 108*, 347–352.

Morgan, K., & Tromborg, C. (2006). Sources of stress in captivity. *Applied Animal Behavior Science, 102*, 262–302.

Ortiga, J., Kanapathipillai, S., Daly, B., Hilbers, J., Varndell, W., & Short, A. (2013). The sound of urgency: Understanding noise in the emergency department. *Music and Medicine, 5*(1), 44–51. doi:10.1177/1943862112471999

Pease, N. J. F., & Finlay, I. G. (2002). Do patients and their relatives prefer single cubicles or shared wards? *Palliative Medicine, 16*(5), 445–446.

Persson, E., Anderberg, P., & Ekwall, A. (2014). A room of one's own—Being cared for in a hospital with a single-bed room design. *Scandinavian Journal of Caring Sciences, 29*, 340–346.

Planning a brand new ED? Study up on acoustics, air quality, and patient wish-lists. (2012). *ED Management*, 6–8. Retrieved from http://search.proquest.com/docview/911718149?accountid=407

Pole, N., Neylan, T., Otte, C., Henn-Hasse, C., Metzler, T., & Marmar, C. (2009). Prospective prediction of posttraumatic stress disorder symptoms using fear potentiated auditory startle responses. *Biological Psychiatry, 65*, 235–240. doi:10.1016/j.biopsych.2008.07.015

Richter, M., Parkes, C., & Chaw-Kant, J. (2007). Listening to the voices of hospitalized high-risk antepartum patients. *Journal of Obstetric, Gynecologic, and Neonatal Nursing, 36*(4), 313–318.

Rothschild, B. (2000). *The body remembers: The psychophysiology of trauma and trauma treatment.* New York, NY: W. W. Norton.

Schelling, G. (2002). Effects of stress hormones on traumatic memory formation and the development of posttraumatic stress disorder in critically ill patients. *Neurobiology of Learning and Memory, 78,* 596–609.

Schelling, G., Stoll, C., Haller, M., Briegel, J., Manert, W., Hummel, T., . . . Peter, K. (1998). Health-related quality of life and post-traumatic stress disorder in survivors of acute respiratory distress syndrome. *Critical Care Medicine, 26,* 651–659.

Shalev, A. Y., Sahar, T., Freedman, S., Peri, T., Glick, N., Brandes, D., . . . Pitman, R. K. (1998). A prospective study of heart rate response following trauma and the subsequent development of posttraumatic stress disorder. *Archives of General Psychiatry, 55,* 553–559. doi:10.1001/archpsyc.55.6.553

Skirrow, P., Jones, C., Griffiths, D., & Kaney, S. (2001). Intensive care: Easing the trauma. *The Psychologist, 14*(12), 640–642.

Stewart, L., & White, P. (2008). Sensory filtering phenomenology in PTSD. *Depression and Anxiety, 25,* 38–45.

Sukantarat, K. T., Williamson, R. C. N., & Brett, S. J. (2007). Psychological assessment of ICU survivors: A comparison between the Hospital Anxiety and Depression scale and the Depression, Anxiety and Stress scale. *Anaesthesia, 62,* 239–243.

van Marle, H. J. F., Hermans, E., Qin, S., & Fernández, G. (2009). From specificity to sensitivity: How acute stress affects amygdala processing of biologically salient stimuli. *Biological Psychiatry, 66,* 649–655.

Wade, D., Howell, D., Weinman, J., Hardy, R., Mythen, M., Brewin, C., . . . Raine, R. (2012). Investigating risk factors for psychological morbidity three months after intensive care: A prospective cohort study. *Critical Care, 16,* 192.

6 CASE STUDIES

In this chapter, we introduce you to three case studies that highlight the factors of medical trauma discussed in Part I. The cases are varied to reflect multiple combinations of risk and protective factors, and their effects on patients' experiences of medical illness and procedures, interactions with staff, and the medical environment. In each case, we explore psychological impacts of medical trauma, including effects on mental health, relationships, well-being, lifestyle, career, and self. Each case is organized similarly, beginning with the patient background and followed by narrative describing the medical trauma and ensuing psychological impacts and secondary crises. We begin by presenting the case of Keith, which depicts a Level 1 Medical Trauma, in this case an outpatient lower back surgery; next we present the case of Sharon, a Level 2 Medical Trauma in which the patient is diagnosed with a life-threatening illness—breast cancer; lastly, we explore the case of Ann, a woman who experiences a life-threatening postpartum hemorrhage, an example of a Level 3 Medical Trauma. Note that the cases are presented as a narrative rather than in a clinical case study format often seen in health care professional education contexts.

LEVEL I MEDICAL TRAUMA CASE STUDY

The Case of Keith

Patient Background

Demographics
Keith is a 48-year-old married Caucasian male with three teenage children ages 17, 15, and 13. He lives on the outskirts of a small, southeastern city that is surrounded by mountains and lakes.

Family Context

Keith has been married to his wife Maria for 22 years. They met in their freshman year in college and were friends for 8 years before marriage. They own their home and live within a 1-hour drive from Keith's parents and two of his siblings. Maria's family lives on the West Coast, and because of the distance they only visit each other twice a year. Keith describes his marriage as supportive and resilient with good communication; however, the relationship was strained for a brief time when Keith returned from deployment to Iraq. Counseling helped rebuild their communication skills and he reports no major conflicts since that time. Keith and Maria also have similar interests and parenting styles and there is no history of past abuse.

Education/Occupation

Keith has an undergraduate degree in history and military science and a master's degree in history. Upon graduation and following 4 years in the Reserve Officers' Training Corps (ROTC), Keith was commissioned as a Second Lieutenant in the U.S. Army and spent 4 years on active duty and 4 years in the reserves with a 1-year deployment to Iraq during the Gulf War. He finished his military obligation with the rank of captain and was honorably discharged. Keith is currently employed in his 15th year as a high school history teacher and also coaches the boys' cross-country team.

Risk Factors

Keith grew up with a judgmental, perfectionistic father with high expectations that caused much anxiety, especially because Keith was only average at most things including academics. Keith also had attention deficit hyperactivity disorder (ADHD) as a child. Always on the go, he participated in multiple physical activities including individual and team sports. His outgoing personality gained him the reputation as a thrill seeker; adventure seemed to be the golden thread to Keith's identity, representing how he participated in many aspects of his life.

Throughout his year-long deployment during the Gulf War, Keith experienced the physical, mental, and emotional hardships that come with leading troops into combat. Although he was never injured, he saw the effects of war in how others tried to cope with stress and injuries. Keith experienced some symptoms of posttraumatic stress disorder (PTSD) following his return home from Iraq, but he never sought treatment or received a diagnosis.

Protective Factors

Keith is a resilient, well-educated man with diverse life experiences and the persistence to overcome life's challenges. Keith has proven that life's setbacks are not long term and believes that with the right attitude, most problems can be solved. He gladly participates in his community and school, and values the bond of friendship he has with so many. Likewise, Keith's family (especially his mother and sister) is very supportive and willing to be a motivating voice when needed. Although Keith's lifestyle is full of adventure, he finds solace in quiet moments by himself or private walks in nature.

Patient Treatment Course

One afternoon last summer, Keith was laying back on the bed with his feet on the floor. Without thinking, he suddenly sat straight up with enough force to propel himself off of the bed. At that moment, he experienced what he described as "the worst pain I've ever felt. It was if someone stabbed me in the lower back with a knife." Keith knew enough about physical injury to suspect that he had herniated or ruptured a disc. He had experienced a similar yet less intense pain 20 years earlier as a student when working out incorrectly on a rowing machine at the college gym. The sharp pain of his previous injury was excruciating and debilitating. All he could do was hobble to the health clinic and begin the muscle relaxant and pain medication he was given, which seemed to work. As time passed, Keith forgot about the old injury and became involved in martial arts, golf, and jogging with no problems to his back.

This time, however, the injury was different. Keith's strategy of simply taking it easy for a few weeks did not work. The constant nerve pain was unremitting. Simply standing in the shower proved difficult because of the constant pain. Even walking and sitting were painful. After a couple of weeks, Keith realized that he needed expert medical attention. His primary care physician ordered an x-ray and suggested a series of cortisone shots to reduce the inflammation of any bulge within the disc.

Medical Trauma Narrative

When Keith arrived for his first injection, he was surprised to find that it was treated more like an operation than simply a quick shot given in the doctor's office. That it was in an operating room with several staff members was a little unnerving for Keith, especially since he had never experienced an operating room as a patient. After the procedure, no one told Keith about what might follow beyond giving him a handout about the medication and setting an appointment for him to get a second injection; Keith had no idea whether his life would return to normal or what to do if things did not improve.

After the first injection, Keith experienced some relief for 24 hours until the nerve pain returned. The second shot proved no better and Keith decided that he would not go back for the third shot. A sense of hopelessness began to creep in as it became apparent that this intervention may have been a waste of time and money. No one from the outpatient clinic called to inquire about the cancellation of the third injection or to answer any questions. Keith cynically surmised that he had been nothing more than an income stream for the doctor and clinic.

Keith did trust his primary care physician, who quickly ordered an MRI with the thought that he may need a microdisectomy surgery. Results showed a ruptured disc in the L4/L5 area with a pushing of the nerve against the facet. Surgery was planned to cut out the ruptured 20% of the disc and route out the facet to give a little more room for the pinched nerve. When Keith heard this news, he was anxious about the surgery but hopeful he would experience complete relief.

In preparation for the surgery, Keith had to attend a mandatory meeting at the hospital with all of the patients who were to get surgery that particular week. This meeting included an overview of the recovery process, at which time the nurse reviewed what to do and not do, and how to take care of oneself to expedite the healing process. The idea of the meeting made sense, yet the topics all seemed to be about taking care of the physical self. These suggestions included such items as, *"Don't walk on hard wood floors in stocking feet"* and *"Follow your dietary recommendations given your respective surgeries."* (Keith would realize later that these concerns would be the least of his worries.) When Keith asked the nurse to comment about the timeline for returning to normal activities, the nurse claimed to have had a similar surgery and was "back running marathons within a year." This was music to Keith's ears. All the sports and activities that he loved were just temporarily on hold.

The day of the surgery was much anticipated, as Keith hoped it would lead to permanent relief and a return to normal life. Prior to being taken to surgery, Keith was visited by the various medical staff who would be helping with the operation. The primary surgeon, however, was running late and would meet everyone in the operating room. A heated blanket was placed over Keith, which he recalled as a most comforting moment. As the stretcher was wheeled down the hallway and into the operating room, Keith was acutely aware of the coldness of the room, and the bright lights and metal instruments—this was a stark difference from the quiet, private, pre-op waiting area, with its dim lights, soft music, and comfortable furnishings.

The operating room reminded Keith of the field hospitals in Iraq he would often visit when one of the soldiers in his platoon was wounded. "Controlled chaos" was the best description he could give. In those moments, it did not seem to be about the person, but the task at hand. Maybe that was how it needed to be? This surgery, however, was not in a war zone, and his life was not hanging in the balance, as far as he knew. Keith, always curious, asked the anesthesiologist just before he went under how the medicine actually modifies the brain. The response was a curt "I don't have time to answer that and you don't have time to hear it." The next thing he recalled was being in the recovery room with his wife by his side. The surgeon stopped in for a brief minute, yet Keith was too groggy to realize his presence. A few hours later, as Keith was wheeled out of the hospital to the curb where his wife waited with the car, the two attendants stated that his operation was "textbook." Keith took this to mean that all would be fine when his wounds healed.

As the days passed, Keith did his best to recover in accordance with medical advice. He was concerned when a blood clot formed over his operation incision: No one had mentioned this and so the follow-up consultation with the surgeon would be a good time to address it. When the appointment day arrived, Keith was called back to the examination room and was met by his surgeon and a young medical student who seemed friendly and eager to learn. The surgeon clearly wanted to be in charge of the visit. The student appeared reluctant to ask any questions and simply took notes as the "post-op consult" continued. Keith was getting more anxious as the visit was coming to an end, as he still had not been asked how he thought his recovery was going. He felt as if his role as a patient was to describe symptoms and defer to his surgeon rather than to be heard. Keith finally decided to ask about the swelling, lifting his shirt so the surgeon and student could see his concern. His question was met with two very different reactions: The surgeon gave a quick glance and a dismissive brush of his hand before mumbling words to the effect that "the swelling will go down—not to worry," while the medical student strained to see the scar area and for the first time spoke. "That must have been troubling to not really know what was happening." Her comment did not fix anything, yet felt more validating to Keith than any other part of the visit. The surgeon seemed slightly annoyed with her interruption and ended the visit with no further instructions or request for another visit.

Keith now felt that he was on his own to manage whatever he experienced, which in his case was anxiety and an inability to participate in many of his previously loved activities. Rock climbing, martial arts, and golf stopped and after a few months were still physically impossible for Keith. "Too much twisting, reaching, and jumping," he told others and himself every time an opportunity to engage in these activities arose. With the pain feeling just beneath the surface, a slow-paced jog proved impossible. As a result of his inability to participate in these activities, Keith experienced changes in many of his relationships: No more weekend golf outings or 5K runs with his children. Rock climbing with his wife could only be watched from the ground. Being a spectator was not how Keith envisioned his life.

Depression began to creep in as Keith pulled back from interactions with others. He stopped taking the initiative to engage in his life fully. Everything that he had come to love about his life was different now. A coworker who had a similar surgery years earlier told Keith, "Welcome to the new normal." This statement terrified Keith which he interpreted as the need to accept that he will never regain the lifestyle he enjoyed just 3 months earlier. How he defined himself and how others knew him must change, but to what? Keith wondered how he could come to grips with the physical limitations he now faced. Where and how would he find life balance? The anxiety of not knowing these answers emerged. Everything seemed different now, and Keith did not feel prepared for what lay ahead.

Questions for Consideration: The Case of Keith

A. How does Keith experience medical trauma? What are the specific psychological impacts and secondary crises in this case?

B. How do Keith's risk and protective factors contribute to his experience of medical trauma? How does his meaning-making affect his perception of his health?

C. What could health care professionals have done differently to help Keith? What aspects of his environment—either his personal environment or the treatment environment—contributed to Keith's response to his health crisis?

D. Without help to manage the psychological impacts of this medical trauma, what are possible long-term consequences for this patient?

LEVEL 2 MEDICAL TRAUMA CASE STUDY

The Case of Sharon

Patient Background

Demographics
Sharon is 55, African American, and widowed with two children. She lives in a quaint neighborhood within the city limits of a midsized East Coast city and regularly attends a nearby Baptist church.

Family Context
Sharon has lived as a widow for 4 years as a result of her second husband's passing from a heart attack. Their marriage had lasted 22 years. They have a daughter together who is now in college. Sharon also has a son from a previous marriage who recently graduated with honors from the local university and now resides 8 hours away in another state. Sharon's parents live nearby and enjoy her visits on Sunday after church. Sharon owns her own home and describes her family as "close knit." She reports a brief history of physical abuse during her first marriage, which partly led to their divorce.

Education/Occupation

Sharon has a bachelor's degree in Business Administration and is employed as the office manager for a mid-sized insurance agency in the city in which she resides.

Risk Factors

Growing up as African American in a small community was not always easy for Sharon. She would say that the toughest part was the high expectation from her parents that she would graduate from college, move to a city with more opportunity, and begin her own family. Sharon was loyal to her family and enjoyed the security of being raised by both parents under the same roof. Going to church and celebrating holidays were the norm and Sharon found such routines and traditions to be predictable and comforting. Unfortunately, plans changed when Sharon became pregnant during her first year in college. Marrying her child's father only seemed to add to her stress and difficulties, and they were divorced a few years later. Sharon noted that her guilt and shame were high during those early years, as the experience of being a young mother and getting divorced were contrary to the values instilled in her. In addition, Sharon experienced a continual stream of verbal and physical abuse from her first husband, which contributed to her feelings of low self-worth. The only support she received at that time was from her parents telling her that she should leave the marriage and that she was "better than all of that."

Protective Factors

As much as Sharon struggled during that difficult time, she claimed to have emerged as an independent, tough-minded woman. After her divorce, Sharon moved back home to rethink her life direction and accepted her parents' help in raising her son. Intent on being self-sufficient, Sharon enrolled in a college closer to home with the determination to graduate and move forward in life. An internship led to the office management job in which she would spend the next 20 years successfully working. Religion was central to her routine and was a daily practice as she began each day with quiet readings and reflection before heading to work. On Sundays Sharon attended the church she grew up in, along with friends and family.

Patient Treatment Course

One morning while Sharon was showering, she engaged her usual weekly routine of checking for lumps in her breasts and found something suspicious. Thankful that she had a mammogram already scheduled for that week, she kept the appointment knowing that this would be the first step in understanding the nature of the abnormality. During the few days leading up to the test, Sharon felt increasingly anxious: Her grandmother had experienced breast cancer years ago, so she was aware of the potential risks for herself and the other women in her family. Sharon had been diligent about getting regular mammograms and was surprised at how fast a lump could develop between annual exams.

Medical Trauma Narrative

Two days later, Sharon arrived at the appointed time for her mammogram. The staff was friendly as usual, and Sharon found herself calmed by the quiet atmosphere that seemed to be designed to reduce stress and worry. "They must see fear every day," Sharon thought, as she was escorted by the technician to a small changing room in which she disrobed and put on a pink hospital gown. Sharon walked herself to the room at the end of the hallway, where the technician waited next to a computer screen.

"Ok, Sharon—I see you've been here many times before, so I'm guessing you know the drill. Any concerns since your last mammogram?" the technician asked while clicking buttons using the computer's mouse.

"I noticed something a few days ago in the shower, in my left breast." She proceeded to discuss what she discovered, pointing to the location of the abnormal area. Sharon noticed that her voice was quivering a bit as she spoke, and her hand was shaking as she pointed to the area in question.

The technician proceeded with the mammogram, taking two extra sets of images of the left breast. After she finished retrieving the images, she reminded Sharon of the procedure.

"Sharon, as usual, we will call you if there is anything questionable in the mammogram. Otherwise, if the results are negative you will get a letter in the mail in about 2 weeks."

Sharon returned to the changing room to remove the hospital gown and gather her things. Before opening the door, she paused in front of the mirror to say a quick prayer, closing her eyes to keep from crying. She had to return to work and did not want to ruin her make-up.

Two days later, Sharon received a voicemail from the testing center. As soon as she heard the woman begin to speak on the message, Sharon's heart started to beat wildly in her chest: She remembered that a phone call meant a positive finding. Sharon immediately called the center for more information, as no details were included in the message. When a staff member answered, Sharon fumbled over her words as she explained the purpose of her call. After explaining herself to the receptionist, she was transferred to a technician. Sharon again had to explain the purpose of her call, but this time she had gotten better control over herself and was able to articulate her words.

The technician accessed Sharon's record quickly, and proceeded to read the test results and indicated that a follow-up appointment would be necessary. Given the speed at which the technician spoke, Sharon had a difficult time catching all of the details. It was as if her brain were in a fog, which is unusual for her—she is typically so on the ball.

"I'm sorry," Sharon interjected, "I didn't catch all that you just said. Can you please repeat the test results? I'm just trying to take some notes and you spoke so quickly. . . ." Sharon's heart was racing, and she could feel her body getting warm to the point of perspiring. Her voice quivered quite obviously as she spoke.

Sharon captured all pertinent information and hung up the phone after speaking with the receptionist to schedule her ultrasound. She was tearful as she scheduled her appointment but held back most of her emotion. Because she was at work, Sharon knew she had to "keep it together" until she got home that evening.

During the next 2 weeks, Sharon received an ultrasound of her left breast, and then a follow-up biopsy. She had agonized over the anticipation of her results but found some solace in her faith and in her relationships with family. When she received a call to schedule a consultation to discuss her biopsy results, Sharon was slightly relieved knowing that at least she would learn something soon. At the appointment, Sharon met with a physician to learn her results.

"Sharon, hi, thanks for coming in today. I'm sure this has been a challenging week for you, waiting for the results."

Sharon sat motionless except for a brief nod in agreement to what she had just heard. The physician sat at the computer terminal and quickly clicked through a few screens on the monitor.

"The results were confirmed positive for breast cancer," the physician said gently and in a matter-of-fact fashion, without looking away from the computer. She then turned toward Sharon.

"The lump was malignant, Sharon, so we'll need to talk about some options." She paused briefly for Sharon to absorb the news. Too much was swirling in Sharon's mind to answer. She heard the words *cancer, malignant,* and *options.* The moment seemed to fragment into pieces, which made it difficult for Sharon to respond in any rational, linear manner. Her emotions collided with questions that she decided to hide in that moment, in part for fear of hearing the answers.

The physician took Sharon's quiet demeanor as determined resolve rather than a traumatic reaction to a life-changing diagnosis. Options were presented in a slow, methodical manner to ensure that Sharon understood the risks, outcomes, and procedures. Sharon took some time to process her diagnosis, and consulted with another oncologist for a second opinion before reaching her treatment decision. Because of the potential spread, aggressiveness of the cancer, and her grandmother's death from breast cancer, Sharon decided to have a double mastectomy.

Sharon began to pray as she sat in the parking lot after leaving the office. It is what she had grown up doing whenever life was hard.

Sharon decided to go back to the first oncologist she spoke with, as she seemed slightly more sensitive and caring than the physician she saw for her second opinion. Sharon felt really vulnerable and raw about the whole process, and she felt she needed health care providers who were kind toward her. The emotions of fear, confusion, and helplessness churned around on a daily basis, and Sharon's greatest concern was for her kids and how this would affect them. More importantly, she worried about how this would affect her ability to participate in their lives and the lives of her future grandchildren.

Telling her family proved more difficult than Sharon could imagine. Their concern for her was reassuring, yet felt awkward. After all, she was the one who cared for others and was unsure of how to let others care for her. The day of the surgery, Sharon's parents and children arrived to offer their love and help. This show of support was comforting to Sharon and lessened the feelings of aloneness that emerged when she was first diagnosed.

The mastectomy procedure itself—from the preparation, surgery, and discharge process—went as expected. The medical staffs were technically proficient and caring toward Sharon throughout the experience. During recovery, she asked every nurse that attended her bedside if they thought the operation went okay. She needed the reassurance.

Discussion of her aftercare included how to manage the physical discomfort and how to care for the incisions. What to expect regarding her drain tube and the different colorations of discharge were explained. How to shower, dress, and simply get around in general were thoroughly reviewed by the staff. Sharon listened closely to her providers about what she could expect in recovery, as she wanted to be as prepared as possible: She did not want to be a burden to anyone.

The hospital provided a bag containing all sorts of information about the physical recovery from cancer, along with several items with the hospital logo, such as a water bottle, magnet, and notepad. Sharon returned home and spent the first few days resting in bed, thinking about all that had just unfolded. At this point all she knew was that she was dealing with something that she had not asked for nor would wish on anyone. Hoping that the hardest part was over, Sharon was ready to get back to life as she knew it.

Postdischarge Recovery Narrative

The first week following the surgery was difficult for Sharon, yet she followed the prescribed care for her pain and for the incision. Daily tasks such as doing the laundry and vacuuming were now a struggle due to her pain and discomfort. Even taking care of her cat was an impossibility, as both the bags of litter and cat food were simply too heavy for Sharon to lift. Family had to help with just about everything and insisted on visiting and bringing meals so that Sharon also did not have to cook.

In the days and months following her surgery, Sharon spent increasingly more time alone, as being with people seemed too overwhelming for her. One activity that brought Sharon comfort was to sit in her sunroom with a cup of coffee and watch the birds at the feeder that she had hung last year. This was a favorite early morning routine along with quiet meditations and biblical readings. Sharon felt now as if she needed these peaceful moments more than ever, yet at the same time was keenly aware of her solitude and loneliness.

Hours spent alone seemed to be taking Sharon further away from the active and engaged life she once knew. Even after returning to work, Sharon felt different and was unable to reconnect with her previous role as the office "go to" person. She had always been one who managed and coordinated everything from business work flow to social functions and family events. Sharon's employer wanted to give her as much time as needed to recover and heal. Although this was a caring gesture, Sharon was concerned that the timing of her diagnosis was not ideal. "After 20 years," her colleagues would say, "you must be ready to retire." A younger coworker who was trained by Sharon was to be the next logical replacement whenever Sharon made the decision to leave. As Sharon grew increasingly aloof at work and isolated herself more at home, her depression led to negative thoughts about her coworkers and slight paranoia that her counterpart would try to supplant her.

In addition to her experience with depression, Sharon also began to notice some existential death anxiety that seemed to grip her in a way that brought a need to hang on to what little she could control. Sharon was unable to shake the almost constant worry about her cancer returning, and yet decided that she would not keep her yearly follow-up appointment with her oncologist, or her appointment for a physical with her primary care physician, for that matter. Sharon felt her anxiety dissipate at the thought of never seeing another doctor again; somehow the prospect of not having to face any more bad news calmed her, even though deep inside she knew that this was not a healthy decision. The unpredictability of life, death, and health seemed too much to bear for Sharon, and she was unnerved by how her own experience with cancer had reopened the deep grief she felt about losing her second husband, as well as triggering anticipatory grief about someday losing her aging parents.

Sharon canceled her follow-up appointment with her oncologist, as well as the appointment with her primary care physician.

Questions for Consideration: The Case of Sharon

A. How does Sharon experience medical trauma? What are the specific psychological impacts and secondary crises in this case?

B. How do Sharon's risk and protective factors contribute to her experience of medical trauma? How does meaning-making affect her perception of her health and of her future?

C. What could health care professionals have done differently to help Sharon more effectively manage her medical trauma? What aspects of her environment—either her personal environment or the treatment environment—contributed to Sharon's response to her health crisis?

D. Without help to manage the psychological impacts of this medical trauma, what are possible long-term consequences for this patient?

LEVEL 3 MEDICAL TRAUMA CASE STUDY

The Case of Ann

Patient Background

Demographics
Ann is a 29-year-old married Caucasian female who recently gave birth to her first child. She lives in a suburb of a midsized Midwestern city, just a 10-minute drive from the suburban hospital at which she gave birth.

Family Context
Ann has been married to her husband John for 7 years, and this is the first marriage for both. They own their home, and live within a 30-minute drive of their parents and extended families. Ann describes her husband and family as supportive with no past family abuse history or significant challenges with communication.

Education/Occupation
Ann has a master's degree in education and currently works in a small suburban elementary school, where she teaches fifth grade math and science.

Risk Factors
Ann was a victim of a sexual assault in college, having been raped by an upperclassman she did not know very well after a party she attended at her friend's sorority house. She was intoxicated during the assault and did not press charges, in part because she was ashamed and afraid of what her

parents would think of her. Ann has always been somewhat perfectionistic and she can have rigid expectations of herself and others. She is also introverted and tends to keep much of her thoughts and feelings to herself. Ann suffers with anxiety but has never spoken to a mental health professional. Her family history is positive for anxiety and depression.

Ann experienced significant anxiety throughout her pregnancy. She and John had difficulty conceiving and spent approximately 1 year attempting to conceive prior to enlisting the help of an infertility specialist. With medical intervention, Ann became pregnant within 6 months. She had a challenging pregnancy in the last trimester, as she was diagnosed with preeclampsia and also experienced significant weight gain (50 lb.) and swelling in feet and ankles. Ann was also very afraid of the birth process, despite her attempts to educate herself and her efforts to prepare. Ann kept much of her anxiety to herself because she did not want to alarm her husband or family. When she shared some of her anxious thoughts about the pregnancy and birth with her OB/GYN, her doctor provided reassurance that "everything would be fine" and that it was normal for first-time moms to be anxious.

Protective Factors

Ann is a well-educated woman who is resourceful and willing to invest time and energy into finding information she believes can help her. She has a stable support system with no major life stressors aside from her difficult pregnancy. She likes her job, her coworkers are supportive, and she enjoys the tasks involved in teaching. Ann has taken time to prepare herself for her upcoming birth experience, especially with respect to relaxation techniques. In the bag she packed for the hospital, Ann included a CD of American Indian flute music and a plug-in air freshener scented with lavender to provide aromatherapy. Ann found these to be quite calming during the prenatal yoga class she took at the local YWCA.

Patient Treatment Course

During the doctor visit 1 week prior to her due date, Ann complained to her OB that she was in constant discomfort from the unabated swelling in her feet, ankles, and legs. She was struggling to carry around the extra weight and experiencing labored breathing. Given her circumstances, Ann's doctor suggested that it might be best to induce her labor. Ann agreed and felt some relief as she talked to her physician about the plan. When her doctor suggested they begin the induction at midnight that night, Ann became slightly anxious but mostly excited that her baby would soon be born: tomorrow she would meet her daughter and begin to heal from this challenging pregnancy.

Medical Trauma Narrative

Just before midnight, Ann arrived at the hospital with her husband John and mother Kathy. After checking in registration, they proceeded to the maternity unit where staff awaited their arrival. Because Ann had completed preregistration, she had only a few forms to complete prior to being taken to her birthing suite. Ann undressed and asked for assistance getting into the bed. She settled in, adjusting the pillows around her back while John pulled up the sheet to cover her legs. Ann asked John to plug in the lavender air freshener, but to wait on the music until after she had gotten started with the induction. Ann's nurse arrived and began explaining the process to Ann, John, and Kathy. She explained each step quickly and asked if Ann had any questions. Ann felt overwhelmed, but said she did not think she had any questions. The nurse then stated she would be right back, but before she walked out she turned to Ann and said, "Oh, and . . . I forgot to mention . . . your doctor is VERY aggressive with Pitocin, so you better hold on for quite a ride!"

Ann smiled and laughed nervously before lying back against the pillows. She quickly tried to reframe what the nurse had just told her into a positive: *that will mean I will see my daughter that much sooner!*

Just as the nurse had forewarned, Ann's labor progressed rapidly. By 3:00 a.m. the contractions came fast and hard, and Ann decided to get an epidural despite her hope that she would have a natural childbirth. (She had weighed the pros and cons of an epidural while creating her birthing plan and had given herself permission to get one if the contractions felt unbearable.) Ann felt her anxiety climb as she waited for the anesthesiologist to position the IV in her back, so she deeply breathed the lavender-infused air, which helped her. John and Ann's mother Kathy were sleeping soundly across the room, and once the epidural began to take effect, Ann felt calmer and even dozed a few times, too.

At 4:30 a.m., Ann was awakened by her nurse, who was standing beside the bed holding an oxygen mask.

"Ann, we've noticed some irregularities in your baby's heart rate—some decelerations. You'll need to wear this oxygen mask, and we'll likely need to reposition you," her nurse explained.

"Is my baby okay?" Ann could feel her heart rate spike as she questioned the nurse in a high-pitched voice.

"Yes, your baby should be fine. It's just a precaution. We'll let you know if anything changes. Try to rest."

After the nurse adjusted the mask on Ann, she made a few notes in the chart and left the room. As Ann lay there, trying to slow her breathing, she decided to pray that everything was going to be okay. She said this prayer to herself several times as she took deep breaths in and out, in and out . . .

By 7:00 a.m., Ann had progressed to approximately 9.5 cm and her nurses decided to let her try to push. Ann was nervous but eager to start the delivery process. The nurse and an aide helped Ann get into position, gently placing her feet in the stirrups. Ann again felt some anxiety when she placed her feet in the stirrups: She never liked these things, and always felt so exposed and vulnerable. After the nurse gave Ann instructions and some encouragement, Ann began to push. *This is not so bad*, Ann thought as she repositioned her body to prepare for the second push. Before she could do so, Ann felt a strong gush of fluid flow out of her. Thinking it must have been the amniotic fluid, Ann once again braced for a second push. She looked up at her nurses but was instantly confused by their horrified expressions.

"Ann, relax. We're not going to push again just yet," her nurse stated, rather haltingly.

At this point, John had reached Ann's bedside, rubbing the sleep out of his eyes. He first looked at Ann's face and seemed alarmed to see an oxygen mask. He then looked down at the sheet between Ann's legs and seemed to freeze.

"What's wrong? Is something wrong?" Ann said, tearing the oxygen mask from her face.

"Ann, you've had some bleeding. I need to call your doctor right away. I'll be right back and let you know our next step, okay?" The nurse left quickly, leaving the young aide by Ann's bedside.

In approximately 5 minutes the nurse returned. Seeming frustrated, she indicated that she was not able to reach her doctor but that another nurse is continuing to call. She proceeded to attempt to calm Ann, John, and Kathy, who had just awoken and was now at Ann's bedside. After 15 minutes, another nurse entered and asked to speak to Ann's nurse in the hallway.

Almost immediately Ann's nurse returned. "Your doctor is on her way." Seems she was playing tennis and did not have her phone with her. Ann's nurse again seemed irritated, which alarmed Ann. *There seems to be some tension between my nurse and doctor*, Ann thought.

Within 30 minutes, Ann's doctor had arrived. She entered Ann's room with the nurse, and explained that she had just gone over the chart to catch up on Ann's progress and current situation. She examined Ann and explained that it would be best to perform a C-section. She stated that Ann may be experiencing a placental abruption and this coupled with the baby's consistent heart decelerations necessitates an immediate delivery.

Ann was simultaneously alarmed and relieved; she was glad to see her doctor but frightened about a C-section. Because of Ann's treatment-resistant anemia during pregnancy, she was told that a C-section would not be the best scenario. Ann quickly put her worries aside, though: She was about to have this baby and the health of her daughter was the most important thing to her at this moment.

An aide arrived with gowns and masks for John and Kathy, as they indicated they would like to be there for the birth. Ann's nurse entered and gave her an indication of the time frame and a little more information about what Ann could expect during the C-section. Before she knew it, Ann was being wheeled down the hall and into the operating room.

Once in the operating room, Ann noticed a flurry of activity all around her. She was nervous about the procedure but anticipated her daughter's birth with great excitement. She was also concerned about her well-being, as she had felt a few more gushes of fluid and hoped it was not blood. The operating room staff placed a drape not far from Ann's face, obstructing her view of her abdomen. Ann felt disconnected from the birth about to take place, but at the same time felt a little relieved that she would not have to watch herself being cut open. Ann felt uneasy as the surgery began; despite feeling no pain, the constant tugging sensation in her abdomen was a disconcerting reminder of what was happening.

Before she knew it, Ann heard her doctor say, "And we have a baby!"

Ann could not immediately see her daughter and could hear nothing, which prompted a spike of her anxiety until she then heard a strong, piercing cry. Relief washed over her and a nurse held the baby within Ann's frame of sight. "She's beautiful!" Ann heard someone exclaim.

Staff took Ann's daughter to a nearby table to perform all initial testing and to clean and swaddle her. John and Kathy were busy watching the baby, looking over at Ann with beaming smiles in order to stay connected to her. John took several pictures while Kathy walked to Ann's bedside, assuring her that everything was fine with the baby and that she should try to get some rest. After Ann was stitched up, she was taken to recovery. She would see her baby in a few hours.

In the recovery room, Ann was wheeled to a spot near the door and told to try to get some rest. She looked to her left and saw a row of three beds on either side of the room—all empty. While normally Ann would not have liked to be in a strange place all alone, she welcomed the peace she felt in that moment. She knew her baby was safe and that her mother and husband were helping her get settled up in the nursery. Ann relaxed her head into her pillow, took a deep breath, and then felt a now-familiar sensation: gush.

Ann's eyes opened in a panic as she raised her head just high enough to see the blood-soaked sheets below her waist. The stark contrast of crisp white cotton streaming with the crimson streaks of her own blood shocked her. Panic-stricken and with no memory of a call button to alert nurses, she did the only thing she could think of, yelling *Help! Help me!*

Ann's nurse must have already been on her way to the recovery room. After seeing Ann, she immediately turned from the doorway to alert staff to the situation before entering the room. She rushed to Ann's bedside, telling her that her doctor was on her way and that they would immediately assess the situation to determine next steps.

Before Ann knew it, her husband and mother were at her side. Kathy looked visibly shaken as John tried to gain his composure. He held Ann's hand and told her that everything would be just fine and that the doctor was on her way. Moments later Ann's doctor arrived and told Ann that she would need to examine her to assess the source of the hemorrhage and attempt to stop the bleeding. She told Ann and her family that she had just ordered a unit of blood to replenish what Ann had lost, and to try to relax as best she could. One of Ann's nurses entered the recovery room carrying Ann's small CD player and air freshener, hoping to create a peaceful environment to help Ann relax.

Over the next 6 hours, Ann's doctor and nurses performed several rounds of interventions to try to stop the hemorrhage. The OB/GYN would repeatedly extract blood clots and attempt to massage Ann's uterus to engage what should have been its natural inclination to contract back to its normal size. In Ann's case, her uterus remained boggy as it constantly filled with blood. At some point during the afternoon, Ann's epidural began to wear off, triggering excruciating pain during the uterine massage and clot extraction. Ann's doctor repeatedly apologized as she performed the necessary tasks while Ann screamed in agony. John and Kathy had been ushered out of the room once Ann's pain became so great, yet they and the rest of Ann's startled family could hear her screams from the waiting room.

As her doctor and nurses managed her medical crisis, Ann began to experience a flood of intense emotions. In addition to the terror she felt at the thought that she could possibly bleed to death, Ann was overcome with grief when she contemplated not surviving to see her daughter grow up. When she was not trying to actively manage her fears about the next round of clot extraction, she was preoccupied with dark thoughts of death and a sadness she could not put into words even if she had wanted to. Ann's state of constant alarm was consistently reinforced by the beeping of her heart rate and blood pressure monitor, which seemed to echo her own heart that beat wildly within her chest.

As the hours wore on, Ann began to feel the odd sensation of being separated from her body, at times able to stare down at herself lying in the bloody sheets beneath her. She felt a strange disconnection from the medical professionals around her as she listened to their conversations with one another and with her husband and mother. In one instance, Ann looked up at a young medical assistant while she was connecting another bag of blood. Ann listened closely to the woman's conversation with a colleague, during which she referenced her weekend plans and a possible dating opportunity. In the moment, Ann sunk into a new level of despair as she recognized she may never again make another plan. She understood with every fiber of her being the likelihood that she might not live beyond this day.

At some point in the afternoon, Ann noticed her feelings toward her doctor beginning to change. While she still looked to her physician to save her, she was also beginning to recoil at the site of her. Seeing her doctor's white coat as she entered the room instantly sent Ann's heart rate skyrocketing, for she knew she was about to endure another round of painful, almost torturous, treatment.

Ann's doctor called another OB/GYN to assist her in managing the crisis, and together both physicians determined it would be best to perform surgery; it was clear that Ann could endure no more, and their efforts to save Ann's life and uterus were starting to feel futile. At this point, Ann had lost 10 L of blood—a massive hemorrhage. John signed the consent forms as Ann struggled to comprehend what her doctor was explaining. It was as if all life had drained from her body. Ann struggled to remain somewhat lucid as the attendants wheeled her down the hallway toward the operating room. She feebly turned her head as her gurney passed the many family members who lined the hallway, hoping to catch a quick glimpse of the faces of those she loved. The last person she saw before entering the surgical suite was her mother, whose face was pale with the stress and shock of the day's traumatic events.

Ann survived the surgery. Her doctor performed a full hysterectomy in order to stop the bleeding, as this became the only option to save Ann's life. Ann had experienced a placental abruption followed by uterine atony. Given the excessive amount of blood Ann lost and the trauma to her body, Ann was transferred to the surgical intensive care unit (SICU) for observation.

When Ann awoke from surgery in the SICU, she was immediately jarred by the bright light and beeping monitors. Thinking she was still in the recovery room and that she had just awoken from unconsciousness, Ann shrieked in terror at the thought that she had succumbed to her body's pull toward death. When Ann saw a nurse she did not recognize, she immediately glanced around the room and noticed her surroundings were different. The nurse told Ann that she was waking up from surgery and that she was now in the SICU.

Ann spent 5 days in intensive care. She developed pneumonia on the second day and felt defeated by her body's fragile state. For most of Ann's time in the SICU, she stared at the wall or out of the window. She resisted nurses' suggestions to watch TV or read, but rather insisted on just *being*. Ann had difficulty sleeping due to the terrifying nightmares, and her body recoiled whenever her doctor or another professional entered the room to examine her. Ann jumped at the slightest noise or movement, and her heart rate remained elevated for the remainder of her hospital stay. She was exhausted and barely able to muster energy or enthusiasm when an attendant brought her daughter into her room. Ann was often lost in thought and overwhelmed by the complex emotions she felt about her birth experience, including the grief of having just lost the ability to give birth to another child. Nurses sometimes noticed Ann's flat affect and low energy and attempted to cheer her up. Ann wondered how her life would now be and how she would heal from all of this. She felt like a shell of her former self.

After spending another 2 days in the maternity unit, Ann and her baby were discharged home. She was given detailed instructions about pain management and physical recovery from a C-section and hysterectomy, as well as a date for a follow-up appointment with her OB/GYN.

Postdischarge Recovery Narrative

In the days and weeks following her childbirth experience, Ann's body slowly began to heal; yet, as her physical strength increased, Ann's emotional well-being began to suffer as she developed PTSD resulting from the trauma. As she settled into life as a new mother and attempted to cope with the difficult psychophysiological symptoms of trauma, her relationship with her husband began to suffer. Ann could no longer be physically intimate with John, and often avoided moments that could potentially lead to an expectation of sex. Because Ann tended to keep her emotions to herself, she had difficulty discussing the trauma with John or with anyone else. Ann began to isolate herself from others, including her friends and family whom she believed could not possibly understand the trauma she had endured. The chasm between Ann and John continued to grow as their attention focused solely on their daughter, and within 2 years they separated and subsequently divorced.

Medically, Ann began to ignore her own needs in an effort to avoid painful triggers of her trauma. Ann decided she could not continue to see her doctor, as the sight of her was a painful trigger of her birth experience. As time wore on, she neglected to find another OB/GYN, rationalizing that since her reproductive organs had been removed, there was little chance of her getting cancer. Ann tended to avoid doctors and medical facilities in general, often neglecting to seek medical attention, either when necessary or for preventive measures.

Emotionally, Ann often felt numb. She pulled herself through each day without much joy to speak of, and often sought solitude because she could control the environment around her. Ann quit her job as a teacher because she found it to be too stressful; she was always on edge, and the bright lights and noise were too much for her to bear on a daily basis. Ann became a private math tutor out of her home, and also did some light bookkeeping for a friend who had a home-based business. When Ann did not have her daughter with her, she would often lie in a quiet, dimly lit room in order to find some peace. She no longer enjoyed the relaxing music she once loved, as it triggered flashbacks and made her heart race uncontrollably. Ann worked very hard to create a life she could live, and this was a struggle nearly every day.

Questions for Consideration: The Case of Ann

A. How does Ann experience medical trauma? What are the specific psychological impacts and secondary crises in this case?

B. How do Ann's risk and protective factors contribute to her experience of medical trauma? How does meaning-making affect her perception of her health and of her future?

C. What could health care professionals have done differently to help Ann more effectively manage her medical trauma? What aspects of her environment—either her personal environment or the treatment environment—contributed to Ann's response to her health crisis?

D. Without help to manage the psychological impacts of this medical trauma, what are possible long-term consequences for this patient?

II | MANAGING MEDICAL TRAUMA

7

PREVENTION AND INTERVENTION: LEVEL I MEDICAL TRAUMA AND PRIMARY CARE

IN THIS CHAPTER, YOU WILL LEARN:

- *The role of patient protective factors in preventing the psychological impacts of medical trauma*
- *Primary care's role in promoting wellness*
- *Current models of integrative medicine that focus on patient wellness*
- *Strategies for screening trauma risk factors in the primary care setting, including the Medical Mental Health Screening (MMHS) inventory*
- *Best practices for integrating mental health professionals into the primary care setting*
- *Using the patient-centered medical home model for medical trauma detection, intervention, and follow up*
- *How to do a quick screen for medical trauma following a planned surgery or intervention using the Secondary 7–Lifestyle Effects Screening (S7-LES) tool*
- *The theoretical models and techniques used by mental health professionals to treat the psychological impacts of medical trauma*

MANAGING MEDICAL TRAUMA IN THE PRIMARY CARE SETTING

The primary care setting has emerged over the last decade as a pivotal site in health care prevention and cost containment. Patients are often first introduced to the health care system through the primary care setting and have grown accustomed to a modality of health care delivery that historically has struggled to coordinate services and practice holistic care. In this chapter, we explore how the primary care setting is shifting toward a more integrative model of medicine. Part of establishing true collaboration is to understand and utilize the talents of professionals from different disciplines and to include them on the primary care treatment team. In examining holistic health, we also review the roles and profiles of mental health professionals and use the Wheel of Wellness model to understand the multiple factors that shape an individual's unique life and health experience. In addition, we mention examples of integrative models that work, along with best practices, in building a team that includes a mental health component and evidence-based trauma interventions.

In an effort to help primary care providers identify the psychological and emotional effects of medical trauma, we also discuss two instruments, the Medical Mental Health Screening (MMHS) tool as a preventive assessment and the Secondary 7–Lifestyle Effects Screening (S7-LES) tool to identify secondary crises that may surface after a medical trauma.

Prevention

Patient Protective Factors

According to the World Health Organization (2014), health is defined as a "state of physical, mental, and social well-being and not merely the absence of disease or infirmary." In order for such a paradigm to work, health care practitioners have been challenged to expand their understanding and inclusion of not only risk factors, but also protective factors that promote wellness. The primary care setting is especially suitable for this approach as it is often considered to be on the frontline of a person's health management. Unfortunately, primary care settings have long held a biased orientation toward the physical/biological aspects of patients' health and well-being. This is partly due to the training focus in the medical sciences and also with what our culture has come to expect from health care professionals—however, this is changing. Over the last decade there have been measurable strides in acknowledging the gap between physical and mental health in the primary care setting and how to best address these needs with patients (e.g., Wolf, Niederhouser, Marshburn, & LaVela, 2014). The idea that patients only visit their primary physician for physical complaints has been challenged with studies showing that upward of 70% of such visits develop from psychosocial issues (Robinson & Reiter, 2007). In other words, mental health concerns are often the root cause of physical symptoms and should be duly noted and assessed during primary care visits. Such efforts are not only being explored, but also being implemented in various ways throughout the country. The patient-centered medical home model, among others, has become a useful framework that encourages collaboration between different disciplined health care providers (we say more about this later in the chapter).

A recent Harris Poll survey found that 90% (*n* = 2,020) of Americans value mental and physical health equally, yet 56% believe that physical health is treated as more important than mental health (Harris Poll, 2015). Furthermore, when asked about the health care providers they visited within the past 12 months, 65% had visited their primary care physician and only 5% had met with a mental health professional—a quite noticeable gap between values and behaviors. On all accounts, it appears that holistic (mind–body–spirit) wellness is valued, and that the primary care setting is a logical and accessible location for a holistic model to be implemented (Vogel, Malcore, Illes, & Kirkpatrick, 2014). When practicing under this model, health care professionals also consider a patient's various life roles along with different life domains such as relationships, career, leisure activities, and civic participation. Working from a biopsychosocial and spiritual framework further allows providers to better understand patients and their unique context, which, as we know, plays a critical role in overall health and wellness.

As we have indicated, there are a myriad of trauma risk factors that patients demonstrate during routine visits with their primary care provider. These risk factors include both the environmental factors (e.g., home and work life, education, access to health care, social networks, culture, and previous medical experiences) and individual factors (e.g., personality, mental illness, coping styles, degree of pessimism). Psychological distress risk factors, which often present as depression and/or anxiety, are common yet often undetected in the primary care setting unless the patient specifically brings them up. In fact, it is the co-occurring psychosomatic symptoms of aches and pains that are typically treated leaving the mental and emotional states unnoticed (Arvidsdotter, Marklund, Taft, & Kylen, 2015).

Patients can also be quite resilient if they possess protective factors that are practiced or developed as preventive measures for well-being. We know, for instance, that persons who choose a healthy diet and regular exercise are living a pattern that fosters not only physical health, but also mental and emotional health, too. Having good relationships with people who matter to us also curtails depression and improves our quality world. Likewise, we are more apt to be in a healthier state of mind when we are engaged in careers in which we feel competent and worthwhile and that meet our interests and values. Further, believing that we are living a purposeful and meaningful life builds our resilience to adversity and gives us hope, providing the optimistic lens we sometimes need to not only shape our well-being but also to be consistent with good habits.

Protective factors for trauma, like risk factors, can develop in our early years in ways that set patterns well into our adult life. They can emerge as a result of circumstances (e.g., loss of job and insurance) or develop with intentional effort on our part (e.g., exercise, diet, and a resilient mindset to adversity). Either way, protective factors provide a counterbalance to the risky dispositions that work against our ability to function optimally. Patients visit their primary care physician with a combination of both risk and protective factors. For some patients, the scale is tilted toward having more risk factors, while other patients are more protected from the potential for traumatic stress responses to difficult circumstances.

Having a framework to consider all aspects of a patient's well-being first begins with understanding the various constructs that make up holistic wellness.

Holistic Wellness

There are a variety of holistic wellness models to consider with much overlap regarding the universal life domains in which we all participate. The Wheel of Wellness (Myers, Sweeney, & Witmer, 2000) provides such a model in that it attempts to account for the complexity of the human experience. As such, this framework gives us a common language to explore wellness as we examine its relationship to medical trauma (Figure 7.1).

Wheel of Wellness

The Wheel of Wellness (Myers et al., 2000; Witmer & Sweeney, 1992) was designed as a multidisciplinary and holistic model of wellness and prevention over the life span. The influence of this concept dates back to the work of famed psychotherapist Alfred Adler (1927) who proposed that the mind and body influence and are influenced by one another. Furthermore, self-actualization (Maslow, 1943) was a goal that characterized meaning and purpose for each individual and contributed to one's complete self. Based on these early ideas, Myers et al. (2000) defined wellness as "a way of life oriented toward optimal health and well-being in which body, mind, and spirit are integrated by the individual to live more fully within the human and natural community" (p. 252). This definition of wellness moves beyond the disease-oriented model of Western medicine and the aged idea that the removal of symptoms should be our ultimate goal. To flourish (Seligman, 2011) is to develop one's best self and requires a responsibility and interest in building a quality world. What that actually looks like is unique to each individual, yet involves some universal factors.

Myers et al. (2000) refined the original model (Witmer & Sweeney, 1992) to present a research-based framework that shows the interrelationship of five major life tasks (spirituality, self-direction, work, friendship, and love) with twelve subtasks associated with self-direction (sense of worth,

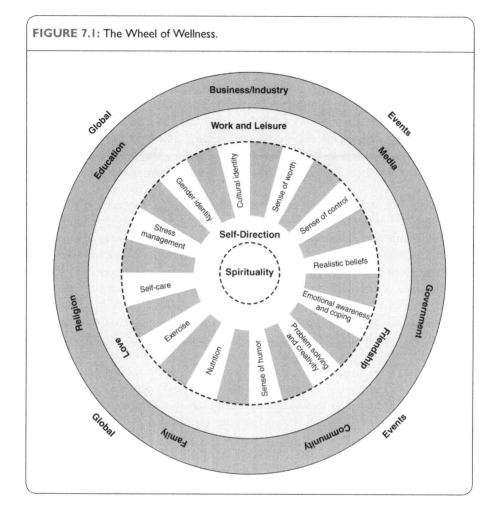

FIGURE 7.1: The Wheel of Wellness.

sense of control, realistic beliefs, emotional awareness and coping, problem solving and creativity, sense of humor, nutrition, exercise, self-care, stress management, gender identity, and cultural identity). The five life tasks interact with various life forces such as family, education, government, media, commerce, and religion. Beyond these life tasks are global events such as wars, terrorism, and economic changes (human origin) or floods, earthquakes, and famines (nature origin). Regarding our examination of the impacts of medical trauma, it may be helpful to take a closer look at a few life tasks that can be affected by traumatic events, namely our spirituality and our ability to engage in meaningful work and leisure.

At the center of the model is the spirituality life task, which is a bedrock for many protective factors of medical trauma. This task represents those personal beliefs that connect us to a greater good with insight and openness toward a sense of the divine. Meaning and purpose reside here along with our moral compass and compassion for others. Hope and optimism are central to our ability to be resilient.

The spiritual core influences the task of one's self-direction, which is a fundamental part of patient-centered care. Being self-directed demands a level of personal attention and initiative toward daily efforts and long-range goals. This is not always an easy process, which we all know. The primary care setting requires a mutual effort between the medical staff and the patient. Each member of the team is tasked with sharing what they know, with the willingness to carry out their respective responsibilities. For the patient, this demands an honest and open dialogue regarding behaviors (e.g., work habits, leisure activities, diet, and exercise patterns), thoughts (e.g., concerns of medical care, self, and stress factors), and emotions (e.g., stress, depression, and anxiety). The health care professional, in turn, listens with the intent to understand the patient's perspective and then shapes treatment from using medical expertise in relation to the patient's behaviors, thoughts, and emotions.

The work and leisure life task represents opportunities for meaning and purpose with economic support. Additionally, social relationships are developed while engaging this life task and these relationships provide psychological satisfaction. Imagine how a medical trauma can impact the job a person holds or their weekend leisure activities. For example, Lisa was scheduled for orthoscopic knee surgery for her combined bone deterioration and arthritis after years of bending and twisting as a landscape designer. Lisa welcomed the relief from pain that this surgery would provide, yet she underestimated the ripple effect of "not working or playing" and did not explore the effects of this surgery with her primary care provider prior to the procedure. Lisa's quality of life dropped as she realized how much value and sense of importance she derived from actually *doing* the landscaping instead of just designing it. Sunday golf was also out, as it placed excessive strain on her knees. Lisa later said how golf was the perfect leisure activity for her because she was surrounded by the beauty that she helped create on a daily basis, and because it gave her a chance to connect with close friends. It was not until she lost these activities that Lisa became aware of just how important they were to her. To provide a more proactive and complete care experience for patients like Lisa, integrative treatment teams comprised of health care and mental health professionals can work in collaboration with patients to provide whole-person care. Let us now take a closer look at models of integrative medicine.

CURRENT MODELS OF INTEGRATIVE MEDICINE

Integrative medicine has emerged within the last decade as a trend in progressive health care that includes many variations of how to best practice its concept (Kinman, Gilchrist, Payne-Murphy, & Miller, 2015). Simply put, integrative medicine means to focus on the patient from a whole-person perspective that embraces health and well-being versus the limited disease-prevention model so prevalent in our Western society (Templeman & Robinson, 2011). The terms *integrated* medicine and *integrative* medicine have both been used to describe the relationship between conventional medicine and complementary practices. An additional term—integrated *behavioral* health care—also represents a collaborative approach used to meet patients' mental (behavioral) health care needs.

The Agency for Healthcare Research and Quality (AHRQ) gives the following definition for integrated behavioral health care (Kinman et al., 2015):

> The care that results from a practice team of primary care and behavioral health clinicians, working together with patients and families, using a systematic and cost-effective approach to provide patient-centered care for a defined population. This care may address mental health and substance abuse conditions, health behaviors (including their contribution to chronic medical illnesses), life stressors and crises, stress-related physical symptoms, and ineffective patterns of health care utilization. (p. 2)

The term *integrative*, as opposed to *integrated*, is believed to be more expansive with an emphasis on wellness and holism using a biological, psychological, sociological, and spiritual framework (Horrigan, 2003). By utilizing both conventional and complementary/alternative approaches, health care practitioners are able to have a broad array of options in designing a wellness plan tailored to each unique patient. Integrative medicine practitioners have been willing to collaborate with various disciplines including mental health, physical therapy, dietetics, body work (e.g., yoga and Pilates), and meditation. Whole-person care can only be accomplished if the whole person is understood in the context of his or her environment and from a *lifestyle* perspective. It would be unfair to assume that one health care professional (i.e., physician) should be responsible for mastering all treatment modalities. The task of doing so would simply be impractical at the very least. Integrative medicine recognizes this and has channeled efforts to break down the silos of health care disciplines, many of which have historically worked independently from one another. Lines of communication are opening up so that the proverbial right hand knows what the left hand is doing.

For example, a physician recognizes symptoms of depression or anxiety in a patient and makes a referral to a mental health professional such as a counselor or psychologist. The mental health professional (therapist), in turn, obtains a release of information from the patient so the therapist can report back to the physician on the progress of their sessions. The therapist might also recognize lifestyle patterns that are contributing to the patient's emotional difficulties and recommend a consultation with a dietician. Upon further exploration, the therapist may also suggest the patient consult with his or her physician about receiving chiropractic care for adjustments and posture corrections. Being aware of and valuing the expertise of different health care professions is the first step in practicing integrative medicine. Collaboration and communication-sharing further builds an integrative, patient-centered foundation (Frenkel & Cohen, 2014).

A more direct way of interprofessional collaboration occurs when professionals are located in the same building or within the same primary care practice (Heath, Wise Romero, & Reynolds, 2013). Even so, challenges can occur regarding confidentiality, recognizing mental health symptoms and referring for mental health treatment, understanding each discipline's unique language and way of conceptualizing a patient's struggle, billing insurance and managed care, and supporting the relationship that each practitioner has with the patient. In a study of primary care physicians and licensed professional clinical counselors, Miller, Hall, and Hunley (2006) also found that both disciplines valued an integrative model using a biopsychosocial framework, and believed any initial challenges were worth the benefits of working together. Fortunately, over the last decade several models have emerged that attempt to connect the various health care disciplines around a common theme: the patient experience. Despite the progress of the integrative care movement, opportunities for improvement remain.

The AHRQ conducted a thorough literature review, "Provider- and Practice-Level Competencies for Integrated Behavioral Health in Primary Care" (Kinman et al., 2015). The authors identify what is required to develop and maintain an integrated primary care setting that embraces a team orientation toward patient well-being. Those identified as providers included primary care physicians, nurses, mental health professionals, care coordinators, and pharmacists. According to the paper, each profession has a unique role to play, yet in general should be knowledgeable in human development, chronic illnesses in primary care, psychotropic medications, and the interaction between biology and behavior. Further, using evidence-based therapies to improve patient functioning is paramount.

Efficiency in any team model requires that communication be seamless and clear. This is especially true in the primary care setting, where time spent with each patient is typically less than 15 minutes; therefore, each provider should attempt to interact with one another and the patient in the most efficient manner possible while still demonstrating empathy and respect. The mental health professional, by training, is skilled in the clinical interviewing and consultation techniques needed to quickly build rapport, which can contribute to a positive patient experience overall (Hooper, 2014). Regarding working with patients who have experienced medical trauma, a real challenge arises if we expect mental health professionals to work within the typical time frames allotted within primary care. As mentioned previously, the primary care setting is a fast-paced environment, with brief interactions and consultations being the hallmark of patient care. Talk therapy, especially as it relates to trauma and posttraumatic stress disorder (PTSD) work, would be severely limited within this time frame. While psychoeducation and screenings for trauma, secondary crises, and/or risk factors can be accomplished relatively quickly, allowing patients to "process" the trauma requires more time. Schumann and Miller (2000) noted that primary care patients with a trauma history are guarded against disclosing anything related to earlier trauma unless they feel safe and supported. Helping patients feel safe enough to risk being vulnerable is the first step in providing holistic care needed in an integrative primary care setting. Cognitive, emotional, and trauma processing takes additional time and requires that the patient continue to feel safe and respected. Feeling rushed could only hinder a patient's ability or willingness to risk self-awareness. True patient-centered care may require more flexibility of the primary care setting, at least as it pertains to trauma work with patients.

Collaboration with both patients and staff is equally important within an integrative care model, in addition to maintaining a degree of flexibility to be able to quickly adapt to changes. The team concept and working alliance can be cultivated by ensuring each provider's role is understood and valued by everyone on the team, and in-service training on a regular basis can help promote collaboration and a shared mission.

Spotlight on an Integrative Care Model: Duke University

Duke University, for instance, has developed a unique approach to holistic care called Duke Integrative Medicine (Horrigan, 2007). Their model is based on a concept of wellness with mindfulness (more on that in Chapter 10) at the core, bringing attention to spiritual, mental, physical, and social well-being. The process begins for patients at a primary care facility, where they first experience an in-depth physician examination and consultation followed by additional consultations with complementary health care practitioners (e.g., fitness, massage, nutrition, and mental health) in order to develop a personal wellness plan. All practitioners work within the same facility, so there is easy patient access for coordinated care. Patients become involved with the Center through different entry points along the health continuum: Some are interested in simply improving their overall wellness while others may become involved after an adverse health event such as a heart attack or life-threatening diagnosis. The model requires flexibility and high quality care in order to stay truly patient focused. Other organizations show similar efforts (e.g., University of Michigan Department of Family Medicine and the Birkenholm Centre in Denmark) with an orientation toward integrative primary care.

Not all primary care settings are able or willing to employ the diverse group of professionals like Duke Integrative Medicine or similar integrative practice. Still, the opportunity to practice using an integrative model exists as long as primary care providers believe that holistic wellness extends beyond Western medicine and they value the contributions of other health care providers.

SCREENING FOR TRAUMA-RELATED RISK FACTORS

Now that we have reviewed some basic concepts related to prevention, including bolstering patient protective factors and improving wellness using an integrative primary care model, let us turn our attention to intervention for medical trauma within this level of care. As with any physical or mental health problem, good intervention starts with good assessment. Screening inventories are used quite frequently within the primary care setting to gain a quick snapshot of a patient's experience, including the patient's perceptions about traumatic life events. This is important to assess because we know that a traumatic experience causes brain chemistry changes that impact a person's health at the biopsychosocial and behavioral levels (Norman et al., 2006). Consequently, trauma-based experiences often present as physical complaints that lead to primary care visits, so it makes sense that we strive to identify specific life stressors to get a more complete picture of the risk factors that contribute to patient health.

Primary care settings that understand this and orient themselves accordingly will be more effective with patients who are struggling due to the effects of a traumatic experience. The National Center for Trauma Informed Care (NCTIC) was initiated by the Substance Abuse and Mental Health Services Administration (SAMHSA) to better prepare organizations in how they understand and interact with persons who have experienced trauma. At a systems level, being trauma-informed means to realize the far-reaching impacts of trauma and the various ways people recover from trauma. At an operational level, organizations respond to this awareness by fully integrating trauma knowledge into policies and procedures so that retraumatization is minimized or avoided. Each provider should be skilled in recognizing the signs and symptoms of trauma in not only the patients, but also in family members and members of the organization (SAMHSA, 2015a).

Screening for trauma, trauma-related symptoms, or risk factors that may predispose a patient to trauma provides medical staff initial insights that can be further explored by a mental health professional. Self-administered checklists are often favored for this purpose, as they may seem less intrusive than a face-to-face interview. In fact, using quick screening instruments to assess for trauma risk factors may be one of the more sensitive ways to *initially* screen for trauma since the topic may bring added vulnerability for the patient. It is advisable to refer patients to a mental health professional if the results of quick screening determine that there are adverse effects from trauma. When patients are more vulnerable, this demands that a "therapeutic orientation" be used, especially when reviewing the results with the patient. Tone and volume of speech, active attending and listening skills, cultural sensitivity, and empathic reflections (Chen & Giblin, 2014) are but a few skills needed when engaged in more in-depth trauma screening or assessment. SAMHSA (2015b) noted that patients should have *time* to complete a trauma checklist or further discuss the results. Difficult emotions may emerge for the patient, and medical staff should anticipate this and be flexible with time beyond the typical per-patient allotment within the primary care setting.

One way to address this would be to implement a two-tiered mental health workflow system in primary care. The initial level would require that the mental health professional use quick screening to assess a patient and determine a diagnosis, intervention plan, and then consult with the primary care provider to ensure coordinated treatment. The second level would require more time as patients who are flagged for risk factors for medical trauma could be scheduled for a standard 60-minute mental health session for further processing. Because psychological and emotional struggles related to medical trauma are often not receptive to the quick-fix assessment and intervention approaches of primary care, recognizing this and adapting accordingly would further ensure tailored interventions for each patient.

There are a number of trauma screening inventories and checklists available for use in the primary setting. In choosing the most appropriate tool, one should consider the purpose (e.g., screen for trauma experiences, PTSD, comorbid mental health issue), population (e.g., adults, children, adolescents, types of trauma experiences), and instrument reliability and validity. Because trauma-related symptoms are often common in a variety of mental health diagnoses (e.g., anxiety, PTSD, depression), it is important to assess a patient from multiple perspectives, which allows interventions to address the unique needs of each patient.

Hooper, Stockton, Krupnick, and Green (2011) advocate using the Trauma History Questionnaire (THQ) in a variety of settings and with populations including medical patients. Likewise, the primary care PTSD (PC-PTSD) screen (Prins et al., 2004) is a brief, four-item tool used to detect PTSD symptoms. Neither instrument, however, is geared specifically to the three levels of medical trauma that we discuss in this book. The Stressful Life Experiences Screening Questionnaire (SLESQ) tool (Goodman, Corcoran, Turner, Yuan, & Green, 1998) does, however, inquire about having either witnessed or experienced a life-threatening illness. Another tool that can be useful in determining how a medical trauma has affected a patient across various life domains is the S7-LES tool, which can be useful for primary care providers in gauging the impacts of specific medical events.

Assessing the Seven Areas of Secondary Crisis

As we have mentioned throughout this book, screening tools serve a critical function at multiple levels of care and can be especially beneficial in identifying the experience of or potential for medical trauma. An important effect of medical trauma beyond developing mental health disorders is the multiple ways in which medical trauma affects every aspect of life, which we call *secondary crises* (Hall & Hall, 2013). Secondary crises, as we mentioned in Chapter 1, are changes in one or more life domains after a traumatic medical event, life-altering procedure, or diagnosis of chronic illness, and can result in unique challenges for the patient and his or her family. Some patients may be predisposed to experiencing secondary crises following a medical trauma, which is especially true for persons who have risk factors for PTSD such as being in the lower 15% of physical and mental health (Seligman, 2011). Unfortunately, secondary crises are often not anticipated nor assessed either in the primary care, specialty care, or hospital setting.

Assessing for medical trauma (and effects such as PTSD, etc.) at the primary care setting builds a bridge between mental and physical health. Assessing for secondary crises is no different, and can be a seamless effort if the resources (i.e., mental health professionals) are available and medical staff is willing to explore this with the patient. Common objections to screening by medical staff might be related to a lack of time or hesitancy to take this responsibility; there can be questions regarding what to do with this information once it is gathered, or a lack of training to "process" the emotional experience of the patient. While we are not suggesting that it is the responsibility of physicians or their staff to process assessment results with patients, we do believe that medical staff can take the opportunity to simply ask patients if there have been any changes in their lives that have occurred since their operation/medical procedure/diagnosis. If patients answer "yes," then medical staff can ensure that adequate assessment and follow-up with mental health resources are part of patients' treatment plans.

The S7-LES tool is designed to quickly assess a patient's perceived level of change regarding the seven life domains following a distressing medical procedure or diagnosis (Appendix B). The tool is self-administered in the primary care setting in the weeks or months following a procedure or diagnosis. Domain responses that suggest a patient has concerns or struggles can be further discussed with a mental health professional. Although the S7-LES is a postprocedure tool, there is merit in asking the patient-related questions *prior* to a medical intervention. For example, it would be helpful to ask questions like 'Is there anything in your life that you're concerned about being affected by this procedure, such as lifestyle changes?' A question similar to this gives the provider a heads up to emerging concerns that could be addressed after the medical intervention by using the S7-LES.

The following is an overview of the seven secondary crises (Hall & Hall, 2013) and how to screen using the S7-LES.

1. *Developmental*—A medical trauma can suspend a person's developmental progression in ways that diminish quality of life. Example: A high school senior who misses graduation with her peers and is delayed in beginning college and/or career aspirations because of an automobile accident. Social, emotional, and mental difficulties arise that could warrant mental health intervention.

2. *Avocational*—Sometimes a medical procedure or diagnosis can create physical limitations that alter how a person participates in leisure activities. Example: A planned surgery to alleviate lower back pain forces a change in exercise routine (e.g., running to swimming). Likewise, one's ability to lift heavy objects could require a change in home life such as carrying groceries and gardening activities.

3. *Existential*—Reflections on the meaning behind a medical trauma can be just as difficult as physical limitations. Awareness of mortality, limits on freedom, and feelings of isolation further complicate how people view themselves and their identity. Anxiety and depression can accompany existential reflections if patients are unable to make sense of their situation in ways that allow them to move forward. Example: A man diagnosed with Parkinson's disease in his late 40s struggles with how his life will change in dramatic and negative ways.

4. *Relational*—A medical trauma can change multiple aspects of a relationship between one or more persons causing them to become closer or drift further apart. Example: A woman who experiences a traumatic childbirth becomes too vulnerable in her sexuality to be intimate with her husband. Communication patterns change as both partners are less open with one another. Feelings of rejection, mistrust, and coindependency begin to emerge as the relationship becomes the point of stress and confusion.

5. *Occupational*—A person's career or livelihood represents a major part of their identity and can be a source of enjoyment, self-worth, and friendships. Medical traumas can become occupational crises when this part of one's identity changes. Example: A surgeon who develops early-onset Alzheimer's decides to step down after contemplating the risk of continuing to perform the complex operations for which she was known.

6. *Spiritual*—Religious and spiritual beliefs are fundamental to many people's faith systems and coping strategies. Faith can also extend to others, oneself, and to the medical system. Medical traumas can bring faith into question and cast doubt on a person's own resilience, the competence of health care professionals, and his or her belief in a higher power. Example: A person who credits God for the gifts he or

she has begins to blame God when they develop a degenerative eye disease thus limiting the use of his or her talents.

7. *Intrapersonal (Self)*—People's self-concept, or how they view themselves, is a fundamental part of mental and emotional well-being. It is part of our identity and influences how we interact with the world around us. Experiencing a medical trauma can cause one to redefine his or her self-identity thus impacting relationships, career, leisure activities, and so on. Example: An assertive, independent, and otherwise healthy man experiences a stroke. Unable to initially care for himself he becomes more passive and dependent in life. Others notice his lack of initiative and adventure, which changes how they relate to him.

These secondary crises do not develop independently or in isolation of each other, as a crisis in one life domain can cause a domino effect of influence in many others. It is also important to remember that there is no specific time line in which these adverse effects will develop or resolve; therefore, it may be necessary for patients to complete the S7-LES at regular intervals following a medical trauma.

While screening for psychological impacts of medical trauma is critical, screening for the purposes of prevention should not be overlooked as an important function within the primary care setting. Another way in which primary care providers can help patients manage possible impacts of medical events is to determine what risk factors a patient might have, as many factors increase their vulnerability for experiencing medical trauma. Let us examine a screening instrument for identifying such factors, or the MMHS.

Medical Mental Health Screening

In an effort to provide a way to focus more specifically on medical trauma and associated risk factors, we have developed the MMHS tool (see Appendix C). This self-administered tool is used as a prescreen to help assess for risk factors that can contribute to adverse psychological responses (specifically, traumatic stress responses) to medical events, illnesses, and procedures. Patients can complete the checklist during preadmission to the hospital for a scheduled procedure, or in a primary care or specialist's office prior to hospital admission. There are five subscales related to being at risk for medical trauma: past trauma history, medical anxiety, current or past mental health issues, personality factors, and lifestyle and coping factors. Each subscale includes questions that if marked "yes" can be further explored with a mental health professional. Administering the MMHS tool prior to a medical procedure can help in prevention, intervention, and postrecovery efforts. Additional screening tools that further aid in building psychological and emotional awareness and healing can be found in Chapters 8 and 9.

USING IN-HOUSE MENTAL HEALTH PROFESSIONALS

So far we have explored various aspects of what integration means with examples of when it is and is not effective. Heath et al. (2013) further clarified the various iterations of integrated care by presenting the model on a continuum representing six levels of collaboration/integration. The first level signifies minimal collaboration among health care professionals, and as the levels increase, collaboration becomes more embedded in the system. Level 6 reflects full collaboration within an integrated practice in which communication and tasks are streamlined and staff members operate using a common, team-oriented, and patient-centered model. The six levels are grouped under three categories of professional interaction: coordinated (emphasizing communication among professionals not located in the same facility), co-located (collaboration within a shared physical proximity), and integrated (close collaboration among professionals within a system that supports integrative care). This model highlights the full range of how primary care settings, along with the various professionals who work in this level of care, can vary in how they view and participate in holistic, patient-centered care. In turn, the quality of the patient experience is affected depending on the structure of the practice, type of professional collaboration, clinical delivery, and the shared mission of all involved. As we have already iterated, highly integrated models that bring together health care and mental health working in harmony are preferred, especially for managing medical trauma.

At the highest level of integrated care there are key elements that characterize best practices in primary care. In this model, not only are health care professionals located in the same space within the same facility, but also they share a culture that values and understands each other's unique contributions to a patient's well-being. Health screenings are standard practice and used to better understand how a patient's past, present, and future can influence interventions and care. Additionally, screenings can serve as indicators of issues (i.e., medical trauma) that would invite more in-depth discussions with health care professionals. The various health care disciplines are also unified in their access to and understanding of these screenings. It is not difficult to imagine how a highly integrated model can benefit patients who experience medical trauma. Incorporating mental health professionals into a practice in ways that promote the visibility of both the professionals and the importance of mental and emotional well-being can decrease the stigma sometimes associated with seeking psychological help.

Let us now examine a highly integrated model that is revolutionizing primary care across the country, and that can have significant impacts on how medical trauma is managed.

PATIENT-CENTERED MEDICAL HOME MODEL

The patient-centered medical home model (PCMH) has evolved over the last decade as a blueprint for excellence in primary care. The AHRQ laid the initial groundwork for the PCMH model and has garnered support from the Patient-Centered Primary Care Collaborative (PCPCC) in defining best practices that create a new paradigm in primary care. The current model emphasizes five core principles to ensure that care is (PCPCC, 2015, p. 1):

1. *Patient centered:* A partnership among practitioners, patients, and their families ensures that decisions respect patients' wants, needs, and preferences, and that patients have the education and support they need to make decisions and participate in their own care.

2. *Comprehensive:* A team of care providers is wholly accountable for a patient's physical and mental health care needs, including prevention and wellness, acute care, and chronic care.

3. *Coordinated:* Care is organized across all elements of the broader health care system, including specialty care, hospitals, home health care, community services, and supports.

4. *Accessible:* Patients are able to access services with shorter waiting times, "after hours" care, 24/7 electronic or telephone access, and strong communication through health IT innovations.

5. *Committed to quality and safety:* Clinicians and staff enhance quality improvement to ensure that patients and families make informed decisions about their health.

Results from implementing the PCMH model are promising, showing a reduction in surgical and medical costs while increasing preventive measures, quality of care, and behavioral health outcomes (e.g., Alexander et al., 2015; Nielsen, Gibson, Buelt, Grundy, & Grumbach, 2014). Each staff member has role to play in the PCMH model and even though they might share in the patient-centered mission, there is still the issue of effective coordination among services. The *patient navigator* is one who can bridge these gaps and serve as the conductor of a well-coordinated orchestra. Patient navigators can help patients understand and choose among health providers and services (including tele-medicine), understand health coverage, help make decisions about treatment, and manage care received by multiple providers (Ferrante, Cohen, & Crosson, 2010). Because of their unique role, patient navigators are also positioned to assess for medical trauma and secondary crises. They could offer the emotional support and encouragement for patients to seek psychological counseling with a mental health provider and monitor follow through. Further, patient navigators can ensure that patients are accessing the care they need, which can reduce the occurrence of medical avoidance which is common in patients who experience severe medical trauma. Overall, this unique role is a valuable resource in promoting a patient's biopsychosocial well-being, and can serve as a template for quality improvement in primary care offices that do not strictly follow the PCMH model.

It is evident that integrative health models are superior approaches to managing medical trauma in primary care, for they ensure that mental health staff members are embedded within the treatment system. But who are the mental health staff members, and what are their roles within primary care? In the next section, we briefly survey the various mental health professions, including outlining unique qualities of each and common settings in which they work.

UNDERSTANDING DIFFERENT MENTAL HEALTH PROFESSIONS

In the primary care setting and community mental health setting, there are a number of mental health practitioners who have distinct differences in training, professional orientation, and roles within health care, as well as striking similarities in their functions within various health care settings. The opportunity exists for medical communities to best utilize this expertise so that patient-centered care is seamless and inclusive, and that assessment and intervention move beyond taking care of physical health. The following is a brief overview of the majority of mental health professions:

- **Psychiatrists:** As medical doctors who specialize in the diagnosis and treatment of mental disorders, psychiatrists have earned either an MD or DO degree, which allows them to prescribe and manage psychotropic medications. Within the hospital setting, psychiatrists often work in the specialized settings of psychological and behavioral health care, providing administrative and clinical leadership to the mental health professional staff and medication management to psychiatric patients.

- **Psychologists:** Practicing psychologists have a doctoral-level, non-medical degree (PhD or PsyD) in areas such as clinical psychology, counseling psychology, health psychology, and many other specialties. Psychologists are skilled in administering and interpreting psychological assessments and in diagnosing and treating mental and emotional disorders. Many psychologists are trained using the medical model and a biopsychosocial framework for understanding pathology and mental illness.

- **Social Workers:** Most social workers who work in the hospital setting have a bachelor's (BSW) or master's degree (MSW), although some have a doctorate (DSW or PhD). Social workers are the largest group of mental health professionals and work in a variety of settings within health care, such as in hospitals, hospice/palliative care, outpatient clinics, and social service organizations. Social workers serve a variety of functions within the hospital, including crisis intervention, acting as an advocate on behalf of the patient, serving as a liaison between the patient and health care staff, and educating the patient and health care staff about the impact of psychosocial issues on an illness or injury. Trained in the ecological perspective, social workers can be helpful allies in managing medical trauma within the acute care setting. Clinical social workers are trained in the diagnosis and treatment of mental and emotional disorders and can provide talk therapy interventions to individuals, couples, families, and groups.

- **Counselors:** Compared to their social worker and psychologist colleagues, professional counselors have typically held fewer positions in hospitals and health care settings, with the majority working in community mental health organizations and private practice. While their specific licenses vary by state (most have some version of a licensed professional counselor [LPC]), professional counselors hold a minimum of a master's degree in clinical mental health counseling or a similar degree, and some have earned a doctorate (PhD or EdD). LPCs are sometimes referred to as clinical mental health counselors, clinical counselors, or mental health counselors. Counselors are trained in diagnosing and treating mental and emotional disorders and understand the medical model, yet the foundation of a counselor's training is developmental, strength based, and holistic. Counselors value wellness, growth, and prevention. Their primary role is providing talk therapy, which can be in modalities such as individual, couples, family, and group therapy.

- **Psychiatric or Mental Health Nurse Practitioners:** Registered nurses can further specialize in psychiatric or mental health nursing and work with individuals, families, groups, and communities to help with mental health needs, often within the hospital setting. The actual title for this discipline, however, can vary by state. Graduate degrees (master's or doctoral) in psychiatric-mental health nursing prepares the nurse practitioner to diagnose and treat mental and emotional disorders across the life span through the use of psychotropic medication and psychotherapy. Policy development and health care reform are additional areas of focus that draw on their expertise in health care.

- **Psychiatric or Mental Health Physician Assistants:** Physician assistants who wish to focus on mental health can seek a Certificate of Added Qualification (CAQ) in psychiatry, which requires documented experience with supervision in psychiatric practice along with an exam. The medical model is highlighted with an emphasis on the *Diagnostic and Statistical Manual of Mental Disorders, Fifth Edition* (*DSM-5*; American Psychiatric Association, 2013) diagnostic criteria and accompanying medication management versus psychotherapy interventions. Settings of employment include mental health agencies, hospitals, and the correctional system.

- **Additional Mental Health Professionals:** Marriage and family therapists and pastoral counselors have many characteristics of some of the aforementioned professions, and focus on counseling for relational wellness, with pastoral counselors being firmly rooted in a faith tradition.

Now that we have briefly reviewed many of the mental health professional disciplines likely to work with patients who experience medical trauma, let us take a closer look at the therapeutic modalities with the strongest evidence for positive outcomes.

MENTAL HEALTH TREATMENT FOR MEDICAL TRAUMA

Treating medical trauma can be difficult for both the patient and the mental health professional because of the patient's vulnerability and the potential complexity of the traumatic experience. Treatment can consist of a combination of antianxiety or antidepression medications and talk therapy interventions. For mental health treatment, specialized training is required and providers should consider all information gathered in the screening process prior to developing a treatment plan; such information includes co-occurring disorders (e.g., substance abuse and mental/emotional diagnoses), trauma history, previous mental health treatment, and contextual background. There are a variety of treatment modalities for trauma in general (e.g., National Center for PTSD, 2015), which would also apply in treating medical trauma and medical PTSD. Regardless of the specific therapeutic approach used, providers should allow time to appropriately process the medical trauma, as well as to treat the psychological impacts of the trauma. Bonanno (2004) emphasized that one session for a patient to tell his or her story and express emotion is not always enough to reduce the risk of developing PTSD; further, adverse outcomes can actually increase for the patient if appropriate time is not given to support the recovery process.

The following methods for treating trauma are just a few of the evidence-based approaches designed to help a patient work through the mental and emotional difficulties that arise following a medical trauma experience. (Additional information about treatment modalities and trauma resources can be found in Appendix A.) Note that there are common themes among the various approaches, including psychoeducation, relaxation techniques, and coping strategies. Because trauma treatment often requires the patient to revisit the event (i.e., retelling the story or trauma narrative) it is important that the patient feels safe and has a degree of life stability (Staggs, 2015).

Cognitive behavioral therapies (CBTs) have proven useful in addressing many problems individuals experience that affect their self-concept, relationships, and behaviors. The basic premise of CBT is that we can learn to change our thoughts so they are more self-affirming, rational, and strength-based versus using the self-defeating distortions such as catastrophizing and blaming (Beck, 2011). At the same time, we can learn to change our behavior toward growth of self and relationships (e.g., new communication strategies, relaxation techniques, exercise, and diet changes). As thoughts and behaviors change for the better, mood begins to lift and one's outlook becomes more hopeful. There are many variations of CBT that can be used as effective interventions by trained mental health professionals. Cognitive restructuring and behavior modification, which are fundamental to CBT, are also integral to trauma interventions.

Staggs (2015) further identified a three-phase protocol that is applicable to a general trauma intervention. Phase One is designed to help a patient move from being in crisis mode to gaining the skills necessary to reduce symptoms and begin a reappraisal of the traumatic memories (Phase Two). To facilitate this, a mental health professional helps the patient improve interpersonal skills, behavioral activities, and thoughts about self, others, and the world. Becoming proficient in emotional self-regulation is also key, as it relates to mindfulness, relaxation, and distress tolerance (Phase Three).

Each patient is different regarding when and how he or she is able to process traumatic memories. Some approaches, such as cognitive processing therapy, trauma-focused CBT, and prolonged exposure therapy, use methods of trauma recall that encourage people to verbalize their trauma narratives and share powerful imagery of the trauma (Monson & Shnaider, 2014). There is a continuum of exposure, from flooding with memories to incrementally desensitizing the experience. Again, the method that mental health professionals choose is dependent upon their training, a patient's mental stability, and the complexity of the trauma.

Another popular method for recalling traumatic memories is eye movement desensitization and reprocessing (EMDR; McGuire, Lee, & Drummond, 2014; Shapiro & Solomon, 1995). EMDR is a unique method to help a patient reprocess unresolved traumatic experiences through bilateral stimulation with body sensations, thoughts, images, and emotions. The patient in effect is guided through the unpacking of the traumatic memories and a mental health professional helps them cognitively "repack" them in ways that allow for PTSD symptoms to abate.

Somatic experiencing (SE) is a newer trauma treatment method generating much interest and promise. Based on the work of Peter Levine (2010), SE emphasizes body movement as a therapeutic intervention. This experiential processing helps release trauma locked or "frozen" within a patient's physical self at the time of a traumatic experience. Levine developed this approach by observing how animals recover from life-threatening events, when the fight-or-flight response does not occur and there is no escape from the traumatic event. He discovered how the body can hold trauma just as easily as the mind and therefore any intervention must assist the body to release and heal.

Mindfulness and mindfulness-based stress reduction (MBSR) interventions are easily accessible to health care practitioners and serve as a powerful addition to evidence-based trauma treatments. Staying in the present moment reorients the mind to avoid past rumination (depression) and future worry (anxiety). The breathing, as well as mental and emotional self-regulation strategies, are beneficial in helping to manage traumatic stress, decrease arousal (Baer, 2003), and provide a greater sense of peace (Williams & Penman, 2011). We will explore applications for mindfulness-based approaches in more depth in Chapter 10.

These are but a few of the interventions that mental health professionals can combine and tailor to patients' needs and lifestyles. Regardless of the method, however, one of the main ingredients contributing to a successful therapeutic outcome is the quality of the therapeutic relationship (Jackson, Nissenson, & Cloitre, 2009). In the end, how we communicate with patients who have experienced medical trauma in the primary care setting becomes one of the most important aspects of patient-centered primary care. It is imperative that health care providers *not* assume that because the majority of episodes of primary care are noncritical in nature that patients are not in need of sensitive, empathic communication. Even in preventive care episodes, patients can be quite vulnerable to trauma triggers, especially in cases of a previous medical trauma. Consider the following episode of care in an OB/GYN office, and how communication and processes can have a detrimental effect on patient health, experience, and satisfaction:

> As I (Michelle) mentioned previously, I experienced medical trauma following the birth of my daughter and subsequent postpartum hemorrhage. Within 3 months of this medical event, I developed posttraumatic stress disorder and sought to avoid many of the reminders of the birth trauma – and this included seeing my OB/GYN. I had many rationalizations for why this was a good idea: *I had a complete hysterectomy, so I shouldn't have to worry about annual screenings for uterine or cervical cancer; I have a lot going on in my life and I don't want to be re-traumatized by having a pelvic exam; my doctor is too strong of a trigger for me—I cannot be treated by her and I don't know of any good doctors in the area.* These were but a few of the excuses I conjured every time I had a thought about going to a doctor. In the back of my mind, I knew it was best that I re-engage in preventive care, but I just couldn't bring myself to do it. I had a primary care doctor (internal medicine) who was willing to prescribe medication for estrogen replacement, so I thought there was no real need for an OB/GYN.

Nearly 10 years later, my doctor retired and my new primary care physician was willing to manage my estrogen *until I found a new OB/GYN*. I panicked at the thought of having a pelvic exam, but I knew that it was in my best interest to do so. I asked my primary care physician to give me a referral because I wasn't all that familiar with the physicians in the area. (Truthfully, I had been researching OB/GYNs online for some time. I just couldn't make a decision about which one seemed the most caring AND clinically competent.) My doctor gave me the name of a practice and told me that they would be calling me to make an appointment.

The next day, a woman from the OB/GYN's office called to schedule my appointment. She asked if I had a preference for a particular doctor in their large group practice as she brought up the schedule on her computer screen. I decided in that moment that I would give the scheduler a little background about me and see if she had a suggestion:

"Well, I'm not familiar with the doctors in your practice. I did want to mention that I experienced a significant birth trauma, and so I would like to see someone who is very caring, and has an excellent bedside manner," I said in a shaky voice.

Without acknowledging a word I had just said, the woman said quickly, "Dr. X has an opening next Tuesday at 1:30. Can you make that?"

Slightly stunned by her aloof response, I quickly checked my calendar and said that I could. She said paperwork would be coming in the mail, and that I should arrive 15 minutes early since I am a new patient. When I hung up, I felt warm tears well up in my eyes, and reminded myself that I was strong and could do this.

The following Tuesday, I arrived for my appointment with paperwork in hand. The waiting room was large, with rows of chairs placed along the perimeter of the room and more seating arranged in a rectangle in the center. Three TVs hung in strategic locations, all playing a daytime soap opera. There were women's magazines scattered throughout. I checked in with the receptionist, who was cold and business-like, barely cracking a smile. She told me that someone would be with me shortly. I picked a chair against the wall as far away from the TV noise as I could get. I took several deep breaths and waited for my name to be called.

Not 10 minutes later, a medical assistant entered the waiting room and called my name. I rose, smiled at her, and followed her to the first small room on the left.

"We are going to stop in here so that I can take your vitals and get your weight and height," she said, matter-of-factly. She proceeded to collect the necessary information, and then sat at her computer monitor to input the data. The door to the little room remained open, and I sat watching people rush by in both directions.

"Any problems you'd like to discuss with the doctor today?" Sitting in the chair opposite the technician, I instinctively knew that I did not feel comfortable in this setting and with this person.

"Nope, nothing," I said haltingly and without emotion.

"Okay, then, I'll walk you to the waiting room and we'll call you back very soon," the technician said as she began to walk toward the hallway.

I followed her back to the waiting room, taken slightly off-guard that I would be returning there instead of going to an exam room. I noticed that I was feeling more vulnerable now than when I first arrived, my heart beating wildly in my chest as I returned to the same chair I occupied previously.

Approximately 15 minutes later, the same assistant called my name once again, but this time she led me down an opposite hallway to an exam room. She motioned to the stack of gowns, grabbing one off of the top.

"You'll need to put this on. Remove all of your clothing. The gown needs to be open in the front. The doctor will be in shortly." The assistant rattled off these instructions mechanically, barely looking me in the eye before she closed the door.

I did as instructed and folded my clothing before placing it on a nearby chair. I then sat at the edge of the exam table lined with crisp white paper, glancing down at the stirrups jutting out on either side. I took several deep breaths and fought back tears as all of the memories of my birth trauma came flowing back, prompting a visceral response throughout my entire body. I glanced up at the bulletin board dotted with photographs of babies dressed as flowers and butterflies, feeling a mix of emotions as I waited for my new doctor to arrive. I read a poster on the wall that detailed the cycle of pregnancy from conception to birth, reminiscing about my own pregnancy and thinking about how I would never again experience giving birth to another child. Before I drifted too far into my own thoughts, I was startled alert by a quick knock and a click of the opening exam room door.

I turned my head and kept my body stationary, not wanting to force open my thin paper gown.

The doctor entered quickly, followed by two other staff members. As she walked across the room to the computer monitor, she barely looked at me as she introduced herself. She did not introduce the staff members who accompanied her.

"Hi, Michelle, I'm Dr. X. Do you have any questions for me today?"

I was speechless, as it seemed an odd and abrupt way to start an office visit, especially with a new patient. Trying to brush it off, I proceeded to try to explain a few of my concerns, starting with my history. As I began talking, the doctor motioned for me to lie back, place my ankles in the stirrups, and slide forward. As I continued talking, I consciously managed the flood of emotions prompted by my body's vulnerable position. I felt the cold speculum enter my body as I began explaining more about my postpartum hemorrhage and subsequent hysterectomy, "Wow!" the doctor exclaimed, snickering. "That's a heck of a way to have a baby!"

I was shocked by her response, and decided in that moment that I just wanted the appointment to end. I knew that this would not be a physician or a practice I would continue with, and at that point all I wanted to do was leave. The doctor commented that everything looked good, and I said I had no questions. The appointment lasted less than 10 minutes.

After she and her staff members left the room, I immediately burst into tears. I got up quickly and reached for my clothes, struggling to see clearly due to my watery vision. I wiped my eyes before opening the door, and then made my way up the labyrinthine hallways to the exit. I stopped at the front desk to settle any payment due, and when she asked if I'd like to go ahead and set up my next annual visit, I declined.

It would be almost 2 years before I worked up the nerve to visit another OB/GYN.

As this example illustrates, patients with a history of medical trauma can experience a recurrence of traumatic symptoms in the primary care setting. Although it should be the practice of *all* staff members in primary care to communicate with *all* patients with sensitivity and respect, it is vital to do so with patients who have increased vulnerability due to risk factors such as prior medical trauma.

Before we bring this chapter to a close, let us take a second look at the case of Keith and explore how his case could have been different had he experienced patient-centered, coordinated care.

TYING IT ALL TOGETHER: REVISITING THE CASE OF KEITH

In Chapter 6 you were first introduced to the case of Keith, a man whose medical trauma developed from a combination of risk factors including vicarious trauma from his military deployment, the ineffective interventions prior to his surgery (microdisectomy), and communication challenges with the medical staff throughout his episode of care. These factors had a culminating effect leading to secondary crises in several life domains, with symptoms of depression, withdrawal, and anxiety resulting from the medical trauma.

There were many chances for medical staff to interact with Keith differently, especially with respect to empathic communication. Prior to Keith's series of cortisone shots, he could have been screened for risk factors using the MMHS, and his providers could have discussed possible lifestyle effects of his injury in more detail. Through this conversation, Keith's primary care clinicians would have noticed Keith's concern regarding the procedural outcome and how his life might be affected. This information could have been passed along to the hospital intake staff so that their communication with Keith could have been further tailored to his needs. When Keith decided to stop the cortisone treatment, a follow-up call from the hospital could have led to conversation about Keith's concerns. Without that call, Keith became more frustrated and cynical about his plan of care.

Keith was hopeful about the effects of his surgery, especially after his presurgery meeting. If the presenter at this meeting would have balanced the talk with some discussion about how changes might occur in various life domains following the surgery instead of giving false reassurance that "Everything will get back to normal," Keith may have been more prepared for these changes and felt more empowered to take some positive actions regarding his mental health. Further, during the moments just prior to Keith's surgery when he asked the anesthesiologist about the effects of the anesthesia, the provider could have attempted to answer Keith's question despite his being close to sedation. Simply put, showing Keith respect as an individual could have offset his negative feelings about his medical care.

You will recall that in the weeks following Keith's surgery, he began to experience the full effects of how his life was changing in his career, activities, relationships, and within himself. A screen for secondary crises (S7-LES) following his medical procedure would have indicated Keith's unique reaction to the effects of his surgery, and prompted a referral to a mental health professional. The mental and emotional impact of this "new normal," as his friend called it, could have been processed in ways that allowed Keith to move forward beyond his perceived limitations. Looking back, there were quite a few things that could have been different in Keith's various levels of care resulting in a more coordinated, holistic, and patient-centered effort.

SUMMARY

Patient-centered primary care settings are unique in their opportunities to provide integrated care in ways that are customized for patients according to their individual needs. When primary care providers focus on wellness and prevention using a holistic lens, they have the ability to influence patient protective factors, which bolster patients' health in mind, body, and spirit. Primary care clinicians are poised to meet the needs of patients who are either prone to experience or who do experience a medical trauma and/or the related effects of secondary crises, and can access tools such as the MMHS and S7-LES to assess for these effects.

There are many examples of integrated models with best practices in place that highlight the need for collaboration with mental health professionals at the primary care level. Treating the psychological impacts of medical trauma is a necessary and challenging process that should be channeled to mental health professionals who have the most appropriate training to provide such care. Furthermore, they are well suited to utilize the many treatment modalities used for trauma healing, making them an integral member of any primary care team.

REFERENCES

Adler, A. (1927). *Understanding human nature*. Oxford, UK: Greenberg.

Alexander, J. A., Markovitz, A. R., Paustian, M. L., Wise, C. G., El Reda, D. K., Green, L. A., & Fetters, M. D. (2015). Implementation of patient-centered medical homes in adult primary care practices. *Medical Care Research and Review*, 72(4), 438–467.

American Psychiatric Association. (2013). *Diagnostic and statistical manual of mental disorders* (5th ed.). Arlington, VA: American Psychiatric Publishing.

Arvidsdotter, T., Marklund, B., Taft, C., & Kylen, S. (2015). Quality of life, sense of coherence and experiences with three different treatments in patients with psychological distress in primary care: A mixed-methods study. *BMC Complementary & Alternative Medicine*, 15(132). doi:10.1186/s12906-015-0654-z

Baer, R. A. (2003). Mindfulness training as a clinical intervention: A conceptual and empirical review. *Clinical Psychology: Science and Practice*, 10, 125–143.

Beck, J. S. (2011). *Cognitive behavior therapy: Basics and beyond* (2nd ed.). New York, NY: Guilford Press.

Bonanno, G. A. (2004). Loss, trauma, and human resilience: Have we underestimated the human capacity to thrive after extremely aversive events? *American Psychologist*, 29, 20–28.

Chen, M., & Giblin, N. J. (2014). *Individual counseling skills and techniques* (2nd ed.). Denver, CO: Love Publishing Company.

Ferrante, J. M., Cohen, D. J., & Crosson, J. C. (2010). Translating the patient navigator approach to meet the needs of primary care. *Journal of the American Board of Family Medicine*, 23(6), 736–744. doi:10.3122/jabfm.2010.06.100085

Frenkel, M., & Cohen, L. (2014). Effective communication about the use of complementary and integrative medicine in cancer care. *Journal of Alternative and Complementary Medicine*, 20(1), 12–18. doi:10:1089/acm.2012.0533

Goodman, L., Corcoran, C., Turner, K., Yuan, N., & Green, B. (1998). Assessing traumatic event exposure: General issues and preliminary findings for the

Stressful Life Events Screening Questionnaire. *Journal of Traumatic Stress, 11*(3), 521–542.

Hall, M. F., & Hall, S. E. (2013). When treatment becomes trauma: Defining, preventing, and transforming medical trauma. *VISTAS Online, 73*, 1–15.

Harris Poll. (2015). *Executive summary: A survey about mental health and suicide in the United States.* American Foundation for Suicide Prevention. Retrieved from http://www.afsp.org/news-events/in-the-news/surveyresults

Heath, B., Wise Romero P., & Reynolds, K. A. (2013). *A review and proposed standard framework for levels of integrated health care.* Washington, DC: SAMHSA-HRSA Center for Integrated Health Solutions.

Hooper, L. (2014). Mental health services in primary care: Implications for clinical mental health counselors and other mental health providers. *Journal of Mental Health Counseling, 36*(2), 95–98.

Hooper, L. M., Stockton, P., Krupnick, J. L., & Green, B. L. (2011). Development, use, and psychometric properties of the Trauma History Questionnaire. *Journal of Loss and Trauma, 16*, 258–283.

Horrigan, B. J. (2003). *Voices of integrative medicine: Conversations and encounters.* St. Louis, MO: Churchill Livingstone.

Horrigan, B. J. (2007). *Best practices in integrative medicine: A report from the Bravewell Clinical Network.* The Bravewell Collaborative. Retrieved from https://www.bravewell.org/current_projects/best_practices

Jackson, C., Nissenson, K., & Cloitre, M. (2009). Cognitive-behavioral therapy. In C. A. Courtois (Ed.), *Treating complex traumatic stress disorders: An evidence-based guide* (pp. 243–263). New York, NY: Guilford Press.

Kinman, C. R., Gilchrist, E. C., Payne-Murphy, J. C., & Miller, B. F. (2015). *Provider and practice level competencies for integrated behavioral health in primary care: A literature review* (AHRQ Publication No. 14-0073-EF). Rockville, MD: Agency for Healthcare Research and Quality.

Levine, P. (2010). *In an unspoken voice: How the body releases trauma and restores goodness.* Berkeley, CA: North Atlantic Books.

Maslow, A. H. (1943). A theory of human motivation. *Psychological Review, 50*(4), 370.

McGuire, T. M., Lee, C. W., & Drummond, P. D. (2014). Potential of eye movement desensitization and reprocessing therapy in the treatment of post-traumatic stress disorder. *Psychology Research and Behavior Management, 7*, 273–283. doi:10.2147/PRBM.S52268

Miller, H. L., Hall, S. E., & Hunley, S. A. (2006). Value perceptions of integrative health care: A study of primary care physicians and professional clinical counselors. *Journal of Contemporary Psychotherapy, 34*(2), 117–124.

Monson, C. M., & Shnaider, P. (2014). *Treating PTSD with cognitive-behavioral therapies: Interventions that work* (Concise Guides on Trauma Care Book Series, viii). Washington, DC: American Psychological Association. doi:org/10.1037//14372-000

Myers, J. E., Sweeney, T. J., & Witmer, M. (2000). The wheel of wellness counseling for wellness: A holistic model for treatment planning. *Journal of Counseling and Development, 78*(3), 251–266.

National Center for PTSD. (2015). *PTSD: National Center for PTSD.* Retrieved from http://www.pstsd.va.gov

Nielsen, M., Gibson, A., Buelt, L., Grundy, P., & Grumbach, K. (2015). *The patient-centered medical home's impact on cost and qualtity: Annual review of evidence 2013–2014.* Patient-Centered Primary Care Collaborative. Retrieved from http:// www.pcpcc.org/download/5499/PCPCC%202015%20Evidence%20Report.pdf

Norman, S. B., Means-Christensen, A. J., Craske, M. G., Sherbourne, C. D., Roy-Byrne, P. P., & Stein, M. B. (2006). Associations between psychological trauma and physical illness in primary care. *Journal of Traumatic Stress, 19,* 461–470. doi:10.1002/jts.20129

Patient-Centered Primary Care Collaborative. (2015). *Defining the medical home: A patient-centered philosophy that drives primary care excellence.* Retrieved from https://www.pcpcc.org/about/medical-home

Prins, A., Ouimette, P., Kimerling, R., Cameron, R. P., Hugelshofer, D. S., Shaw-Hegwer, J., ... Sheikh, J. I. (2004). The primary care PTSD screen (PC-PTSD): Development and operating characteristics. *Primary Care Psychiatry, 9,* 9–14.

Robinson, P., & Reiter, J. (2007). *Behavioral consultation and primary care: A guide to integrating services.* New York, NY: Springer Science & Business Media.

Schumann, L., & Miller, J. L. (2000). Post-traumatic stress disorder in primary care practice. *Journal of the American Academy of Nurse Practitioners, 12,* 475–482. doi:10.1111/j.1745-7599.2000.tb00159.x

Seligman, M. (2011). *Flourish: A visionary new understanding of happiness and well-being.* New York, NY: Free Press.

Shapiro, F., & Solomon, R. M. (1995). *Eye movement desensitization and reprocessing.* New York, NY: John Wiley & Sons.

Substance Abuse and Mental Health Services Administration. (2015a). *Trauma-informed approach.* Retrieved from http://www.samhsa.gov/nctic/trauma-interventions

Substance Abuse and Mental Health Services Administration. (2015b). *Trauma-informed care in behavioral health services: A Treatment Improvement Protocol (TIP 57).* Retrieved from http://www.store.samhsa.gov/shin/content//SMA14-4816/ SMA14-4816.pdf

Staggs, S. (2015). *Psychotherapy treatment for PTSD.* PsychCentral. Retrieved from http://www.psychcentral.com/lib/treatment-of-ptsd

Templeman, K., & Robinson, A. (2011). Integrative medicine models in contemporary primary health care. *Complementary Therapies in Medicine, 19,* 84–92.

Vogel, M., Malcore, S., Illes, R., & Kirkpatrick, H. (2014). Integrated primary care: Why you should care and how to get started. *Journal of Mental Health Counseling, 36*(2), 130–144. doi:10.17744/mehc.36.2.5312041n10767k51

Williams, M., & Penman, D. (2011). *Mindfulness: An eight-week plan for finding peace in a frantic world.* New York, NY: Rodale.

Witmer, J. M., & Sweeney, T. J. (1992). A holistic model for wellness and prevention over the life span. *Journal of Counseling & Development, 71,* 140–148.

Wolf, J. A., Niederhauser, V., Marshburn, D., & LaVela, S. (2014). Defining patient experience. *Patient Experience Journal, 1*(1), 1–14. Retrieved from http://pxjournal .org/journal/vol1/iss1/3

World Health Organization. (2014). *Mental health: Strengthening our response.* Fact sheet No. 220. Retrieved from http://www.who.int/mediacentre/factsheets/ fs220/en

8

PREVENTION AND INTERVENTION: LEVEL 2 MEDICAL TRAUMA AND SPECIALIST CARE

IN THIS CHAPTER, YOU WILL LEARN:

- *How medical trauma manifests in the management of chronic, life-threatening medical illnesses*
- *The role of specialized, interprofessional treatment and support centers in promoting health and well-being for patients with chronic illness in order to prevent more serious consequences of medical trauma*
- *Examples of support resources for patients who live with chronic, life-threatening medical illnesses*
- *Strategies for health care and mental health professional collaboration for specific medical disorders and the role of physicians, nurses, allied health professionals, and mental health professionals in the interprofessional network*
- *Specific interventions for managing the psychological impacts of medical trauma and secondary crises*
- *Examples of best practices for integrated care among specialists in primary/ acute care settings for the management of medical trauma*

HIGH-QUALITY CARE FOR CHRONIC ILLNESS

Chronic, life-threatening diagnoses remain an immense burden on the health care system and can have far-reaching effects on the lives of patients and their families. Aside from the obvious costs associated with missing work, medications, testing, and office visits to manage chronic illnesses, living with a life-threatening diagnosis can have consequences that are less easily quantified but nonetheless impactful. You will recall in Chapter 3 that the prevalence rates of mental health issues such as depression, anxiety, and posttraumatic stress disorder (PTSD) related to chronic illnesses are significant. Secondary crises are also a concern for patients who struggle with diseases such as cancer, diabetes, and heart-related illnesses, especially given the lethality of these disorders. It is not difficult to understand how these illnesses can lead to other health and mental health-related concerns, especially for the increasing numbers of patients who, for various reasons, have difficulty complying fully with medical treatment. When we think of these patients—those with chronic illnesses and other biopsychosocial concerns—getting fragmented, piecemeal treatment from health care and mental health professionals in a noncoordinated way, it is not difficult to imagine how patients can suffer. In this disjointed system, providing treatment can be akin to playing a game of whack-a-mole, which is frustrating for care providers, and potentially deadly for patients.

Thankfully, in many organizations, methods of treatment delivery for patients with chronic illness are becoming more coordinated in an effort to provide higher quality care. Many of these efforts reflect the six dimensions of patient centeredness as outlined by the Institute of Medicine (2001), which suggest that providers should:

1. Be respectful of patients' values, preferences, and expressed needs

2. Provide care that is coordinated and integrated

3. Provide information, communication, and education

4. Ensure physical comfort

5. *Provide emotional support to relieve fear and anxiety*

6. Involve family and friends when appropriate

While these dimensions provide the foundation for patient centeredness for *all* medical care, they are especially critical for patients who experience medical trauma as a result of receiving a life-threatening diagnosis and living with the many effects of such an illness. One important step in ensuring that these dimensions are acted upon is to build an interprofessional team who can support each aspect of this mission. In cases in which patients struggle psychologically as a result of living with a life-threatening illness, the services of mental health professionals are necessary to ensure that patients receive the support and education they need to restore emotional well-being. While physicians and nurses can certainly be sensitive and supportive to patients throughout treatment, it is important to note that medical trauma requires the specialized knowledge and skills of mental health professionals, too.

An ongoing challenge to providing whole-person care for patients who live with chronic illness rests with our ability to identify and fill gaps within treatment systems. In cases of medical trauma, a highly coordinated system of providers that includes mental health creates a safety net in which to catch patients who experience psychological distress from their chronic illness diagnosis. The patient-centered medical home (PCMH) model of integrated and coordinated care delivery is a promising step toward ensuring that illness management, mental health treatment, and wellness promotion are all part of one seamless plan rather than disparate pieces of a fragmented approach to patient care. As mentioned in Chapter 7, the PCMH model utilizes a centralized approach in which the primary care provider and patient care coordinator/patient navigator orchestrate care based on the unique needs of the patient. In cases of medical trauma under this approach, the patient coordinator or primary care provider could identify when a patient could benefit from mental health services and link patients with mental health professionals. The PCMH model can, in theory, provide a safety net for patients whose medical trauma might otherwise go undetected. While this does not solve the issue of managing the psychological impact of Level 2 Medical Trauma (accurate assessment and patient follow-through with mental health treatment are both required for this), it certainly helps. The bigger challenge might in fact be: What do we do for patients with a chronic, life-threatening diagnosis who do not currently benefit from this coordinated care model?

In this chapter, we explore the management of medical trauma in the outpatient, specialist level of care. In doing so, we examine how integrative models of disease management make for successful and effective programs, exploring the role that adjunct support services play in filling gaps left when treatment has a singular focus on the body. Additionally, we more closely examine how treatment centers coordinate care from diverse professionals and how this care integration benefits patients holistically. Before we traverse the treatment landscape for managing medical trauma at the specialist level, let us first take a closer look at how medical trauma from chronic illness affects patients.

IDENTIFYING LEVEL 2 MEDICAL TRAUMA

How Medical Trauma Manifests in Patients With Chronic Illness

There are a number of ways in which people first learn that they have a serious medical diagnosis: They may hear the words *"You have X"* spoken by a physician, after waiting for results from perhaps several rounds of tests; they may first experience a life-threatening medical event out-of-the-blue that requires hospitalization for stabilization, only to learn later that their condition is chronic and will require life-long management; they may have been born with a physical vulnerability and have been anticipating a worsening of their condition. Regardless of the exact circumstances in which patients hear the news, learning that one has a chronic illness is shocking, potentially devastating, and most certainly life-altering. In other words, it can be traumatic. As we have already explored, the lived experience of medical events and illness is highly subjective, and as such we know that some patients do not perceive a life-threatening medical experience or diagnosis of chronic illness as traumatic; however, regardless of where patients fit on the continuum of distress, we can safely assume that all patients could benefit from an integrated approach to care management in order to promote optimal wellness and disease management.

Before we examine some of the strategies within this approach, let us first consider the many ways in which patients can respond psychologically to living with a diagnosis of chronic illness. Many physicians and possibly nurses witness the actual moment when patients first hear that they have a serious illness, and they have likely seen a wide variety of reactions ranging from highly emotional to calmly stoic—and everything in-between. While providers may deliver this kind of news several times weekly or even daily, for patients this may be the first time ever hearing that they have a serious medical issue. Upon leaving the provider's office after receiving a life-threatening diagnosis, patients face a barrage of thoughts and emotions, many of which they may keep to themselves—*especially if they do not have caring, supportive individuals around them to process these reactions.*

In addition to the plentiful and varied actions that patients with chronic illness must take in order to manage their disease, many will likely face any number of the following:

New responsibilities

New routines

Altered capabilities

Altered meaning-making

Fear

Depression

Uncertainty

Discomfort

Pain

Burdens: Financial, personal, social, physical

Altered goals: Personal, career, financial

Altered relationships

Disconnection from or a new fear of the body

These experiences can create tremendous stress in the lives of patients and their families, especially if patients do not have adequate support. Patients without such support may find themselves feeling isolated and unsure of how to proceed in a life that has become redefined by illness; additionally, without the support and perspective of a mental health professional, patients may not recognize the signs of acute psychological distress that often accompany the physical burdens of chronic illness. When patients do not recognize the signs of psychological distress and specialist care providers do not screen patients for distress and secondary crises associated with chronic illness, medical trauma goes unnamed and more importantly, unnoticed. Thus, screening for medical trauma at the specialist level of care is critical.

Specialist Care for Chronic Illness: Opportunities for Detecting Medical Trauma

Many chronic illnesses have the potential to threaten the lives of patients if they are not managed effectively. Just as the physical implications of chronic illness can be dire if the disease is not well managed, the psychological, emotional, and relational implications of medical trauma can lead to poor quality of life for patients and their families, which can negatively impact physical health. Because the origins of chronic illness are located within the body, we naturally turn to medical professionals who specialize in these physical diseases—in many cases, connecting with specialists is an automatic step in the process of managing the disease. Before we explore how interprofessional teams can synergistically manage the physical and psychological aspects of chronic disease, we start by reviewing the medical specialties typically involved in ongoing care of patients with these illnesses. In many cases, treatment of chronic, life-threatening illness requires specialized care beyond treatment from the primary care physician. These specialist providers are typically physicians (MD or DO) with advanced training in internal medicine and in a specific area of the body or group of illnesses (e.g., cardiologist). In Table 8.1, we highlight the specialties in internal medicine. In addition to physicians, physician assistants (PAs) can specialize in internal medicine, in addition to many other specialties.

Nurses also play a key role in the care of patients with chronic illness. Registered nurses (RNs) can specialize according to the specific patient population with which they work (e.g., cardiovascular nursing, perinatal nursing), whereas nurse practitioners (NPs) specialize according to setting and level of care (e.g., acute care or primary care). Like physicians, nurses are well versed in prevention and disease management, and understand the importance of including psychosocial support in the treatment of chronic illnesses.

Physicians and nurses within specialized areas of medicine commonly work side by side to provide ongoing care and disease management, whether in a hospital/clinic setting or group practice. As we will soon see, care for patients who experience medical trauma as a result of their chronic illness can also benefit from integrated treatment that includes the expertise and support of

TABLE 8.1: SPECIALTIES IN INTERNAL MEDICINE

Specialties in Internal Medicine	
Advanced heart failure and transplant cardiology	Interventional cardiology
Cardiovascular disease	Nephrology
Clinical cardiac electrophysiology	Oncology
Critical care medicine	Pulmonary disease
Endocrinology, diabetes, and metabolism	Pulmonary disease and critical care medicine
Gastroenterology	Rheumatology
Geriatric medicine	Sports medicine
Hematology	Transplant hepatology
Hematology and oncology	
Infectious disease	

Source: *Association of American Medical Colleges.*

mental health professionals. In the next section, we explore multiple methods for connecting patients who experience medical trauma with mental health services, examining diverse health care settings across the collaboration/ integration continuum (Heath, Wise Romero, & Reynolds, 2013).

INTERVENTION IN LEVEL 2 MEDICAL TRAUMA: COLLABORATION FOR CHRONIC DISEASE MANAGEMENT

Integrated Care in Leading Health Care Organizations

As the health care system strives to improve itself vis-à-vis patient safety, patient outcomes, and the patient experience, several organizations have risen to the top in terms of demonstrating their effectiveness across a variety of domains. It is no secret that the business of health care is competitive. Rankings are crucial in a hospital's ability to attract patients from all across the country and even the world. Gone are the days of the neighborhood single-building hospital serving the health care needs of the surrounding community: Many of today's hospitals have become lucrative, mega-health care systems encompassing all levels of care with locations across large regions and rosters of patients from every corner of the globe. While all health care organizations strive to be the best in something, whether in their city or region, in treating a particular condition, or in serving the health needs of a particular population (e.g., women's health), a few have been noted as the nation's best of the best. Names such as Massachusetts General, Johns Hopkins, Mayo Clinic, UCLA Medical Center, the Cleveland Clinic, and Brigham and Women's have become synonymous for excellence—but why?

Let us take a closer look at one of these leading health care organizations to see how its approach to patient care has created a reputation of being one of the best hospitals in the world.

Spotlight on a Leading Health Care Organization: The Cleveland Clinic

Located in Cleveland, Ohio, with offices and satellite centers around the country and the world, the Cleveland Clinic has become one of the nation's leading multibillion dollar health care organizations with a vast network of hospitals and research and treatment centers spanning the entire continuum of care. With specialized institutes focusing on a wide range of complex illnesses (e.g., cancer, cardiac diseases, digestive diseases) and patient populations (e.g., pediatric hospital, women's health), the Cleveland Clinic employs a highly successful model of patient care with impressive clinical outcomes. In fact, the Cleveland Clinic has been named the nation's best hospital for cardiac care by *U.S. News & World Report* for the last 21 consecutive years, with high rankings in other specialties as well (e.g., number 3 in diabetes care, number 2 in gastroenterology, and number 2 in rheumatology). Clearly, the Cleveland Clinic has "cracked the code" for delivering high-quality clinical care and a positive patient experience—so what is the secret?

Turns out, it is not so much that the Cleveland Clinic has a secret, but rather that the organization as a whole maintains a steadfast commitment to providing the best possible experience to patients. Their model of patient care, which has become a template and ideal for many health care organizations, rests on the basic belief that patients come first. They have been successful in operationalizing this belief, partly because they seem to continually ask the question "What do patients need?" Simply put, the Cleveland Clinic is empathy in motion.

In his book detailing the Cleveland Clinic's model for excellence in health care, CEO Delos (Toby) Cosgrove, MD, outlines how his organization has tackled the challenges posed by a changing health care system by adhering to guiding principles of efficiency and effectiveness. In *The Cleveland Clinic Way*, Cosgrove (2014) shares these principles, which reinforce that *health care* should be integrated, collaborative, customized, innovative, holistic, healing, and focused on *health*. Even in a 5-minute navigation of the organization's website, you can quickly see these ideals in practice: from the Office of Patient Experience in which the hub of services is focused on enriching patients' experience with an emphasis on empathic communication for every staff member of the organization; from perusing more than

15 integrative treatment options as part of the Wellness Institute, including alternative therapies like acupuncture and reiki to mental health (labeled "holistic psychotherapy"); from learning about the Center for Connected Care, which helps patients transition from the hospital to home or postacute care; and from reading about their annual conference, the Patient Experience: Empathy + Innovation Summit. These are but a few examples of how the Cleveland Clinic differentiates itself among the top health care systems in the world.

While the foundation of the Cleveland Clinic's success seems to be built on caring and empathic communication, another important aspect of the organization's success in treating patients with chronic illness is its culture of integrating multiple professionals across disciplines and specialties in order to restore the health of patients. It is their interpretation of *restoring health* that seems to be another of the Cleveland Clinic's greatest strengths, for staff members at every level seem to understand that health extends far beyond curing the body.

While many of the qualities of the Cleveland Clinic are shared by the other top health care systems—especially with respect to collaborative care and focus on health of the whole person—we chose to highlight the Cleveland Clinic because of its explicit focus on the value of empathy and empathic communication (a video on the organization's website speaks to its keen understanding of the emotional impacts of medical trauma and is worth viewing: www.communicatewithheart.org). Later in this chapter, we revisit empathy and its importance in managing the psychological impacts of Level 2 Medical Trauma. First, let us continue our discussion of the types of organizations that serve patients with complex chronic illnesses and how they address the experience of medical trauma.

Specialized Treatment Centers and Co-Located Coordination

Specialized treatment centers, which may or may not be affiliated with larger health care organizations, have become a desirable treatment option for millions of people living with chronic and potentially life-threatening diseases such as diabetes and cancer. As comprehensive treatment centers engaging in clinical research, medical care, patient education, and health and wellness programs related to a specific complex disorder or group of disorders, specialized treatment centers offer medical care and adjunct care seamlessly under one roof. In addition, like large health care systems, treatment centers have the benefit of shared culture, information and records management systems, and staff training and development opportunities. They are large enough to house all of the specialists (including mental health professionals) necessary to meet patients' medical and nonmedical needs related to living with their chronic illness, while small enough to be nimble and supportive of strong, collaborative treatment teams that are highly skilled in their specialty. Examples of specialized treatment centers include Cancer Treatment Centers of America with five hospital locations throughout the United States, and Joslin Diabetes Center in Boston. Specialized treatment centers for cardiac disorders are also quite common, with most connected to larger health care systems (e.g., the Heart and Vascular Institute at the Cleveland Clinic).

Centers that specialize in treating a particular disease employ clinicians who are competent in understanding the complicated effects of living with that disease, as well as how to best help patients by providing services from diverse professions. In cases of medical trauma stemming from a diagnosis of a chronic, life-threatening illness, specialty treatment centers with integrated teams including mental health professionals can provide appropriate care assuming they screen for psychological impacts and secondary crises and initiate care protocols to address patients' mental and emotional needs (more about screening for medical trauma can be found in Chapter 9). While smaller specialized treatment centers are not on par with the mega-health care organizations such as the Mayo Clinic or Cleveland Clinic in terms of infrastructure and resources, many are making important inroads in research and in providing excellent patient care. One example of such a place is the Joslin Diabetes Center in Boston.

Spotlight on a Leading Specialized Treatment Center: Joslin Diabetes Center

Founded over 100 years ago by Elliot P. Joslin, MD, as a private practice focusing on caring for patients with diabetes mellitus, the Joslin Diabetes Center has grown into an internationally recognized center for diabetes research, education, and clinical care. As an organization that recognizes the value of caring for the whole person, Joslin Diabetes Center employs a system of integrated treatment drawing upon the expertise of professionals from a wide range of disciplines. Joslin is a good example of best practices in collaborative care; patients can access not only the medical attention so crucial in managing a chronic disease such as diabetes, but also the resources and services that can help patients adjust to and even flourish while living with diabetes. Information about mental health services (termed "behavioral health") is featured prominently on its website, with emphasis on the psychological impacts of living with diabetes. Patients at Joslin can connect with one of its mental health professionals or access the professionally monitored discussion boards for peer support. By locating mental health professionals with expertise in the psychosocial effects of diabetes on-site, Joslin Diabetes Center increases the likelihood that patients who experience distress as a result of their illness will receive the mental health care they need in order to improve functioning in every area of life.

Examples of specialized, integrated care such as the Cleveland Clinic and Joslin Diabetes Center demonstrate the best practice of including a variety of practitioners relevant to the care of patients with chronic illness—especially with respect to mental health. While it certainly helps to have medical professionals and mental health professionals under one roof and as part of a system of integrated, cooperative care, many hospitals and treatment centers are not large enough to support the resources needed to realize such a goal. In order for these facilities (e.g., smaller hospitals, treatment centers, specialist practices) to provide whole-person care to patients who experience medical trauma as a result of their chronic, life-threatening illness, they must rely on external mental health resources and referrals and, in some cases, nonmedical supportive care centers. In the next section, we take a closer look at this type of care center and how these organizations can be an important adjunct to medical care in the treatment of medical trauma.

Nonmedical Adjunct Support Services and Coordinated Care

Following a definitive diagnosis of a serious, chronic medical disease such as diabetes or cancer, or discharge from the hospital after a life-threatening medical event such as a heart attack or stroke, patients often turn to organizations that provide support and services that augment their traditional medical care. These supportive care centers can offer a wide range of services to patients living with a specific disease, from education and resources; wellness activities such as yoga, tai chi, nutrition classes, and relaxation/mindfulness; lifestyle enrichment; and individual/group counseling and peer support. As an adjunct to medical care, supportive care centers may or may not be affiliated with a specific health care system. For example, the Cancer Support Community (CSC), a national nonprofit supportive care center offering the services mentioned previously for its members living with cancer, has many stand-alone locations as well as some sites located within hospital and health care facilities. Let us take a closer look at how the CSC helps patients manage the psychosocial impacts of living with cancer.

Spotlight on an Adjunct Support Organization: The CSC

In 2009, two large cancer organizations merged to become what is now the CSC, a nonprofit that strives to support people living with cancer. According to the CSC website, the organization has centers throughout the country and affiliates and partners around the world, and it is the largest employer of psychosocial oncology mental health professionals. As a nonmedical support organization, CSC provides many of the adjunct services beneficial to people living with cancer. According to the CSC website, they help "complete the cancer plan" by providing "essential, but often over-looked" services to patients, including peer and professionally led support groups, counseling with mental health professionals specially trained in psychosocial oncology, educational workshops and resource centers, and healthy lifestyle programs including yoga, exercise, and nutrition—all free of charge for CSC members.

In addition to the many support services offered, CSC uses web-based and mobile applications to help members manage the emotional and lifestyle impacts of living with cancer. Their mobile app *My Cancer Manager* enables users to access educational resources, connect with other cancer survivors through the online support community, and monitor thoughts and feelings through its journaling function. To help connect members with professional resources to manage the psychological distress from living with cancer, the CSC has created *CancerSupportSource*, which integrates distress screening, referrals for mental health services, and follow-up care. Using this program, patients first complete a 25-item, web-based survey (either at home or in a provider's office) that screens for distress, and then generates a personal-ized plan and referrals for psychosocial support and mental health services. Providers receive a patient distress management report that alerts them to patient distress, keeping them apprised of patients' ongoing emotional health and well-being.

The CSC is an example of best practices related to managing the psycho-logical effects of Level 2 Medical Trauma. By incorporating screening for psychological distress, systems of referral for professional mental health ser-vices, and a community of support and education, the CSC fills in the gaps created by traditional health care approaches.

Whether a health care organization integrates mental health profession-als into their treatment teams to provide whole-person care in a seamless package, or uses the robust adjunct resources offered by a support organiza-tion, it has become clear that services that support the psychosocial health of patients with chronic illness play a vital role in successfully restoring health in mind, body, and spirit. For more examples of support services for chronic illnesses such as cancer, diabetes, and heart disease, see the list of resources in Appendix D. In the following section, we highlight tips for managing medical trauma in specialist care group practices, including communication strategies and ideas for integrating mental health professionals into treatment protocols.

SPECIALIST CARE PRACTICES: STRIVING TOWARD INTEGRATION

While it is true that most specialist care practices do not have the resources to provide services on par with the Cleveland Clinic and similar large orga-nizations, there are a number of ways in which medical practices of every size and type can improve care to those patients living with medical trauma due to chronic, life-threatening illness. In this section, we explore a number of strategies to increase sensitivity to medical trauma at a systems level, including improving communication, screening efforts, and referral and follow-up for mental health services. We begin with one of the most important: empathic communication.

Ensure That Entire Staff Has Empathic Communication Training

Patients who live with chronic illness are vulnerable. They are vulnerable physically and also emotionally as they live each day with the responsibilities of treatment regimens and the uncertainty of future health and well-being. They take more medication, get more testing, and have more contact with health care providers on average than those without serious health problems. While some patients develop a degree of acceptance of a chronic illness and learn how to cope with and even thrive emotionally despite the prospect of ill health, others experience distress as a result of their diagnosis, ongoing treatment regimen, and looming threats to well-being. Given this, it is critical that staff members throughout specialty care practices receive thorough and regular training on empathic communication in order to ensure that interactions with patients are sensitive to the unique vulnerabilities within this population. While using patient-centered communication should be the goal of every medical professional, it is also equally important that frontline, nonmedical staff receive such training given the frequency and nature of their interactions with patients. Let us take a closer look at important aspects of staff communication, and review some tips for ensuring interactions are sensitive to patients who have experienced medical trauma.

Receptionist/Scheduler/Office Staff

When patients first make contact with a specialist's office, they often speak to a member of the office staff to schedule a first appointment, receive additional information about the practice, or occasionally to learn that test results have returned. In many cases, when patients call for the first time they have just learned of their diagnosis, or they have just been given a referral from their primary care physician to get more testing. Regardless of the specific context, patients who make first or subsequent contact with a practice are likely feeling a mix of emotions, including fear, worry, dread, and uncertainty. As the "face" of a specialty practice, office staff members have a special role and responsibility to communicate with sensitivity, compassion, and understanding.

When speaking with patients, office staff should remember to do the following:

- Speak in a warm, friendly tone of voice—never let your own mood, frustrations, or stress impact your interactions with patients.
- Speak clearly and slowly, especially when giving instructions or information about a patient's condition—never approach interactions in a mechanical way. You may give test results to patients 100 times throughout the day, and this may be the first time a patient learns he or she has a health issue.
- Listen to patients without interrupting, even if they are verbose and take more time than you think is necessary.
- Be calm and understanding if patients seem irritable, impatient, or nervous—always keep in mind the context of the patient's experience.
- Keep communications focused on the patient—avoid sidebar conversations with other staff while interacting with patients.

Medical Staff

Medical staff, including physicians, nurses, assistants, and technicians, handle highly sensitive information and interact with patients during moments of great vulnerability. While many medical professional education programs include training in patient-centered communication, it is important to ensure that ongoing continuing education includes "refresher" training in empathy skills. As the leaders in specialty care practices, physicians and nurses have a responsibility to model patient-centered communication and to encourage all staff (medical and nonmedical) to participate in communication training.

In addition to ensuring that communication is empathic and patient centered, it is also imperative that processes are sensitive to the unique vulnerabilities of patients living with chronic illness. Consider the following example of patient-centered, sensitive communication and procedures:

On a recent visit to the Ohio State University (OSU) Wexner Medical Center, we had the opportunity to observe patient–staff interactions in the waiting area of the Ross Heart Hospital. As we sat near the bustling entrance in one of many small booths aptly colored in OSU scarlet and gray, we observed several communications between staff members and patients who ostensibly were waiting for their appointments.

If you weren't closely paying attention, these exchanges would have seemed unremarkable: Every few minutes, a staff member entered the bright, airy lobby, walked up to a seated patient who was there to receive cardiac care, spoke to the patient, and walked with him or her through the clinic doors to begin the appointment; however, when examining these interactions through the lens of patient vulnerability, they were special.

First, staff *walked to the patients* rather than standing at the clinic doors, calling names to beckon patients to them. Second, each staff member, upon saying what I can only surmise as the patient's name, smiled—not a superficial or obligatory smile, but one that communicated a deep sense of welcome and warmth. Third, rather than leading patients—which would require them to match the pace of staff—they waited for each patient to rise, then walked side-by-side through the clinic doors. All of these interactions took place amid the soothing sounds of a piano, which created an air of dignified calm for patients, their families, and staff alike.

A few days after observing this, I shared my perceptions with Susan Moffatt-Bruce, MD, PhD, Chief Quality and Patient Safety Officer, and asked her if the manner in which the medical staff approached patients and communicated with them was intentional and a result of their specific training at OSU Medical Center. Dr. Moffatt-Bruce's reply was a resounding "absolutely," as she reiterated how important these kinds of processes are in creating a positive patient experience. As this example illustrates, using patient-centered procedures, warm communication, and soothing environmental elements are all important when caring for patients seeking care for chronic, life-threatening illness.

In the next section, we explore how developing protocols for responding to patient distress within the specialist care setting can help in the management of medical trauma.

Develop Protocols for Responding to Patient Distress

Like the example of OSU Medical Center highlighted previously, the most successful medical organizations have clear protocols for providing health care that is *consistently* efficient and effective. Managing medical trauma in the specialist care setting also requires that guidelines be established for medical and nonmedical staff to alert providers when medical trauma is suspected. Office staff members who interact with patients and witness emotional responses to simple exchanges (such as scheduling an appointment) could have a method for entering a note for the patient's provider so that the medical professional can ask targeted questions about the patient's emotional well-being during the appointment. Consider the following example: A patient calling a specialist care office speaks to a member of the office staff to schedule an appointment for her biopsy. During the call, she at first seems irritable and then chokes up when speaking to the scheduler. After the call, the scheduler enters a note to the provider, who is then prompted to ask the patient follow-up questions about how she is doing emotionally during their appointment together, and also asks the patient to complete a screening for distress. As this example illustrates, it is important to consider how to systematize responses to these kinds of interactions, for they can be indicative of patient distress and impairment due to the stress of a serious medical condition. Formal training is ideal for office and paraprofessional staff members who interact with patients regularly, and could include educating them on the following signs of patient distress:

- Tearful or visibly upset when scheduling appointments, or when discussing medical circumstances

- Irritable or impatient with administrative tasks associated with managing care

- Angry or hostile toward staff or family members while in the presence of staff

- Visibly shaken, worried, or anxious regarding any aspect of their medical care

- Exasperated or stressed about their health or the impacts of their illness on quality of life, family members, career, and so on

While maintaining empathy and developing clear communication protocols among staff are necessary aspects of effective health care delivery and positive patient experience, they are not sufficient for managing the psychological impacts of medical trauma. In order to successfully manage these emotional effects, organizations must implement processes for screening, intervention/referral, and follow-up.

Perform Regular Screenings for Patient Distress

Clearly, training nonmedical staff and paraprofessionals to identify signs of patient distress should not be considered a fail-safe approach to identifying patients who experience medical trauma. Specialist care practices can employ regular screenings for patient distress, whether using instruments developed specifically for distress associated with a particular illness (e.g., Diabetes Distress Scale, Polonsky et al., 2005; NCCN Distress Thermometer for Patients, National Comprehensive Cancer Network) or general distress screenings for depression (e.g., Patient Health Questionnaire [PHQ-9], Kroenke & Spitzer, 2002) and anxiety (e.g., Primary Care PTSD Screen [PC-PTSD], Prins et al., 2003). Screening for patient distress should be performed as part of the regular treatment protocol in specialty care practices. While some specialties are quite advanced in incorporating screenings for patient distress or medical trauma on a regular basis (e.g., oncology), specialist practices without specialized screening instruments or who may not routinely screen for distress (e.g., orthopedics may screen for distress in patients who were injured in an accident, but may not screen patients who require surgery because of wear and tear) can use general screenings for distress as part of the treatment protocol for every patient. By employing regular screening for patients, specialists take the first important step in providing whole-person care; however, without a clear plan for intervention/referral and follow-up, screening would be pointless. Caring for patients who experience medical trauma, therefore, requires that providers include mental health resources as part of patients' plans of care, and this can be accomplished through referral to an in-house mental health professional, affiliated mental health professional, or by connecting patients to supportive care centers if applicable.

Hire an In-House Mental Health Professional With Specialized Knowledge

One common characteristic of health care organizations that successfully care for the holistic needs of patients is the inclusion of mental health and adjunct specialists as part of integrated treatment teams. While this can occur through networks of professionals at multiple locations (i.e., coordinated care), ideally such professionals work together closely, building strong collaborations that benefit patients (integrated care). Given this, it may be worthwhile for practices to consider hiring a mental health professional with knowledge and training in the disease process and psychological impacts of a particular chronic disease or specialty area in order to provide psychosocial support, individual and group counseling, assessment, and psychoeducation for patients and their families experiencing distress. These professionals—clinical mental health counselors, clinical social workers, or psychologists—can be a valuable part of treatment teams and contribute to the overall health and well-being of patients. Beyond working with medical trauma and helping patients manage the many effects of their disease on all areas of life, mental health professionals can also help patients who struggle to follow their health care regimens by employing motivational interviewing techniques in addition to the trauma-informed interventions used with patients experiencing traumatic stress.

Research Adjunct Services in the Area and Connect Patients

For those smaller specialty practices unable to hire a mental health professional, it would be helpful to create a list of resources for patients to access in their local community for help in managing the emotional effects and other distressing impacts of living with chronic illness. This list could include local and online supportive care organizations (e.g., CSC), local mental health professionals who specialize in working with people living with chronic illness, and holistic health centers that include services such as yoga, reiki, massage, and mindfulness meditation. For patients who express interest in learning more about mindfulness-based stress reduction and other practices to manage stress, consider providing a list of books and websites such as the example in Appendix E.

Make Efforts to Destigmatize Mental Health Services

All of the efforts to integrate mental health professionals, screenings for distress, and referrals for mental health treatment become futile if patients are unwilling to follow through with providers' recommendations. While health care professionals readily understand the value of mental health in contributing positively to patients' overall health, some patients are bound to view recommendations for mental health services as inherently negative and therefore unwanted. Efforts to make mental health professionals more visible to patients, either as part of a regular screening process or through psychoeducation (e.g., practice newsletters) can help demystify the profession by putting a face to it. Further, when providers normalize the process of working with a mental health professional by explaining the benefits and rationale to patients, patients may be more likely to agree to participate. When patients view these services as a beneficial part of their overall health plan rather than indications of serious psychological/characterological deficits, they will likely be more inclined to follow through with suggested services.

Before wrapping up this chapter, let us briefly revisit the case of Sharon to explore how some of the strategies we discussed could positively impact this patient's experience of Level 2 Medical Trauma.

TYING IT ALL TOGETHER: REVISITING THE CASE OF SHARON

If you recall from Chapter 6, Sharon was diagnosed with breast cancer and experienced significant medical trauma as a result of her diagnosis and treatment, the consequences of which included depression and avoidance of medical care. In revisiting Sharon's case, we can see a number of opportunities to directly address signs of medical trauma in an attempt to prevent the significant depression Sharon experienced.

First, staff members could have used empathic communication strategies and alerted Sharon's providers to her signs of distress. From the technician performing Sharon's mammogram to the receptionist speaking with Sharon about scheduling her biopsy, office staff and technicians encountered numerous signals that Sharon was struggling—at the very least in that moment—with the prospect and eventual realization of her serious medical condition. In her communication, Sharon demonstrated a strong emotional response to the possibility of having breast cancer; however, with no procedure in place for staff to inform providers of this, Sharon remained on her own to manage her feelings. Once Sharon met with her provider and received her definitive diagnosis, she demonstrated signs of shock that were again overlooked. If Sharon's provider had included as part of the standard treatment protocol a mental health screening, an appointment to "process" the emotions with a mental health professional, and a referral to an organization such as CSC, this would have created an emotional safety net of support and resources to help Sharon protect her mental health as she dealt with the trauma and challenges inherent in cancer treatment. If these resources had been built into the treatment process, then even a patient like Sharon—stoic, independent, and sensitive to burdening others—would have likely engaged the help that could ultimately have prevented the grave consequences of her untreated medical trauma. Without regular distress screenings and an outlet to both process her emotions and to learn and engage healthy coping strategies, Sharon was left alone to make sense of a life event that has the power to destroy the mind and spirit as well as the body.

Sharon, like so many others who live with serious psychological impacts of medical trauma, could have had a dramatically different experience had communication and treatment protocols been sensitive to her emotional reactions. In cases of chronic, life-threatening medical illnesses, health care and mental health professionals must work together in collaboration with patients in order to address emotional health and overall well-being—ideally intervening at the first signs of emotional distress.

SUMMARY

In this chapter, we explored medical trauma in the specialist care setting, including how it manifests in patients with chronic illness and how health care and mental health professionals can work together to ensure that patients receive integrated care. From highly integrated organizations such as the Cleveland Clinic that provide world-class, whole-person care, to neighborhood specialist practices employing patient-centered communication and comprehensive screening, intervention, and follow-up processes, we examined multiple avenues for addressing the mental health needs of patients who experience Level 2 Medical Trauma. Finally, by revisiting the case of Sharon we illustrated how some of the strategies discussed throughout this chapter could positively impact how a patient experiences chronic illness.

REFERENCES

Association of American Medical Colleges. (2015). *Careers in medicine*. Retrieved from https://www.aamc.org/cim/specialty/list/us

Cosgrove, T. (2014). *The Cleveland Clinic way: Lessons in excellence from one of the world's leading health care organizations*. New York, NY: McGraw-Hill.

Heath, B., Wise Romero, P., & Reynolds, K. (2013). *A review and proposed standard framework for levels of integrated health care*. Washington, DC: SAMHSA-HRSA Center for Integrated Health Solutions.

Institute of Medicine. (2001). *Crossing the quality chasm: A new health system for the 21st century*. Washington, DC: National Academy Press.

Kroenke, K., & Spitzer, R. L. (2002). The PHQ-9: A new depression and diagnostic severity measure. *Psychiatric Annals, 32*, 509–521.

Polonsky, W. H., Fisher, L., Earles, J., Dudl, R. J., Lees, J., Mullan, J., & Jackson, R. A. (2005). Assessing psychosocial stress in diabetes. *Diabetes Care, 28*(3), 626–631.

Prins, A., Ouimette, P., Kimerling, R., Cameron, R. P., Hugelshofer, D. S., Shaw-Hegwer, J., … Sheikh, J. I. (2003). The primary care PTSD screen (PC-PTSD): Development and operating characteristics. *Primary Care Psychiatry, 9*, 9–14.

9

PREVENTION AND INTERVENTION FOR LEVEL 3 MEDICAL TRAUMA: THE HOSPITAL SETTING AND BEYOND

IN THIS CHAPTER, YOU WILL LEARN:

- Characteristics of effective interprofessional teams in the acute care setting, including good communication, mutual respect, and shared patient-centered goals

- Protocols for integrating mental health professionals into interprofessional treatment teams to manage medical trauma, with a focus on roles before, during, and after acute medical events

- Strategies for screening patients for trauma risk factors prior to scheduled surgeries and medical procedures, and tools for identifying signs of acute stress disorder (ASD) in the hospital setting

- How to assess the impacts of environmental stressors using the Experience of Medical Trauma Scale (EMTS)

- Discharge planning that includes information and resources for managing the psychological impacts of medical trauma, including linkages to primary care providers and mental health services

- The business case for managing the psychological impacts of medical trauma

MANAGING MEDICAL TRAUMA IN THE ACUTE CARE SETTING

Hospitals are ground zero for medical trauma. When critical incidents occur, patients, their families, and providers can be at risk for experiencing traumatic stress and short- and long-term psychological impacts that can range from mild distress to mental disorders, such as depression and posttraumatic stress disorder (PTSD). In earlier chapters, you learned about the many factors that contribute to medical trauma and how a person's unique history and risk factors can influence his or her experience of an illness or medical event, the medical environment, and interactions with providers. Armed with this understanding, we can now consider interventions to help patients, their families, and staff members manage the serious effects of a medical trauma, and in some cases to prevent the longer term psychological impacts of traumatic medical experiences. For these interventions to be effective, they will require teams of health care and mental health professionals working together for the expressed purpose of protecting both the physical and mental health of patients.

In the previous two chapters, we emphasized the importance of collaboration among health care and mental health providers in order to meet the unique needs of patients who experience medical trauma. While integrated care has posed a challenge within the primary care setting—due in part to providers' differing locations, electronic records platforms, and patient goals—health care professionals working together is certainly more the norm in critical care settings. Ostensibly, interprofessional work in the hospital setting would not have many of the challenges encountered in primary and specialized care, but this does not mean that team-based care is without its obstacles. Although health care professionals of nearly every ilk may be housed under one hospital roof, working within the same culture, and using the same care management software, the challenges posed by hierarchies, turf wars, interpersonal conflicts, and siloed treatment approaches to care can often impede health care and mental health professionals from working together harmoniously to meet the holistic needs of patients.

Recognizing these and other impediments to operating highly effective interprofessional teams within acute care, many have taken up the task of improving providers' team-based skills and developing care protocols that optimize the expertise of various disciplines in order to provide the best possible treatment. In this chapter, we explore the interprofessional health care team in acute care to uncover the current gaps in how medical trauma is managed and, more important, to propose new resources, protocols, and roles for mental health professionals within this environment. We begin by exploring interprofessional treatment teams in acute care, including how they are formed, structured, and managed and the efforts to improve them.

Treatment in the Acute Care Setting: A Team Sport

Delivering good health care in the hospital setting requires the orchestration of complex tasks by a dizzying array of diverse professionals with synchrony, sensitivity, and the utmost competence. Over the past several decades, the culture within many hospitals has begun to shift from a paternalistic, physician-centered model to a collaborative, team-based, and patient-centered model—and this has not been without many bumps in the road. Teamwork in health care is wrought with challenges, many of which stem from communication issues, whether from a lack of clarity, misperception, lack of trust or respect—or from any other typical impediment to good communication. When teamwork fails, leading to medical errors, then patients suffer: It is estimated that 400,000 people die annually from preventable medical mistakes in the United States alone (James, 2013). Just as poor teamwork can lead to catastrophic consequences for patients and their families, good teamwork saves lives, and even better teamwork in critical care ensures that patients leave hospitals with not only their lives, but also with a plan for restoring psychological well-being in cases of medical trauma. In this section, we discuss characteristics of that "even better team" and how we can continue to build them to ensure support for the mental health needs of patients.

What Are Interprofessional Treatment Teams?

It might be helpful to begin our discussion by defining "interprofessional teams," as this term may be new to some readers. Before doing so, let us take a closer look at the term "interprofessional." In the introduction to this book, we discussed a core problem with health care delivery: fragmentation. Professionals operating in disciplinary silos provide fragmented care, and this approach does not meet the holistic needs of patients. The response to this rather disjointed status quo has been to change the paradigm for how professionals are trained (i.e., interprofessional education) and how professionals work together to deliver care (i.e., interprofessional practice). D'Amour and Oandasan (2005) define "interprofessionality" as a response to the fragmentation of health care delivery, stating that it is "the development of a cohesive practice between professionals from different disciplines. It is the process by which professionals reflect on and develop ways of practicing that provides an integrated and cohesive answer to the needs of the client/family/population" (p. 9). Some could argue that nowhere is interprofessionality needed more than in acute care, for it is at the hospital where stakes are at their highest and patients have the most to gain from care providers working in unison on an effective interprofessional team.

Before we dive into the characteristics of effective interprofessional teams and the competencies required for high-functioning teams, let us first look at the structure of a work team within the acute care setting. Generally speaking, a work or clinical team in the health care setting would be any group of professionals who work in harmony to achieve shared goals, with shared responsibility to patients and their families and with shared accountability to the larger organization. In cases within acute care, the first shared goal is often to stabilize a patient or save the patient's life, and each professional understands his or her role in meeting this goal. Beyond these characteristics, there are other factors that differentiate various types of work groups in health care. In *Understanding Teamwork in Health Care*, Mosser and Begun (2014) examine team structure using several additional characteristics, such as the group's purpose, the stability of its membership, its leadership, and whether the group has shared responsibility. The authors explore four main types of clinical teams, their strengths and vulnerabilities, as well as their most appropriate applications. The following is a brief summary of each type of team:

- **True team**: A true team has stable membership and a formalized leader with clearly defined roles and responsibilities for all of its members. In this type of team, members can build trust and knowledge of one another, ideally forming a strong bond that enhances the team's overall effectiveness. The execution of tasks can become synchronized and intuitive in a high-functioning team with strong leadership. True teams can often be found in ambulatory surgery centers, outpatient testing centers, specialized group practices, and in primary care.

- **Template team**: As the name would suggest, a template team uses a stable framework—or template—for professional roles and responsibilities needed within the team, yet the actual personnel varies from one treatment episode to the next. Like true teams, template teams have shared goals and formalized leadership. When template teams employ evidence-based, standardized protocols (including communication processes), they can be quite effective. Template teams can often be found in emergency departments and in other surgical and nonsurgical departments within acute care.

- **Knotwork**: A knotwork is a group of professionals coming together with the shared purpose of providing coordinated care to a specific patient with a specific need. While all members of this group share responsibility in the patient's care, knotwork members do not often have a working knowledge of each other's roles and responsibilities, nor do they have a clearly identified leader. Membership in knotworks is unstable, and the collaborative could be thought of more as an ad hoc group than as a team. Knotworks often connect professionals across multiple locations, such as when a patient is diagnosed with a cancer requiring surgery and chemotherapy: In this case, the patient's primary care physician, oncologist, and cancer treatment center staff collaborate on behalf of the patient to provide the best care possible.

▪ **Network:** The most loosely connected of all teams, networks are collectives of professionals and organizations that have similar interests and value being connected, but do not have stable membership, shared responsibility, or clear leadership. Whereas knotworks function to help specific patients, networks are more generalized and often focus on systems of care.

While most true teams and template teams within acute care consist mainly of physicians and nurses of varying specialties, teams often consult with staff from professions outside of medicine, nursing, and pharmacy—in other words, with allied health professionals. "Allied health professionals" are professionals who work to support patients in achieving their health goals, from promoting recovery, preventing disease, and realizing greater well-being and overall health. Examples of allied health professionals include therapists of varying specialty (e.g., physical, speech, respiratory, occupational, art and music), mental health professionals (e.g., clinical psychologists, social workers, mental health counselors), medical assistants and technicians, dieticians, and athletic trainers. This is just a sampling of the many professionals who support patients by completing the puzzle of whole-person care.

When you think of all possible variables that exist within the dynamics of an interprofessional team—from members' diverse knowledge, skills, and values to the different personalities, temperaments, and communication styles—it is astounding that so many teams function as well as they do. Recognizing how vital teamwork is to the delivery of health care, many hospitals invest greatly in training, supports, and resources to assist staff in learning effective teaming skills. To get a better sense of these skills, let us take a closer look at the competencies of interprofessional collaboration.

Interprofessional Collaborative Practice: The Domains of Competency

As the need for interprofessional collaboration has become increasingly clear to health care leaders and educators around the country, health care professional organizations have mobilized to develop and adopt mutually agreed upon standards for competency (which is itself a great interprofessional collaboration!). The Interprofessional Education Collaborative (IPEC), which includes the national educational associations for medicine, nursing, dentistry, pharmacy, and public health, outlined four broad competencies for interprofessional collaborative practice in its published report (IPEC, 2011). These competencies, which focus on the values of interprofessional practice, roles and responsibilities, interprofessional communication, and interprofessional teamwork, lay the foundation for effective collaboration with the expressed purpose of improving patient care and patient outcomes. The following is a brief summary of each competency:

Values/Ethics for Interprofessional Practice

As elucidated in the IPEC report, the bedrock of effective interprofessional practice is a commitment to providing *safer, more efficient, and more effective patient care.* Pick up any white paper on effective health care delivery in this country today and you will see at least a nod to this commitment. While quality health care must begin with this intention, the intention alone is not sufficient for realizing effective interprofessional teamwork: Good teams require mutual respect, and trust among members and across professions with the charge of promoting health and wellness, preventing illness, and providing care for the whole person. With these values driving every interaction, interprofessional teams can navigate even the most challenging medical events provided that team members respect and trust one another, and that there is clarity and acceptance of each member's role and responsibility.

Roles and Responsibilities

As previously mentioned, many interprofessional health care teams are formed with staff from a variety of disciplines, including medicine, nursing, pharmacy, and allied health professionals. Professionals are expected to understand their roles and responsibilities in any given treatment scenario and be able to communicate these to staff from other professions; further, professionals should have clarity with regard to the boundaries of their competence and understand how and when to collaborate with other professions in order to meet the needs of patients.

Interprofessional Communication

When a student becomes a professional, he or she learns to speak the language of that profession; this jargon, which is mutually understood between members of the same profession, can create barriers to effective communication when working interprofessionally. Recognizing this issue is one important step in learning to communicate effectively across professions. Another important skill of interprofessional communication is assertiveness coupled with mutual respect, which enables all members of an interprofessional team—regardless of hierarchy—to have a voice and to feel safe enough to use it appropriately, especially when concerns arise.

Teams and Teamwork

The last competency domain entails having an understanding of the structure of teams and the nature of teamwork. Regardless of the type of team, successful interprofessional teamwork requires that members respect one another, accept interdependence, be willing to flex when necessary, and recognize team leadership and the overall goals of the team. Sharing the values of interprofessional teamwork, knowing one's and others' roles and responsibilities, and using effective interprofessional communication can help ensure competent interprofessional collaboration. This last characteristic, interprofessional communication, is the focus of a team-training program that is widely used across health care systems nationwide.

Training in Interprofessional Communication: TeamSTEPPS

TeamSTEPPS, or Team Strategies and Tools to Enhance Performance and Patient Safety, is a training program to support team building and communication skills within health care settings (Agency for Healthcare Research and Quality [AHRQ], 2014). Developed by the Department of Defense and the AHRQ, TeamSTEPPS training provides a foundation for collaboration across diverse health care providers using a modular curriculum of team-based communication and teamwork skills. The overarching goal of the program is to increase quality of care and patient safety by decreasing medical errors due to communication issues. In a sense, a program like TeamSTEPPS provides the tools to realize the IPEC competencies in that it teaches professionals *how* to build sound team structure, value interprofessional collaboration, demonstrate mutual respect, communicate clearly and assertively, and work in concert with others toward shared goals. The original version of the program addresses team strategies and tools for teams within acute care; subsequent modules have been developed for long-term care facilities, primary care, and dental care.

The TeamSTEPPS curriculum can be accessed and learned in a number of ways. Entire health systems, departments, and even individual teams across the United States have committed to implementing the evidence-based program in order to improve patient outcomes. The train-the-trainer model allows representatives from facilities to receive training in the program and then teach others in their organizations. There is a wide-scale implementation project with supports to help organizations be successful in adopting the skills. The curriculum—the core of which focuses on team structure, communication, leadership, situation monitoring, and mutual support—is modular, concrete, and easy to access and understand. Perhaps the most valuable aspect of a team skills program like TeamSTEPPS (or another popular team training program, Crew Resource Management; criticalcrm.com) is that it fosters a shared language and structure that every team member can understand and implement, thus creating more cohesion among otherwise disparate professionals.

One module of the TeamSTEPPS curriculum that is of special interest to our discussion of medical trauma is the *situation monitoring* component because it introduces specific skills to help team members actively scan unfolding treatment situations to understand the status of patients, fellow staff, and the environment around them. Using the acronym "STEP" (**S**tatus of the patient, **T**eam members, **E**nvironment, and **P**rogress toward goal), professionals are trained to look for important changes and concerns that may need the attention of one or more team members. For example, when teams in acute care are trained to look for signs of mental and emotional distress, they can engage the help of a mental health professional immediately.

There are a number of questions team members can ask themselves in order to better assess a situation in terms of medical trauma, and to discern the most appropriate steps to ameliorate the patient experience when necessary. When team members "check in" with themselves periodically, they could ask questions such as:

- What is the quality of our team's communication? Of my and others' communication? Are we communicating to each other and to the patient in a respectful, calm, and sensitive manner?

- Are we demonstrating sensitivity to the patient's experience of this medical event?

- How am I feeling right now—am I managing my own emotions in a healthy way? Do my team members seem to be managing their emotions in a healthy way? If not, what should I do to intervene?

- Is the treatment environment calming for the patient? If not, what can our team do to minimize stressful stimuli around the patient? Is someone asking the patient about his or her stress level, and what he or she needs in order to feel safer, more relaxed, and more comfortable?

- If I notice anything that is emotionally unsafe for the patient, how and when should I intervene?

These are a few questions that all team members can ask themselves in order to take the "emotional temperature" in the room.

One important aspect of TeamSTEPPS is the egalitarian nature of team structure. While this can be a challenge in hospitals that have a strong hierarchical culture, it is imperative for the effective management of medical trauma that every team member has a voice and the ability to raise others' awareness of any situation in which a patient becomes emotionally unsafe. When mutual respect and understanding are cultivated among hospital staff and interprofessional teams, this can go a long way in ensuring that patients get the quality of care that they need—especially in cases of medical trauma.

Tools such as those provided in training programs like TeamSTEPPS can be quite effective in helping interprofessional teams deliver quality care with decreasing errors; however, tools are not all that is needed in order to effectively manage the psychological impacts of medical trauma in the hospital setting. In order to effectively manage medical trauma, one first has to *see* it, and then address it with the appropriate staff as part of the treatment team. In the next section, we discuss how interprofessional teams can leverage the expertise and services of mental health professionals in order to meet the psychological needs of patients who experience medical trauma.

Management of Medical Trauma: An Interprofessional Endeavor

Managing the psychological effects of medical trauma in the hospital setting requires a well-prepared team of health care and mental health professionals who have clearly defined roles and responsibilities, as well as a shared vision for the health and well-being of patients. In this section, we discuss specific roles of physicians, nurses, and mental health professionals in identifying signs of psychological distress, intervening on behalf of patients in distress, and in ensuring linkages with mental health resources at discharge to help prevent more serious decompensations in mental health. We present a template protocol that can be customized to a variety of treatment situations, as well as screening tools to help providers detect signs of emotional distress.

Strategies for Health Care Providers

The patient-centered treatment movement has taken hold of modern day health care, and at no other time in our history have patients been more empowered than they are today. Generally speaking, patients today are more knowledgeable, and as health care consumers, patients expect excellent care from caring professionals. In other words, they want a good *experience*. In a recent article in the trade publication *The Hospitalist*, physician Thomas McIlraith writes that patients judge their medical experiences not based on cognition or cold, hard facts (e.g., Did I survive? Was I healed?), but rather on how they *feel* about the encounter emotionally (e.g., Was my doctor caring? Did my doctor listen to me?). It makes sense when you think about it, because medical experiences—especially traumatic ones—are very emotional for patients and their families. McIlraith argues that it is imperative that physicians and nurses connect emotionally with patients by listening actively, demonstrating compassion, and taking the time to show that they care. He also reminds us that when health care providers do these things, patients remember.

When medical traumas unfold in acute care, they are often in response to life-threatening crises in which health care providers have to act swiftly, with little time to think about how the patient is experiencing the intervention. The goal in that moment is to save a life, and emotional implications of necessary medical actions are often after-thoughts in the minds of medical professionals. It is quite a tall order indeed to ask medical staff to attend to patients' psychological needs *while* health crises unfold, and many professionals meet this challenge by employing sensitive and clear communication skills while simultaneously providing excellent health care. These skills are at the center of many conversations about improving patient satisfaction and the patient experience in health care *in general*, and are perhaps even more vital when managing medical trauma. In the next section, we outline the most important tasks for health care professionals in managing the psychological effects of acute medical events.

Training the Lens to See Medical Trauma

It goes without saying that in order to manage the effects of medical trauma one must first see that a trauma has occurred and that a patient is in some state of distress. As we discussed in Part I of this book, medical trauma is a subjective experience, and what can seem like a benign procedure to one patient (and provider) could be terrifyingly threatening to another patient. In order to better understand patients' subjective interpretations of medical events, we must train our lens to see the signs of a traumatic stress response and to ask patients a few simple screening questions to gauge their level of distress.

Physicians, nurses, and many other health care professionals are well aware of the physical signs of traumatic stress or of activation of the sympathetic nervous system. What can make detecting medical trauma elusive is that the many signs of fight-or-flight—such as tachycardia (rapid heartbeat), perspiration, dilated pupils, and difficulty sleeping—occur commonly in a wide range of medical disorders and can be misread and misunderstood as a result. When these and other signs of traumatic stress are noted, health care professionals should investigate whether they are due to a patient's physical state, emotional state, or a combination thereof. Patients' responses should be reported accurately in the chart. Later in this chapter, we explore how health care and mental health professionals can more precisely gauge patients' emotional states following a life-threatening medical event. First, we take a closer look at the communication skills within the acute care setting, as well as the importance of empathy in every treatment interaction.

Using Good Communication

In all corners of the health care system, good patient–provider communication is the foundation of effective care. But what is good communication? Regarding the communication skills of effective health care providers, we know that when clear, direct, frequent, honest, and complete information is exchanged between health care providers working together on a treatment team, patients benefit by receiving care that is synchronized. Good communication is at the center of patient safety—we know this from research in medical errors. However, in order to effectively communicate with patients who have experienced medical trauma, health care providers need to move beyond the characteristics described earlier and develop communication styles that take into account the acute emotional vulnerability of patients. Developing a keen sensitivity to patients' emotional states and adjusting one's interaction style to meet those states is one important step toward communicating effectively with patients and their families. The following are a few suggestions for providers in acute care to help ensure that communication skills are a help rather than a hindrance to patients:

- **Use empathy**: This can be difficult during times of crisis, because health care providers often attempt to shut off their emotions in order to stay sharp intellectually. While this style of coping can certainly aid some professionals in performing tasks effectively, the unintended consequence is an aloof, clinical, and cold demeanor that is not helpful for patients. Further, when providers are cut off from their emotional experience, they may be less likely to identify when patients are struggling emotionally. Maintaining empathy means that you are choosing to attempt to feel what others feel—that you are putting yourself in their shoes—in order to better understand their situation. As frightening as this may be during such a critical time, maintaining empathy helps professionals remain aware of their demeanor and communication style when patients most need their sensitivity and caring. An unintended consequence of staying emotionally connected, however, is that providers may be more likely to experience vicarious traumatization; we explore interventions for this in Chapter 10.

- **Avoid sidebar conversations**: It is extremely important that professionals avoid sidebar conversations when in front of patients. Essentially, a sidebar conversation is any conversation that is not directly related to patients' care. When professionals are in the process of managing a medical crisis, communication should remain solely focused on the tasks involved in caring for the patient, and conversation between staff members should remain respectful, professional, and cordial. Avoid any communication that alienates patients and their families, or that suggests an over familiarity between staff members (i.e., a personal relationship between staff members). Perhaps a good rule of thumb should be that if there is any possibility of encountering a patient, then personal conversations between staff members should be avoided altogether.

- **Speak slowly and clearly**: When people experience trauma, their ability to comprehend even basic information can become greatly diminished. It is important to slow down when giving updates or instructions to patients, and make sure that you enunciate clearly when speaking. While this can apply to anyone who has experienced a trauma, it is especially important when communicating with children, older adults, patients whose native language is not English, or patients with specific disabilities that affect auditory processing or hearing.

- **Bring warmth to every interaction**: It goes without saying that some people are naturally more "warm" than others, but it behooves all health care professionals to work to achieve some level of warmth in their interactions. The medical literature is replete with examples of the power of warm, caring professionals in the lives of patients, and time and time again we hear about how treatment of others matters. We also hear about the damage incurred when health care professionals are cold, uncaring, and disconnected from patients. In life-threatening medical situations, it is crucial that staff maintain warmth, which translates as a friendly tone of voice, steady eye contact, genuine positive regard for others, patient and calm demeanor, and respectful language.

- **Manage your own emotions**: As challenging as it can be during a medical crisis, it is important that health care professionals try to avoid showing strong emotions. While it is normal for staff to feel a wide range of feelings during a medical event, it is more helpful to the patient and his or her family if staff express those emotions outside of the treatment room. Showing strong emotions during the management of a medical crisis can lessen patients' and families' confidence in a professional's ability to maintain composure and stay sharply focused on the patients' care. Do not assume that by showing strong emotion to patients that you are showing you care. These emotional expressions by staff can most assuredly backfire, prompting some patients to feel uneasy about expressing their own emotions, or to think they have to console staff in some way. Having said this, it is critical for staff to get the support they need following a medical crisis, for vicarious traumatization is a very real issue that should be addressed with the help of a mental health professional *outside* of the treatment context with the patient.

- **Minimize staff-splitting**: When staff members turn on one another, whether due to a disagreement in how care is conducted, conflicts in personality, or for a wide variety of other reasons, then the quality of care is diminished. It is important that professionals work together as a cohesive team, especially during times of medical crisis when the stability of those managing the crisis is imperative. If conflicts arise during an episode of care, they should be addressed after the patient is stable in a constructive manner following established protocols.

- **Inquire about the patient's emotional state, too**: Health care professionals are well versed in assessing all relevant aspects of a patient's physical state, relying on monitors that give them second-by-second updates and other tests that provide quantitative measures of biological functions. Unfortunately, there are no equivalent methods for gauging a patient's emotional state, so health care professionals must seek feedback from patients about their emotional status and rely on assessment instruments and appraisals from mental health professionals.

- **Contextualize the patient**: In Chapter 5, we discussed one important element of the experience of medical trauma, and that was the role of the medical environment itself. Remembering that the hospital environment is not the patient's normal context, it can be helpful if health care professionals seek to understand a patient's uniqueness in order to bring greater humanity and familiarity to an incredibly vulnerable and potentially disorienting experience. One simple example of contextualizing is to use a patient's preferred name instead of generic labels such as "Honey/Hon," "Sweetie," or "Sir/Ma'am." While these appellations may seem innocuous, they do little to contextualize the patient. Consider employing the following questions in an intake so that professionals can quickly get up-to-speed on the patient's context:

    N—Name: What does the patient prefer to be called?

    A—Activities: How does the patient spend most of every day (e.g., career, hobbies)?

    M—Most Important People: Who are the important people in the patient's life?

    E—Environment: What are aspects of the patient's typical home environment? Does the patient live in the city, suburb, or in a rural setting? In a house or apartment? Alone or with others? Does the patient have any pets?

When health care providers know answers to questions in these four areas, they can more readily establish rapport and continue to humanize and personalize patients even though they remain decontextualized while in the hospital setting.

By employing sensitive, caring, and empathic communication, health care professionals can potentially buffer some of the adverse effects of a medical trauma; however, while empathy on the part of health care professionals is a necessary ingredient in managing the psychological impacts of medical trauma, we would argue that it is not sufficient. Because health care professionals are on the front lines with patients, they are often in the best position to assess mental status in order to appraise whether a mental health professional may be needed on the treatment team. In the next section, we examine several assessment instruments that could be utilized to determine the presence of psychological distress. While the feasibility of including such assessments should be examined by clinical teams for each unique treatment scenario, if patients are open to the screening process (and most are; see Rayner et al., 2014), then efforts should be made to help protect their mental health during and after a medical crisis.

In the following section, we explore some of the assessment tools most relevant to medical trauma, beginning with tools that measure general distress and ending with an instrument that captures a more detailed picture of the sources of traumatic stress. Note that the focus here is on the content of the assessments rather than on the method of administration; we examine the use of technology in managing medical trauma in Chapter 10.

Using Tools for Assessing Patient Distress

Subjective Units of Distress Scale

Perhaps one of the simplest scales for measuring patient or client distress, the Subjective Units of Distress Scale (SUDS), uses a numerical scale ranging from 0 (which indicates an absence of stress, discomfort, etc.) to 10 (which indicates the most amount of distress, turmoil, misery, etc.). The midpoint on this scale, or 5 on a 0 to 10 scale and 50 on a 0 to 100 scale, typically indicates a moderate level of stress, anxiety, depression, and so on. Developed in 1969 by psychiatrist Joseph Wolpe, the SUDS has been a popular instrument in health care and mental health treatment, most likely due to its ease of use and simple concept. Its popularity is perhaps also due to its ultimate goal, which is to discover a person's subjective distress. Beyond providing a quick snapshot of the severity of distress one feels in the present moment, it tells us nothing more, thus requiring additional investigation in order to ascertain the specific experiences causing or exacerbating a patient's distress, as well as the nature of the distress (e.g., anxiety, depression, general stress).

Regardless of its brevity and simplicity, the SUDS can be used as a rapid screening device for physicians and nurses to determine the need for a mental health professional consultation, and this makes it a valuable part of the toolkit for managing the psychological impacts of medical trauma.

Breslau Scale

Another scale that has some utility in measuring medical trauma in the acute care setting is the Breslau Scale (Breslau, Peterson, Kessler, & Schultz, 1999), which consists of seven questions addressing the symptoms of PTSD according to the *Diagnostic and Statistical Manual of Mental Disorders, Fourth Edition* (*DSM-IV*; American Psychiatric Association [APA], 1994) criteria. The administration instructions for the scale suggest that it only be administered following a qualifying traumatic event, which can be problematic if patients' subjective experience of a medical event as being traumatic does not match with staff members' objective interpretation of the event (i.e., if staff do not recognize the trauma, they may not screen for a traumatic response). Another potential issue with using the Breslau Scale in the hospital setting following a medical crisis is the potential for false negatives due to administering the measure too soon after a medical event. For example, questions that determine decreased interest in enjoyable activities or a decreased interest in planning for the future are not necessarily relevant for a patient in the intensive care unit following a heart attack experienced 2 days prior; further, since the scale screens for PTSD rather than acute stress disorder (ASD), which is the traumatic stress response that can occur anytime from just after a traumatic event up to 1 month following the experience, it can lack sensitivity when used in the acute care setting. Rather than wait a month to screen for PTSD in the primary care setting using a scale such as the Breslau, it can greatly benefit the patient if staff recognize signs of acute stress—and this requires using tools sensitive enough to capture indications of emotional distress within the hospital context.

Recognizing Signs of ASD Tool

As mentioned in the discussion of the Breslau Scale, some instruments meant to detect PTSD can have limited relevance for the acute care setting, especially for those patients with shorter lengths of stay prior to discharge. It does make sense to screen for signs of acute stress while patients are hospitalized, provided that the screening tool used is appropriate to the setting. Screening for acute stress can allow providers to customize discharge plans to patients' unique circumstances by including linkages to mental health providers in the community or to mental health resources within the hospital system.

When a mental health professional is part of the interprofessional treatment team in acute care, he or she can take the lead in assessing the psychological impacts of medical events and can administer screening instruments appropriately. If treatment teams do not include mental health professionals, this responsibility falls to physicians and nurses who can use rapid screening tools such as the SUDS to determine the level of patient distress. Treatment teams can also review several instruments for measuring PTSD and ASD using a compilation of assessment tools such as Orsillo (2001). Once again, the clinical staff would need to be prompted to administer such a screening instrument and this would require that they actively look for and recognize the signs of acute stress.

   Mental health professionals can assist health care workers in learning the signs of acute stress within the hospital setting by providing regular consultation and support. Resources that specialize in a specific population within the hospital, such as postpartum women, can aid hospital staff in recognizing how acute stress can manifest (i.e., how might patients look, behave). An example of such a resource is the Recognizing Signs of Acute Stress Disorder in Postpartum Women in the Hospital Setting tool (Hall, 2014; Appendix F), which includes each symptom of ASD according to *DSM-5* (APA, 2013) criteria, but presented within the context of a woman who has just given birth and who experienced trauma during the event. Any resource that can provide context for the signs and symptoms of ASD within the hospital setting can be helpful to staff as they work to ensure that patients receive the treatment and care they need. Bundled toolkits published by professional associations that include mental health resources can be a good place to look for assessment tools customized to specific patient populations and illnesses/medical events (e.g., the tool mentioned previously for postpartum women appears in the Patient, Family, & Staff Support toolkit bundle published by the Council on Patient Safety in Women's Health Care, 2015).

Screening for Impacts of Environmental Stressors

Experience of Medical Trauma Scale

While the aforementioned scales can provide real-time measures of psychological responses and patient distress, they tell us little about the sources of such distress. Given what we know about the influence of environmental factors on traumatic stress, it seems useful to have a method for teasing out specific triggers for these psychological responses. The Experience of Medical Trauma Scale (EMTS; Hall, 2015a; Appendix G) is an ecological assessment tool meant to be used in the acute care setting to screen for patient distress in response to a wide variety of discomforts within the hospital environment. Initially developed as a mental health resource tool for obstetrical trauma as part of the Council on Patient Safety in Women's Health Care toolkit bundle, the scale can be used for general medical trauma within the acute care setting. The EMTS, which uses a Likert scale to measure 46 items on a continuum from 0 (not distressing/not experienced) to 4 (extremely distressing), covers categories of patient stimuli, such as communications with staff, physical pain and discomfort, environmental discomforts, and emotional discomforts. In addition to ratings of discomfort, the EMTS directs the interviewer to capture qualitative remarks from patients for items scored a 2 (moderately distressing) and higher in order to gather additional detail about the patient's subjective experience. The tool then requires the provider to craft a response and plan to ameliorate the patient experience of the distressing stimuli.

The EMTS can be administered by a health care professional following a serious medical event, or by a mental health professional who is part of the interprofessional treatment team. The team should have prepared protocols for using the EMTS, which should include sample action plans based on specific items within the scale. For example, if a patient indicates that the sound of a beeping monitor is causing moderate distress, then staff should have a protocol for silencing the monitor and for communicating the patient's request to subsequent team members. It would be helpful for team members to familiarize themselves with the tool and become comfortable discussing solutions for these factors within the treatment environment. It will also be important that staff involve patients and family members in discussing options for improving the care environment whenever appropriate.

One challenge to using the EMTS is a lack of time to administer the tool. While it only takes approximately 10 minutes to complete the measure, it can be difficult for busy physicians or nurses to carve out that time when working in a critical care unit. One solution would be to task a mental health professional with the responsibility of overseeing the tool's administration and of convening a huddle to discuss potential changes to the treatment care environment to reduce patient distress. Because we cannot assume patients will recognize the sources of their distress without prompting and share their distress with staff members, it seems important to address these issues in a timely, constructive manner; this approach can help staff improve the care environment and can assist patients in their recovery efforts by decreasing stress and feelings of vulnerability.

The tools we highlighted previously can be administered by a health care professional such as a physician or nurse, but as mentioned, this could create an unfair burden on professionals whose primary task is to attend to the physical health needs of patients. Rather than suggest that physicians and nurses expand their roles to include mental health concerns, we feel it is more expeditious and effective to collaborate with a mental health professional. In order to most effectively manage the emotional impacts of trauma from life-threatening medical events in acute care, health care professionals need to work in conjunction with mental health professionals to accurately assess and quickly intervene in order to prevent serious, longer term distress. In the next section, we present ideas for creating a template team in acute care that includes mental health professionals in order to support the psychological needs of patients who experience medical trauma.

Collaborating With Mental Health Professionals

As we have discussed in this and earlier chapters, integrating mental health professionals into existing health care models can be challenging for several reasons, many of which are outside the scope of this book. While the medical and nursing professions have long recognized the need for allied health professionals as part of interprofessional treatment teams, this recognition has not always translated into action—especially with regard to mental health. Some of the ideas regarding integration of mental health that we present may have obstacles to being realized, and therefore, we present them as a template for best practice and as a vision for what may be possible if professionals work together. In this section, we explore the current roles of mental health professionals before presenting a protocol that includes ideas for expanding such roles. Additionally, we highlight several tools for assessing the emotional status of the patient who may have experienced medical trauma, and we include some of these tools in the appendices at the end of this book.

Current Roles of Mental Health Professionals in the Hospital Setting

Exploring new roles for mental health professionals in the management of medical trauma may require loosening the ties to existing beliefs about what mental health professionals *can* and *should* do in the acute care setting. When we asked a sample of health care and mental health professionals the question, "What do mental health professionals do in hospitals?" the answers did not surprise us:

- They provide services and medication for patients who are suicidal, homicidal, psychotic, or manic.

- They help patients who have financial, legal, social, or other support needs to connect with resources (social workers).

- They connect with patients and families in the grief process, especially when a death occurs.

- They work in psychiatric or psychological services departments, providing services such as individual and group therapy for specialized topics and populations (e.g., bereavement, eating disorders, depression, PTSD).

This list represents the major themes from the answers we heard, and are all accurate descriptions of typical roles of mental health professionals in acute care. The last bullet point represents the most *siloed* role of mental health professionals, whereas the first three suggest a more integrated role wherein a mental health professional works more closely with physicians and nurses on a true team or template team. Before we discuss how the roles of mental health professionals could be expanded within acute care to manage the psychological impacts of medical trauma, it might be best to revisit a list of mental health professionals *typically found in the hospital setting* (described in more detail in Chapter 7):

Psychiatrists

Psychologists (clinical, counseling, health psychologists)

Social workers

Counselors (clinical mental health, pastoral, or chemical dependency counselors)

Psychiatric/mental health nurse practitioners

Psychiatric/mental health physician assistants

You recall from Chapter 7 that each of these distinct mental health professions has unique characteristics and areas of expertise within the field. Psychiatrists, psychiatric nurse practitioners, and psychiatric physician assistants typically serve the needs of patients who have comorbid, serious psychiatric disorders, such as schizophrenia, bipolar disorder, and major depressive disorder, by providing expertise in medication management. Psychologists also work with such patients, but do not prescribe medication; psychologists are highly skilled in assessment and treatment (talk therapy) for psychological disorders, and in crisis intervention. While bachelor's-level social workers often work in roles that highlight patient advocacy and resource connection, master's-level clinical social workers are able to provide treatment for psychological disorders and are also highly skilled in crisis intervention, advocacy, and processing grief. Clinical mental health counselors or licensed professional counselors—like their psychologist and clinical social worker colleagues—also provide treatment for psychological disorders, perform crisis intervention, and are skilled at processing grief. While psychologists likely have more training in clinical assessment and social workers likely have more training in accessing community resources and navigating complex systems, clinical mental health counselors have a strong emphasis in empathic talk therapy, conceptualizing people in terms of strengths and wellness, and in emphasizing holistic (mind, body, spirit) growth. With few exceptions, all mental health professionals (regardless of discipline) value prevention, education, and collaboration, and are skilled in recognizing patient distress, in communicating effectively, and in working collaboratively within a team environment.

In the next section, we explore expanded roles for mental health professionals within the hospital setting. While all of the mental health disciplines described previously may be suitable for the roles we discuss, we want to emphasize that the roles are best suited for those mental health professionals with strong empathic communication skills and significant experience in providing talk therapy.

EXPANDED ROLES FOR MENTAL HEALTH PROFESSIONALS IN MANAGING MEDICAL TRAUMA

Preadmission: Screening for Risk Factors of Medical Trauma

When patients complete the admission process for planned surgeries and procedures, there is an opportunity to screen for vulnerabilities that may increase the likelihood of adverse psychological reactions to medical care. Whether the admissions protocol includes a more extensive instrument, such as the Medical Mental Health Screening (Appendix C) discussed in Chapter 7, or simply a few general questions to gauge a patient's anticipatory anxiety (i.e., "How are you feeling about your upcoming surgery?"), screening for mental health concerns prior to admission can ensure that mental health professionals are included in treatment teams.

A mental health screening can be given as part of the regular admissions process as long as clear instructions are provided to administrative staff about how they can best communicate with mental health professional staff about any concerns noted by patients. When risk factors are present, a mental health professional can make a connection with the patient for a brief consultation to determine if the patient is open to discussing his or her concerns prior to the procedure.

Prevention: Mental Health Coaching

In cases of planned surgeries or procedures, consultation with a mental health professional prior to treatment can help patients prepare mentally and emotionally for the upcoming medical event. Whether to process their anxiety about the procedure or recovery, or to receive coaching for stress management (such as mindfulness-based stress reduction techniques) in order to help patients actively cope with their anxiety, a preprocedure meeting with a mental health professional can put patients and their families at greater ease before a potentially stressful event such as major surgery.

There are a number of ways that mental health professionals can assist patients prior to procedures, although time will likely be limited once patients are admitted to the hospital. When risk factors are determined early (i.e., with a patient's primary care treatment team or in a specialist's office prior to scheduling the hospital procedure), there is greater opportunity for a mental health professional to help patients prepare psychologically and to make a plan for managing potential secondary crises. Regardless of when a mental health professional is alerted to a patient at risk of experiencing medical trauma, the important thing is that the professional is in place as part of the interprofessional treatment team.

Crisis Management: Roles During Medical Treatment

In many cases, medical traumas occur with no warning. Heart attacks, strokes, car accidents—these experiences catapult people into the patient role with the prospect of losing their lives. As mentioned previously, it is imperative that health care providers recognize the signs of acute stress and activate a team protocol that employs the expertise of a mental health professional. It would be advisable for some specialty teams or departments to automatically include a mental health professional trained to manage medical trauma, especially when there is a high likelihood of traumatic stress. Examples would be template teams in emergency departments, cardiovascular and cerebrovascular treatment teams, and maternity care teams. Whether hospitals and medical centers invest in training mental health professionals specifically for working in specialized teams (e.g., cardiac trauma) or as members of a pool of mental health professionals trained in general medical trauma, health care professionals would benefit from having strong connections to mental health staff and a familiarity with the process of employing such staff in the event of a medical trauma.

Once a mental health professional is alerted to a medical trauma, he or she can serve the interprofessional treatment team in a variety of ways. Simply put, when a mental health professional is in the treatment room with health care staff who are attending to the immediate medical needs of the patient, the mental health professional can attend to the patient's unfolding mental and emotional needs. This can include any number of interventions, including but not limited to (Hall, 2015b):

- Providing accurate assessment and charting of patients' mental status

- Administering instruments to gauge the sources and level of patients' emotional distress

- Identifying sources of environmental stress for patients and working with staff to ameliorate these factors

- Providing emotional support for patients and their families throughout the medical experience

- Acting as a skilled, empathic communicator who takes the emotional "temperature" in the room to gauge stress levels of patients, family members, and staff

- Coaching patients in stress management techniques

- Helping patients verbalize their sensory experience in order to engage the brain's executive functioning and process the trauma

- Being a witness to events in order to more effectively facilitate debriefing meetings with patients, family, and staff at a later date

▪ Recognizing signs of vicarious traumatization in family members and staff and providing needed support

▪ Calling a huddle when necessary to share concerns about patients' emotional safety and providing suggestions regarding environmental or communication needs that may improve the patient experience

These are but a few of the specific tasks a mental health professional can perform when working with health care professionals to manage a medical trauma. Team leaders should work with professionals knowledgeable about developing treatment protocols to create task flows and identify specific roles in order to implement integrated plans for patients. An example of suggestions for roles and tasks of mental health professionals in managing medical trauma can be found in Appendix H (Hall, 2015b; Council on Patient Safety in Women's Health Care Safety Bundle).

Addressing Medical Trauma at Discharge

As part of interprofessional treatment teams or as ad hoc consultants, mental health professionals can play a vital role in managing medical trauma throughout a patient's hospital stay. Whether functioning as a coach and advocate for patients, support for family and staff, and/or as a team member able to make an accurate assessment of the emotional state and safety of patients, mental health professionals can provide several services throughout patients' medical experiences. Another critical role for mental health professionals comes as patients are readied for discharge, as this is an opportunity to provide additional resources, support, and linkages to ensure that patients get the psychological services they may need to help restore mental health and promote healing of mind, spirit, and body following a medical trauma.

In our examination of general discharge protocols used within acute care, we found a gaping hole when it comes to mental health. In our own personal experiences and from talking with numerous former patients, verbal and written instructions often focus solely on care for and healing of the physical body: Tips about caring for wounds, instructions for administering medications, dietary guidelines, a timeline for resuming limited and normal activities, and warning signs that may indicate a worsening of physical symptoms or disruption in recovery are typically shared as patients prepare to leave the hospital. In the standard discharge forms we reviewed, items ostensibly meant to prompt a social worker's involvement focus on psychosocial red flags, such as limited or poor social supports and/or housing options, financial concerns, lethality risk (i.e., harm to self or others), addiction concerns, or inability to adequately meet one's needs. In cases of medical trauma, it would be helpful to expand the discharge process to include educational resources about possible effects of medical trauma and linkages or referrals to mental health services.

When a mental health professional is part of the interprofessional treatment team working with a patient who has experienced medical trauma, he or she can provide resources that focus not only on the signs of anxiety, PTSD, and depression, but also on wellness and strategies to boost protective factors. The ultimate goal is to prevent the more serious psychological impacts from the traumatic medical event, and one of the best ways to do this is to take a proactive approach. Another benefit of the involvement of a mental health professional throughout the episode of care within the medical setting is the possible decrease in the stigma of seeking mental health services after discharge. When mental health professionals make empathic connections with patients during vulnerable times and perhaps demonstrate the value of processing emotions and gaining new skills, patients may be more likely to seek the help of a mental health professional in the future.

In cases where mental health professionals are not available or are not an active part of a treatment team, it is still possible to improve the discharge planning process to include resources and linkages. In consultation with a mental health professional, hospitals can develop resources that provide information about what patients might experience in different life domains following a particular procedure, including signs of secondary crises and mental disorders—as well as resources for additional help if they need them.

Patient Education at Discharge

Developing an educational resource that addresses common psychosocial and emotional concerns following a specific procedure can be one way of destigmatizing mental health concerns and empowering patients with information beyond facts about their physical bodies. In many cases, patients are left on their own to sort through the sometimes complex feelings that arise after a life-threatening medical event. By providing education that specifically addresses patients' concerns and potential experiences postdischarge, hospitals are providing a valuable resource and service to their patients. Mental health and health care professionals can work together to develop such resources, or work with consultants who specialize in developing these materials. It can also be helpful and empowering to enlist the help of former patients, as they are experts in the lived experience of specific medical events. An example of this type of resource is the tool titled Understanding the Emotional Effects of a Difficult Childbirth Experience (Hall, 2015c) located in Appendix I. In this tool written for obstetric patients who recently experienced a birth trauma, the complex feelings that can arise from this kind of medical event are discussed, in addition to warning signs of secondary crises and mental health concerns (published as part of a safety bundle for the Council on Patient Safety in Women's Health Care).

Linking to Primary and Specialist Care Providers

In Chapter 7, we discussed the concept of integrated care and the importance of using a systematized flow of information between providers. While it is seemingly easier for providers to connect when they work within the same health network (i.e., a health system consisting of interconnected hospitals, subacute care centers, specialists, testing centers, and primary care providers using shared technology platforms, marketing and financial resources, and branding), it can be substantially more challenging to initiate linkages between acute care and community providers when those systems are not in place, especially when community providers are mental or behavioral health professionals. Currently, when patients are discharged from the hospital following treatment for an acute medical issue, linkages for follow-up care target the patient's primary care physician or specific specialists, treatment centers, and/or allied health professionals whose purpose is to provide ongoing treatment, rehabilitation, and monitoring of the patient's condition. Often these linkages do not include referrals for mental health—and this is a missed opportunity to advocate for the overall health and well-being of patients.

When medical trauma occurs in the hospital and patients experience traumatic stress as a result, providers should provide clear instructions regarding follow-up care postdischarge that includes a referral to a mental health professional—one who is affiliated with the patient's primary care office, specialist's office, or specialized treatment center, or one who is part of a community mental health practice office. While it goes without saying that a patient cannot be forced to seek the services of a counselor, health care professionals can normalize the option by providing referrals just as they would for physical therapy following an injury or for a cardiologist and dietician following a heart attack. If the end goal postdischarge for patients who experience medical trauma is to help them improve overall health and prevent another acute medical event, then including mental health in the linkages at discharge seems to be just what the doctor ordered.

When Acute Medical Trauma Is Managed Effectively, Everybody Wins

Pick up any health care trade magazine in this day and age and you will likely see at least one article devoted to improving the patient experience, shoring up patient safety, increasing patient satisfaction, or ensuring patient-centeredness (occasionally you will see all of these!). A main reason these concepts are so central to the discussion of improving health care is because, aside from being respectable goals, they are keys to positive patient outcomes. Another reason these goals remain a focus of health care improvement efforts is the effect they have on the bottom line: It may go without saying, but a hospital or medical center that creates an excellent patient experience by providing care that is safe and patient-centered will discharge satisfied patients who would be willing to return in the future and who would refer others desiring the same excellent care. In other words, the hospital is profitable, satisfaction is high, and national, regional, or local rankings follow suit. For many patients, effects of medical trauma may not surface until after discharge from the hospital setting, making identification and assessment more difficult. As part of the assessment protocol for medical trauma, postdischarge assessment that includes pointed questions about emotional well-being related to the hospital experience, in addition to the standard consumer survey Hospital Consumer Assessment of Healthcare Providers and Systems (HCAHPS or CAHPS; Hospital Consumer Assessment of Healthcare Providers and Systems, n.d.), could help hospitals better understand what they are doing well and what improvements need to be made.

A link exists between creating an excellent patient experience with safe and patient-centered care and the integrated, interprofessional management of the psychological impacts of medical trauma. When we demonstrate we care for patients—even after they walk out of the hospital doors—by ensuring they understand the possible mental, emotional, spiritual, and lifestyle implications of the medical experience they just had, and by linking them with professionals who can help them rebuild a sense of normalcy and strength, we provide a patient experience that goes above and beyond "good enough."

When Acute Medical Trauma Is Ignored, Everybody Suffers

The alternative to managing medical trauma effectively, which unfortunately likely occurs more often than not, is to ignore the emotional experience of the patient in favor of a myopic focus on the physical body. In these instances, no one assesses the emotional response to the acute medical crisis, no one intervenes to offer mental health services, and no one empowers the patient with information and referrals at discharge. When patients leave the hospital traumatized, they reenter their lives traumatized: their relationships, careers, parenting, and social worlds bear the brunt of a trauma that may remain unnamed and untreated. A compelling question to ask regarding medical trauma is: Who is ultimately responsible for the psychological effects of traumatic medical experiences? If a recent lawsuit against an Alabama health care organization filed by a woman who experienced medical trauma ("obstetrical violence") is any indication of the road ahead, motivations for helping patients manage the complex emotions arising from such experiences move beyond altruistic and become financial (see *Malatesta v. Tenet Health*). As patients become more empowered to speak out against a health care system that has harmed them psychologically (e.g., "Exposing the Silence" Project, www.exposingthesilenceproject.com), that system needs to be ready and willing to care for them.

TYING IT ALL TOGETHER: REVISITING THE CASE OF ANN

Think back to the significant trauma, psychological impacts, and secondary crises Ann experienced as a result of her postpartum hemorrhage. From PTSD and depression, detrimental consequences for her marriage and career, and significant impacts on overall quality of life, Ann's experiences represent the devastating effects of untreated medical trauma. Ann's case also highlights how multiple factors contribute to a patient's experience of medical trauma, including patient risk factors (anxiety and trauma history), medical staff (communication and task performance), medical environment (harsh stimuli and decontextualization), and diagnosis/procedures (postpartum hemorrhage and uterine massage). Given the assessment strategies, protocols, and resources discussed in Chapters 7 to 9, we can envision a different outcome for Ann—and a revised treatment approach that addresses her medical trauma before, during, and after her childbirth experience.

In cases of a planned medical intervention such as childbirth, providers have the opportunity to engage preventive measures that give patients tools and resources to help them manage their health care experience. Following the sample protocol in Appendix H (New Roles for Mental Health Professionals Before, During, and After Severe Maternal Events), Ann's OB/GYN could have assessed her risk factors for experiencing medical trauma using the Medical Mental Health Screening (Chapter 7; Appendix C). Given Ann's predisposition for anxiety, a mental health provider could have worked with Ann prior to childbirth to shore up her coping skills. Ideally, the same mental health professional would reconnect with Ann at some point during her medical trauma and at the very least visit her in her hospital room following the event, once Ann was stabilized. In order to gauge the effects of the trauma and determine factors that contributed to Ann's distress, medical staff could have administered the EMTS (Appendix G) in order to identify stressful stimuli and a screen for signs of ASD. Medical staff could have also been more watchful of Ann's emotional state, using the Recognizing the Signs of Acute Stress Disorder (Appendix F) tool as a guide, and they could have been more mindful of their communication, refraining from sidebar conversations and comments suggesting tension among staff members.

Beyond addressing the medical trauma in the hospital, staff could have ensured that Ann had mental health resources at discharge, including a referral for follow-up care with a mental health professional. Providing resources to educate Ann about the possible effects of medical trauma could have helped her recognize the downward spiral she experienced, and with information about supportive services in her local area, Ann could have been more willing to reach out for support. If Ann had received a referral directly from her OB/GYN, then her doctor could have followed up to make sure that Ann was getting the mental health support that she needed. In the end, what Ann truly needed was an integrated treatment team that included a mental health professional, medical staff sensitive to the traumatic nature of her experience, and follow-up resources to help guide Ann through the painful (and sometimes lonely) process of recovery.

SUMMARY

As you have learned, managing the effects of medical trauma requires the coordinated efforts of an interprofessional team. In this chapter, you learned the qualities of effective interprofessional teams working in acute care, as well as how health care and mental health professionals can work together in new ways to help prevent or minimize traumatic stress responses in patients, intervene to better manage medical trauma as it unfolds, and plan for interprofessional intervention and for providing mental health resources at discharge. You also became acquainted with screening instruments to help professionals assess patients' mental health within the hospital setting, including a tool for addressing distressing factors within the treatment environment, the EMTS, and a guide to help staff recognize the signs of ASD. Finally, you explored why it is important to manage medical trauma in the acute care setting and to provide interprofessional, whole-person care.

REFERENCES

Agency for Healthcare Research and Quality. (2014). *TeamSTEPPS 2.0 core curriculum*. Retrieved from http://www.ahrq.gov/professionals/education/curriculum-tools/teamstepps/instructor/index.html

American Psychiatric Association. (1994). *Diagnostic and statistical manual of mental disorders* (4th ed.). Washington, DC: Author.

American Psychiatric Association. (2013). *Diagnostic and statistical manual of mental disorders* (5th ed.). Washington, DC: Author.

Breslau, N., Peterson, E. L., Kessler, R. C., & Schultz, L. R. (1999). Short screening scale for DSM-IV posttraumatic stress disorder. *American Journal of Psychiatry*, *156*, 908–911.

Council on Patient Safety in Women's Health Care. (2015). *Patient, family, and staff support after a severe maternal event patient safety bundle*. Washington, DC: Author. Retrieved from http://www.safehealthcareforeverywoman.org

D'Amour, D., & Oandasan, I. (2005). Interprofessionality as the field of interprofessional practice and interprofessional education: An emerging concept. *Journal of Interprofessional Care*, *19*(Suppl. 1), 18–20.

Hall, M. F. (2014). A guide to recognizing acute stress disorder in postpartum women in the hospital setting. In C. Morton, M. Price, & A. Lyndon (Eds.), *Women's experience of obstetric hemorrhage: Informational, emotional, and physical health needs.* Stanford, CA: California Maternal Quality Care Collaborative.

Hall, M. F. (2015a). Experience of Medical Trauma Scale. In *Patient, family, and staff support following a severe maternal event.* Washington, DC: Council on Patient Safety in Women's Health Care.

Hall, M. F. (2015b). New roles for mental health professionals before, during, and after severe maternal events. In *Patient, family, and staff support following a severe maternal event.* Washington, DC: Council on Patient Safety in Women's Health Care.

Hall, M. F. (2015c). Understanding the emotional effects of a difficult childbirth experience. In *Patient, family, and staff support following a severe maternal event.* Washington, DC: Council on Patient Safety in Women's Health Care.

Hospital Consumer Assessment of Healthcare Providers and Systems. (n.d.). Baltimore, MD: Centers for Medicare & Medicaid Services. Retrieved from http://www.hcahpsonline.org

Interprofessional Education Collaborative Expert Panel. (2011). *Core competencies for interprofessional collaborative practice: Report of an expert panel.* Washington, DC: Interprofessional Education Collaborative.

James, J. T. (2013). A new, evidence-based estimate of patient harms associated with hospital care. *Journal of Patient Safety*, *9*(3), 122–128. doi:10.1097/PTS.0b013e3182948a69

Mosser, G., & Begun, J. W. (2014). *Understanding teamwork in health care.* New York, NY: McGraw-Hill.

Orsillo, S. M. (2001). Measures for acute stress disorder and posttraumatic stress disorder. In M. M. Antony & S. M. Orsillo (Eds.), *Practitioner's guide to empirically based measures of anxiety* (pp. 255–307). New York, NY: Kluwer Academic/Plenum.

Rayner, L., Matcham, F., Hutton, J., Stringer, C., Dobson, J., Steer, S., & Hotopf, M. (2014). Embedding integrated mental health assessment and management in general hospital settings: Feasibility, acceptability and the prevalence of common mental disorder. *General Hospital Psychiatry*, *36*, 318–324.

Wolpe, J. (1969). *The practice of behavior therapy.* New York, NY: Pergamon Press.

10 MEDICAL TRAUMA AND THE FUTURE OF HEALTH CARE

IN THIS CHAPTER, YOU WILL LEARN:

- *The role of technology in managing the psychological impacts of medical trauma, from mobile applications, integrated and dynamic electronic medical records, telehealth, and more*

- *How interprofessional education (IPE) can dramatically reshape and retool an integrated health workforce capable of providing efficient, effective, and patient-centered care for the whole person*

- *The role of mindfulness-based techniques in bridging physical and mental health to manage medical trauma*

- *The importance of taking care of staff who experience vicarious traumatization, and an example of how one medical center incorporates integrated approaches that help professionals to manage the emotional impacts of medical trauma*

- *The need for more assessment and research to better identify and understand the psychological impacts of medical trauma*

There is no doubt that the health care system is changing at a staggering pace. With the advancement of new technologies in the diagnosis and treatment of diseases to the ways in which health care workers are trained and reimbursed—it seems that change is the only constant in an industry tumbling toward its goals of becoming ever more efficient, effective, safe, and accessible. However, in the midst of all the innovation, progress, and fine-tuning, a few simple ideas have emerged as being central to the mission of health care: Treat people kindly, work together to provide the best care possible, and take responsibility for the care that we provide. The explosion of patient-experience associations, professionals, research, and resources are a testament to this mission as the industry strives to become more patient-centered. Helping patients manage the psychological sequelae of medical trauma relates to this mission because doing so requires empathy, interprofessional collaboration (IPC), and a new level of responsibility to ensure that patients leave the health care setting with the support they need to address the emotional consequences of their medical experience. In this section, we explore some of the new frontiers in health care and how advances in technology, education, and mental health can be leveraged to help patients heal in mind, body, and spirit. Let us begin by exploring an area that has become synonymous with advancement and innovation, and that dominates nearly every aspect of our lives: technology.

TECHNOLOGY'S ROLE IN MANAGING MEDICAL TRAUMA

Nearly all of us experience multiple forms of technology, especially regarding how we collect and use information. Knowledge is power in that it keeps us informed of nearly every aspect of life in order to better prepare us for making informed decisions. This is certainly true for phone apps that map the fastest, least congested route to a weekend destination or that provide us with weather alerts that influence what we choose to wear. Having information keeps us from guessing, which in turn reduces our anxiety. With technology, patients have become better informed through sites such as WebMD.com, the MayoClinic.com, and a dizzying number of other sites replete with health-related information. Having access to these outlets can influence patients' confidence in the questions they ask medical staff and in the responsibility they take for their own care.

In addition to the many ways in which individuals use technology to manage their health, health care organizations are using technology to better address patient needs in their quest to provide high-quality care, education, and cost transparency (Workman, deBronkart, Quinlan, & Pinder, 2014). Patients value care that is personalized to them and that is delivered in a safe, dignified, and empathic way. They want their care to be coordinated, with less fragmentation between providers while still maintaining appropriate confidentiality. On the surface, these efforts seem to be good logical practice, and the telemedicine movement is trying to meet this need by changing the landscape of health care. Health care organizations are also using technology to help reduce patient anxiety related to their medical visits, to manage patient and staff expectations as well as ongoing patient well-being, and to collect data for satisfaction reports.

As we have already established, when patients experience a traumatic procedure or life-threatening diagnosis, their stress, uncertainty, and confusion can be compounded. Managing medical trauma first requires that it be identified, and technology can play an important role in this process. Each setting in which patients interact with medical staff (e.g., primary care, specialty care, or hospital) has an opportunity to maximize patient engagement in communication using technology as a pivotal tool. This includes not only assessing for and imparting information about medical trauma, but also coordinating, treating, and following up with patients in a proactive way. Let us begin our exploration of technology's role in managing medical trauma by considering ways in which wearable technology and in-room software can help patients and staff members address anxiety and stress related to medical care.

Using Applications and "Wearables" to Manage Medical Trauma

Mobile technology in the form of applications has exploded as accessible and inexpensive methods for patients to track progress in lifestyle changes and symptoms related to health concerns. Health information technology (HIT) efforts are joining the popularity of apps by offering patients portals to their health records and mobile health management. This includes innovative methods to transfer patient information through blue-button technology so that multiple caregivers have the most current information about a patient.

Examples of mobile patient engagement platforms include Anthelio Engage, GetWellNetwork, and CareCloud, which are designed to provide multiple points of access to patients and their providers. The applications allow for appointment scheduling, information updates, prescription refill requests, review of lab and test results, educational material, and secure access to providers. Care transitions are also bridged in a more seamless manner with lower costs. This type of technology infrastructure fits well with the various personal health care devices available to consumers and medical communities. One of the most popular forms of personal health technology is wearables.

Wearable health monitoring devices have surged in recent years as real-time ways to track everything from fitness progress, heart rate changes, sleep patterns, and chronic disease management. Data from these wearables can be shared so that a patient is not alone in the monitoring and interpretation of his or her health data. Clinicians around the world are beginning to integrate wearables as early warning detection devices so that intervention can be more timely and preventive when concerns arise. In fact, many studies predict that mobile health technology will revolutionize health care management and delivery within the next decade (e.g., GlobalData, 2012).

Within the hospital setting, wearables such as the IntelliVue MX40 are used to monitor patients during transport or as they walk around the health care setting. Medical staff can quickly gauge a patient's vitals and intervene as needed. The emphasis of the monitoring, however, on biometric data such as heart rate or blood pressure is often interpreted through a physical rather than an emotional lens. While spikes in heart rate are likely caused by a patient's medical circumstances, they can also be indicative of anxiety or panic. Given this, it would be important to widen the lens when interpreting biometric data retrieved from wearables. Speaking of which, let us take a look at a few scenarios in which wearable technology can be integrated into the management of medical trauma.

Imagine, for instance, a hospital that provides patients with wearable heart rate monitors that interface with the nursing station and with the in-room television display. Suppose a patient began to feel anxious about an upcoming surgery or test, which causes his or her heart rate to elevate. The wearable device would then send two signals: one to the nursing station and the other to the television screen, which displays a question such as, "Would you like to do a relaxation activity?" If the patient agrees, the screen shifts to a soothing visual with sound, and a prompt for the patient to begin a simple guided-breathing exercise to help lower the heart rate. Breathing in through the nostrils for a count of four and slowly exhaling through pursed lips for a count of eight activates the parasympathetic nervous system, which helps the patient relax. Upon finishing this activity, the patient can explore other relaxation prompts on-demand.

In addition to the preprogrammed relaxation prompts provided by the hospital, patients could also personalize their menu to include statements, mantras, or reminders that soothe them, and these could be programmed to appear on their in-room screen as a means of relaxation or contextualization in times of stress or when patients feel uneasy. Statements such as "You are stronger than you think you are" or "Get better for Jim and the kids" could be potent reminders of one's resilience and motivation to recover. Patients could also upload pictures from a mobile device to scroll across the screen as a means of emotional grounding. When patients elect to view these, an alert could be sent to the nursing station, which could prompt a staff member to check in to see if any additional mental health resources are needed, such as aromatherapy, breathing exercises, or time with a mental health professional.

Using Technology for Aftercare

Patients who become lost in the complexity of the dos and don'ts of aftercare are often unmotivated to follow through with instructions, in part because they may feel incompetent to handle the tasks expected of them. For instance, one study found that 42% of patients had doubts about managing their medications (Stempniak, 2014). The study noted additional issues as well, such as patients having difficulty retaining information and varying levels of understanding of the information provided to them. Imagine if these patients had also experienced a traumatic medical event and it is easy to understand how people struggle to follow aftercare instructions.

Patient engagement portals can be highly effective in helping patients manage the psychological impacts of medical traumas. The personalized sites can include linkages to wearable devices that monitor biometric indicators of distress as well as to assessment instruments that can give patients and their providers more insight into the effects of a particular medical experience. For example, portals could link to the Medical Mental Health Screening tool and the Secondary 7–Lifestyle Effects Screening tool to help patients and providers determine the risks for and effects of medical trauma. If primary care providers, specialty care providers, and mental health providers were linked within this system, communication regarding integrated patient care could be seamless and promote effective IPC.

Wearable devices for home use could help a patient track and intervene when stress or panic sets in. For example, if an elevated heart rate is detected, the device could signal the patient through a buzz or beep. A question prompt would then appear on the device asking the patient if his or her heart rate rose purposefully (i.e., due to exercise) or because of anxiety or panic. If the patient indicates an experience of anxiety, a guided diaphragmatic breathing intervention could follow. The device could log the frequency and duration of panic attacks or anxiety and patients could opt to upload those data to their patient engagement portal as an alert to a health care or mental health provider. Patients could also access online educational materials through a mobile app or through their patient portal. Such linkages between patients and providers can help patients manage their emotional health following medical traumas, as well as help professionals intervene quickly when psychological or secondary crises arise.

There are also many applications for mobile phone and electronic devices that are designed to help the user self-assess for, learn about, and work through posttraumatic stress disorder (PTSD). An example of this is PTSD Coach, developed for the National Center for PTSD and the National Center for Telehealth and Technology. This app enables people to self-monitor in-the-moment symptoms (e.g., anger, disconnected, worry) and participate in mindfulness and cognitive behavioral interventions. If an experience is too overwhelming, people can access immediate help from a mental health professional. Currently, there are no applications that focus specifically on medical trauma and its unique considerations, such as secondary crises and specific triggers related to receiving medical care, but this kind of app could be helpful to patients who struggle emotionally as a result of their medical circumstances.

Speaking of medical contact triggering trauma, let us take another look at medical avoidance, and how telehealth can serve as an alternative for patients who disengage from health care due to medical trauma.

Using Telehealth for Medical Avoidance

As you learned in Chapter 3, medical avoidance is a potentially dangerous and costly consequence of untreated medical trauma. When people, and any conscious living thing for that matter, experience a trauma, it is a natural instinct to seek to avoid reminders of the traumatic experience. Unfortunately for those whose trauma unfolds within a healing environment, this avoidance can sometimes mean refusing to get medical treatment, even in cases in which the consequences of *not* getting treatment may be dire. We know that patients who develop PTSD following critical medical events can take significantly longer to recognize a health issue and to intervene on their own behalf, if they intervene at all. For some, it may be that they seek to avoid the medical setting, but given the advances in telehealth technology, it is not a stretch to use this technology to our advantage when treating patients with medical trauma.

Telehealth (or telemedicine) has become an integral part of the health care landscape and is continually building on the use of technology in everyday life. Pretty extraordinary things are happening with telemedicine, including using telecommunications (and glass technology) to increase access to specialist care for rural populations, enable consultation with experts from around the world, and link health care professionals with each other and with patients in order to provide efficient and effective care. Never before have health care professionals been more empowered to provide care remotely, with methods of transmitting biodata in real time, and even the prospect of using drones to carry medical equipment to remote or inaccessible places in order to provide critical care through a video link. Aside from the capabilities for remote specialist and critical care, another important function of telemedicine is its use in the primary care setting.

Because of its efficient and cost-effective model, telehealth for primary care is becoming a viable option for patients who need immediate help for nonlife-threatening health issues, and who cannot or prefer not to visit a primary care provider. Insurers are either providing direct telehealth care options, or are contracting with telehealth organizations to provide care remotely. Using this option, patients can simply log in through their computer, tablet, or smartphone to the telehealth organization's app, and within minutes can be connected to a primary care provider trained to provide assessment, diagnosis, and treatment—and this transaction happens within the comfort and privacy of patients' homes. This method of health care delivery can be a viable alternative for patients who develop fears of or reluctance to visit the medical setting for primary health care. Further, if telehealth provider organizations perform a quick screen prior to each telehealth visit in order to assess the patients' motivations for choosing telehealth, they can determine if patients have experienced medical trauma or have an aversion to visiting health care settings for some other reason. If patients indicate any fear or reluctance to see a primary health care provider, telemedicine professionals can provide a referral to a mental health professional (who could also be available for online counseling). While an overall goal would be to help patients reintegrate into the traditional health care system, telehealth, and online mental health services represent a critical stop-gap solution for patients who might otherwise slip between the cracks.

It is clear that technology has an intriguing role to play in helping health care staff and patients manage the psychological impacts of medical trauma, from monitoring and assessment to allowing for remote access to primary care. Let us now examine another trend that plays an important role in how we provide whole-person care: IPE.

IPE: TRAINING A COLLABORATIVE HEALTH CARE WORKFORCE

A main premise of this book has been that health care is best delivered by diverse professionals working collaboratively in teams, especially in cases of medical trauma when patients require the dual perspective of health care and mental health professionals. As we know from our own personal and professional experiences, it is not always easy to work with others— especially under stressful circumstances when the consequences for making mistakes and working ineffectively can be serious and even deadly. With this understanding, many health care organizations employ formal training in team-based skills (such as TeamSTEPPS or Crew Resource Management) in order to improve patient safety and clinical outcomes. Building highly effective health care teams can be challenging, in part due to the paradigm shift required for some health care and mental health workers who are used to working independently and in the silos of their own professions. In addition, when we consider the hierarchical culture found in many health care organizations and in smaller practices, it can seem like a momentous task to transition to a more egalitarian, collaborative way of working. There are certainly additional challenges to functioning in health care teams (e.g., personality conflicts, communication barriers, concern for professional liability), yet in this section we focus specifically on shifting the culture of health care practice to a team-based model; perhaps one of the most effective ways to do so is to teach team skills and model IPC during the educational process.

While not a new concept, IPE has gained tremendous momentum in the past few decades and has become the gold standard in training health care professionals. Members of the 1972 Institute of Medicine (IOM) Steering Committee recognized that the best way to train the health care workforce was to educate professionals to work in teams (IOM, 1972), and since then health care educational associations (through the Interprofessional Education Collaborative [IPEC]) have taken the lead in promoting IPE to health care educators; teaching the knowledge, skills, and dispositions of IPE; and in supporting research efforts to measure the many effects of IPE. Desiring to further the spread of IPE at universities and encourage IPC throughout practice settings, governmental institutions such as the Health Resources and Services Administration (HRSA) provide large competitive grants to support such efforts. It seems that never before have universities been more supported in implementing opportunities for students from diverse health professions to work together to solve health care problems. By engaging students in the collaborative learning process early and often, the hope is that this shapes future behavior by creating a new template for professional practice that includes an openness and ability for health care and mental health professionals to work well together.

IPE is a key to breaking down the silos of the health care and mental health professions, which is critical if we are to successfully manage the psychological impacts of medical trauma. By providing students of diverse professions the opportunity to learn with, from, and about each other, educators increase interprofessional understanding and mutual respect while normalizing the collaborative process. When students from health care and mental health learn team-based communication and conceptualization skills together, they become more in tune with explicit and nuanced differences among their professions, which can lead to increased understanding and more effective collaboration. Perhaps one of the most important aspects of IPE as it relates to medical trauma is that it allows for the sharing of professional perspectives in order to get a multidimensional view of a patient.

Problem-based learning (PBL) exercises that present medical trauma cases can allow for insightful collaborations among health care and mental health students, as well as increase the understanding of other professions and improve overall attitudes about IPE and IPC (Goelen, De Clercq, Huyghens, & Kerckhofs, 2006). Further, PBL activities can provide an opportunity for students to discuss every aspect of a medical trauma case, from prevention, interprofessional intervention using treatment protocols, and aftercare. During case discussions, mental health professionals can share perspectives about the psychological impacts of specific medical interventions and the longer term mental health implications of illnesses and injuries. Educators can use case studies as part of a full IPE course taken by students from various professional programs or as one component of a non-IPE course in order to provide a collaborative experience. Medical trauma case studies could be relevant to students from many professional programs depending on the nature of each case, but those who would likely benefit the most from collaborative discussions would be students from nursing, medicine, and mental health (e.g., social work, counseling, psychology).

Moving beyond case discussion, simulation training can provide an opportunity for students to put their team skills into practice (VanKuiken, Schaefer, Hall, & Browne, 2016). Real-world simulations depicting a medical trauma (e.g., obstetrical or cardiac trauma) could require health care and mental health students to follow the steps of treatment protocol, which would provide them valuable practice using team-based communication and leadership skills. Educators can provide realistic simulation experiences by using established resources (e.g., Council on Patient Safety in Women's Health Care Safety Action Series tool on Obstetric Hemorrhage Drills [Council on Patient Safety in Women's Health Care, 2015]) and by ensuring that students from all relevant professions are present for the simulation. For example, medical and nursing students studying a specialty (e.g., obstetrics and gynecology) can be grouped with mental health students (e.g., social work and counseling) to perform a simulation depicting a birth trauma. Students would prepare for the simulation by becoming familiar with protocols and by discussing the case with their team members, and they would debrief on the simulation experience following established guidelines. When simulation drills are part of an IPE course, students can also practice communication and leadership skills they learn through a curriculum like TeamSTEPPS. Beyond the experiential learning benefits of interprofessional simulation drills, they also have a positive effect on students' attitudes about other disciplines and about IPE and IPC (Titzer, Swenty, & Hoehn, 2012).

Thankfully, IPE is already happening at many universities across the country—at least to varying degrees, and IPE has also become a focus of the WHO as a way to improve health care across the globe (World Health Organization, 2010). It would be important for health care and mental health professional education programs to continue to explore ways of bringing their students together to ensure continued collaboration and integration in diverse practice settings. Using medical trauma cases and simulations can not only provide a bridge between the professions, but can also sensitize students to the possible psychological effects of medical procedures, experiences, and illnesses—and give them the tools to address the complex needs of these patients. Speaking of tools, let us turn our attention to another zeitgeist within the health care and mental health professions that has tremendous applicability for medical trauma: mindfulness.

THE MINDFULNESS REVOLUTION IN HEALTH CARE: APPLICATIONS FOR MEDICAL TRAUMA

If you wander the self-help section of any local bookstore you are bound to see the words "mindfulness" or "mindful" within 20 seconds of scanning the shelves. It seems there is a mindfulness book, app, video, or website devoted to nearly everything that ills us, from anxiety, depression, and chronic pain to relationship problems and low self-esteem. There are mindfulness resources for children, adolescents, and adults; women and men; and individuals, groups, and classrooms. In health care, mindfulness plays a central role in many integrated health and alternative therapy programs focused on holistic care for patients with issues related to chronic illness, depression, anxiety, smoking cessation, alcohol and drug treatment, and overall health and wellness. Leaders in the mindfulness movement, specifically Dr. Jon Kabat-Zinn, who founded the Center for Mindfulness in Medicine, Health Care and Society at the University of Massachusetts Medical School, have been strong proponents of integrating mindfulness into the health care experience. So, what is mindfulness and how can it benefit patients who experience medical trauma?

What Is Mindfulness?

Simply put, mindfulness is paying attention in the present moment without judgment (Kabat-Zinn, 1982). Rooted in Buddhist and Eastern traditions, mindfulness encourages compassion, flexibility, and acceptance of each unfolding moment. It promotes regulation of affect, cognition, and behavior, which makes it efficacious for a wide variety of problems and as a contributor to overall health and well-being. In mental health, mindfulness is a component of a number of distinct therapies, such as dialectical behavior therapy (DBT) and acceptance and commitment therapy (ACT), as well as the foundation of approaches, such as mindfulness-based stress reduction (MBSR) and mindfulness-based cognitive therapy (MBCT). In health care, mindfulness had grown in popularity and has become a mainstay of integrative, mind–body medicine programs at hospitals around the country. Mindfulness meditation, a stand-alone practice as well as a component of MBSR (a more extensive 8-week program), focuses on diaphragmatic breathing, which engages the parasympathetic nervous system. Beyond the obvious benefits of being more centered and relaxed, mindfulness can promote an increased tolerance for pain and discomfort by reducing emotional reactivity as well as attachment to beliefs, thoughts, and expectations. As a powerful tool for managing anxiety and depression in addition to tolerating pain and discomfort, mindfulness seems a viable intervention for medical trauma and has several applications within the medical setting (Ludwig & Kabat-Zinn, 2008).

The Effects of Brief Mindfulness Interventions

While an 8-week MBSR program has significant empirical evidence to support its effectiveness with a number of psychophysiological disorders, not everyone has the time, resources, or inclination to participate; further, there are many circumstances that arise within the health care setting that call for immediate intervention to help patients cope with distress associated with actual or anticipated pain/discomfort, or with strong emotional reactions to a diagnosis or procedure. For these situations, brief mindfulness-based interventions may be necessary to assist patients with coping— and studies have demonstrated that such interventions, despite being brief, are effective. Mindfulness-based interventions can be used to help patients cope with the pain that accompanies chronic illness, which can in turn help lower anxiety and depression related to chronic pain. For example, patients with chronic pain experienced greater pain relief after doing a 10-minute mindfulness-based body scan compared to the control-group in a clinical setting (Ussher et al., 2014). Garland and Howard (2013) found that participants with chronic pain who engaged in mindfulness-oriented coping demonstrated lower pain attentional bias (meaning they did not selectively pay attention to the pain as often) as well as lower reactivity to distressing thoughts and emotions about the pain they experienced compared to participants in the control group. Mindfulness interventions can also help patients *before* they have a procedure by reducing anticipatory anxiety and increasing pain and distress tolerance. In a study comparing a mindfulness-based coping strategy with two other conditions (participant-chosen, spontaneous coping strategy, and distraction as coping strategy), researchers found that the participants who used the mindfulness-based strategy experienced significantly less distress and had a higher pain tolerance compared to the other coping styles (Liu, Wang, Chang, Chen, & Si, 2013). Recent studies also demonstrate the efficacy of mindfulness in reducing pain (Zeidan, Grant, Brown, McHaffie, & Coghill, 2012), with the most recent study demonstrating its superiority over placebo analgesia (Zeidan et al., 2015). These are but a few significant findings related to mindfulness—there are literally hundreds of studies that demonstrate the power of this intervention. Let us take a look at how one health care organization employs mindfulness-based interventions with its acute care population.

Spotlight on Mindfulness in Acute Care: Urban Zen at Ohio State University Wexner Medical Center

We recently met with Beth Steinberg, MS, RN, Director of Nursing, Critical Care and the Associate Director of Integrative Nursing at Ohio State University (OSU) Medical Center, to learn more about how this large academic medical center manages medical trauma and helps patients handle the emotional experience of receiving medical care for critical illnesses. Within the first 5 minutes of our conversation, Beth mentioned that she was trained in MBSR at the 7-day Residential Professional Training by Jon Kabat-Zinn's group, is a certified yoga instructor, and is trained in reiki—all of which told us that this director of nursing knows a thing or two about treating patients holistically.

Currently, OSU Wexner Medical Center is a clinical site that offers the Urban Zen Integrative Therapy Program (UZIT; www.uzit.urbanzen.org) to hospitalized patients, their families, and staff from a variety of units within the hospital (e.g., trauma, vascular surgery, hospitalist) who request a visit from a trained integrative therapist, all of whom are nurses. Staff trained in UZIT can provide yoga (gentle movement, guided meditations, and focus on the breath), aromatherapy with essential oils, reiki, nutrition consultations, and contemplative care. At OSU Medical Center, results from the over 750 patients and family members treated have shown significant benefits including anxiety relief and lowering of blood pressure, specifically for patients who have experienced stroke and other neurological disorders (B. Steinberg, personal communication, November 12, 2015). Given the positive results from and overwhelming satisfaction of the UZIT sessions (9.1 on a 10-point scale), the medical center hopes to expand the program by training additional staff and including more hospital units.

The UZIT sessions demonstrate the effectiveness of integrative therapy modalities in creating a more relaxed patient experience in the hospital, and show us that these kinds of interventions are possible in the acute care setting. Programs that incorporate mindfulness, such as UZIT, along with sound assessment protocols for identifying the psychological impacts of medical trauma are an intriguing example of how we can ensure that people are cared for in mind, body, and spirit while engaged in the health care system. Regarding integrating mindfulness interventions in health care, health care and mental health professionals are really only limited by their own creativity as there are a number of ways in which mindfulness can be utilized to improve patient well-being (see Appendix E for mindfulness resources).

Applications for Mindfulness in Treating Medical Trauma

There are a number of ways in which mindfulness interventions can assist patients who experience medical traumas. In the primary care setting and for Level 1 Medical Traumas, mindfulness can serve as a major component in prevention, intervention, and aftercare. When patients have planned or routine medical procedures and experience anticipatory anxiety (which can be identified using a tool such as the Medical Mental Health Screening), health care and mental health staff can teach mindfulness strategies to help them cope with any distress they may experience. Likewise, staff can coach patients in using a mindfulness technique during a procedure, such as helping them stay grounded with breathing techniques to help them tolerate the pain associated with their treatment or discomfort of their surroundings. Mindfulness skills are also a useful addition to any aftercare and wellness plan, and can help patients build an acceptance of physical and emotional changes they experience as a result of their medical care or of living with chronic illness (Level 2 Medical Trauma). For traumatic medical events or Level 3 Medical Traumas, MBSR can help patients manage acute distress by facilitating activation of the parasympathetic nervous system, encouraging a mind–body connection to minimize dissociation and encourage pain tolerance, and exposing them to new tools they can use after discharge as they continue to recover both physically and emotionally. In addition to one-on-one mindfulness coaching with staff, patients can also benefit from accessing mindfulness resources via personal technology or through resources embedded within the health care setting.

The majority of this book has been devoted to helping patients cope with the heavy emotional consequences of medical traumas, but we would be remiss if we did not revisit a topic crucial to our ability to effectively care for patients: how we care for staff members who have experienced vicarious traumatization.

CARING FOR THOSE WHO CARE FOR PATIENTS: MANAGING VICARIOUS TRAUMATIZATION

It may go without saying, but we *must* take care of our caregivers. It is not lost upon us that in the examples of patients' experiences of medical trauma that we have provided throughout this book, there were people on the other end of those interactions who bore witness to them—people who tried furiously to save lives and preserve health while attempting to maintain calm exteriors and professional perspectives. In the end, despite their clinical approach and level-headed demeanor, health care staff members are human beings who deeply care about others and have strong emotional responses to some of the patients with whom they work. While we call these intense emotional reactions "vicarious" trauma, they are nonetheless very real, very personal, and can directly impact caregivers' lives in numerous ways.

Just as we advocate for an established protocol for identifying and intervening with patients who experience medical trauma, we also believe in implementing similar programs for staff members who provide direct clinical care. Health care organizations have a duty to normalize help-seeking among staff members who experience traumatic stress, and to build a culture of mutual support in order to ensure that staff—and by proxy, patients—receive the best care possible. Organizations large and small can implement staff education to help professionals recognize signs of stress and impairment, as well as a sound process for referring staff for confidential mental health services, either through an Employee Assistance Program (EAP) or affiliated trauma resource center. Consider the following example of a multifaceted program for supporting staff developed by the OSU Wexner Medical Center and Ohio State Department of Psychiatry.

Spotlight on Programs for Supporting Staff and Patients Touched by Medical Trauma: The STAR Program

The Stress, Trauma, and Resilience (STAR) Program at the OSU Wexner Medical Center is an integrated support program for patients, health care staff, and members of the community who have experienced trauma. Specific to staff support, the program's clinic offers trauma support services or brief therapeutic support for staff members who have experienced vicarious traumatization, as well as resiliency training that includes mindfulness-based skills for boosting coping strategies and overall mental and behavioral wellness. The culture within the medical center also encourages resiliency, relaxation, and stress-reduction through symposia, forums, and other educational opportunities in order to support staff members' overall health and well-being.

Within the umbrella of services to support staff members' emotional health and healing following a medical trauma, the OSU Medical Center has initiated Schwartz Center Rounds (www.theschwartzcenter.org), which provide an important outlet for staff (physicians, nurses, allied health professionals, and students) to debrief about patient cases that elicit strong emotions and to provide mutual support in a safe environment conducive to sharing. According to Beth Steinberg, MS, RN, attendance at the rounds has steadily risen with some meetings being standing room only.

The STAR program at the OSU and others like it can serve as a model for staff support for health care organizations around the world. By encouraging holistic self-care for staff, we increase the likelihood that they will be fit enough in mind, body, and spirit to provide the very best care to patients, even in the most traumatic of circumstances.

MEDICAL TRAUMA AND IMPLICATIONS FOR FUTURE RESEARCH

The primary purpose of this book has been to assemble some of the puzzle pieces of medical trauma in order to examine how best to serve the needs of patients. Our personal experiences of medical trauma, coupled with the many stories shared with us by clients, colleagues, friends, and family, have informed our perspective of the phenomenon; our training as academicians and mental health professionals has informed the lens through which we view medical trauma, and armed with this perspective we have stitched together many previously disparate pieces to create a new whole. It would be a valuable endeavor for future research to focus on the validity of the model of medical trauma for multiple populations, as well as the efficacy of the many protocols and assessment tools we have presented here. Additionally, research investigating the effectiveness of technological applications in managing medical trauma, as well as research already underway that explores the effects of mindfulness-based interventions for patients who experience medical trauma, will lead to unfolding insights about how best to care for people who suffer emotionally as a result of their medical circumstances. In many ways, we are entering a brave new world with regard to how we deliver the best medical care possible, and research will help us fine-tune our approach along the way.

THE BUSINESS CASE FOR HIRING MORE MENTAL HEALTH PROFESSIONALS

Programs like STAR at the OSU Medical Center that provide intensive trauma-focused support and resources are really only possible with the help of mental health professionals. The many approaches to identifying and treating medical trauma require that mental health professionals be an integral part of treatment teams. We have spent the majority of this book discussing how and why medical events become traumatic for some patients, and what health care and mental health professionals can do together to prevent and treat the distress and complex consequences that can accompany this type of experience. We have advocated on behalf of increasing the roles of mental health professionals in health care in order to realize greater collaboration and improved patient outcomes; however, without articulating a business case for implementing these ideas, they could remain just that—ideas. While many of the prevention and intervention strategies that we outline require new behaviors from existing staff, for those hospitals and practices without sufficient mental health professional staff, putting these strategies into action may require hiring additional resources. So why should health care organizations invest in a mental health workforce dedicated to managing the psychological impacts of medical trauma?

First and perhaps most important, mental health professionals are highly trained in the communication, assessment, and trauma intervention skills necessary to provide the level of care required for managing the many effects of medical trauma. They have the education and experience to consistently offer patients the empathy, sensitivity, and perspective necessary to provide those who experience medical trauma—as well as the family members and staff affected by patients' experiences—holistic care. By employing mental health professionals to perform many of the assessment and intervention tasks we have described, health care professionals can attend to the physical health needs of patients knowing that their team members are attending to the emotional needs, thus providing care for the whole patient and improving the overall patient experience.

It is likely that mental health professionals are currently underutilized in many health care organizations, and it can make good business sense to reevaluate how the skills of these staff members can be leveraged to meet the holistic needs of patients, their families, and staff. In addition to the diverse roles mental health professionals can perform within interprofessional treatment teams at all levels of care, many can also serve a vital function as part of a patient-experience office, as a member of a team focused on organizational quality, or as a training and development professional who teaches empathic interprofessional communication. Depending on their unique skills and qualities, mental health professionals can serve health care practices and organizations in a wide variety of ways—all of which can have a positive impact for patients in general, not just for those who experience medical trauma.

Lastly, in terms of protecting the overall health of patients, providing easy access to mental health services at all levels of care is important. From what we know about the negative effects of PTSD and chronic stress on physical health concerns, such as coronary artery disease, hypertension, hyperlipidemia, obesity, sleep disorders, gastrointestinal diseases, diabetes, arthritis, autoimmune disorders, and pain sensitivity (Gupta, 2013; Husarewycz, El-Gabalawy, Logsetty, & Sareen, 2014; McFarlane, 2010), it makes good sense to ensure that patients are receiving care that is well-coordinated and comprehensive.

SUMMARY

Throughout this chapter, we have explored many trends that will influence the trajectory of health care delivery for the foreseeable future, and how each of these trends can assist in our endeavor to manage medical trauma. We have only scratched the surface of the role of technology, IPE, and mindfulness-based interventions in helping health care staff achieve safe and effective whole-person care for patients; indeed, each of these topics could be books unto themselves. Perhaps the most salient idea woven throughout this chapter is that current innovations and trends within the health care system can be leveraged to meet the holistic needs of patients and their families. In fact, aside from the many tools we present in this book, much of what is needed to manage the psychological impacts of medical trauma are resources and strengths already in place in many health care organizations and practices around the country. Perhaps what may have been missing is the lens through which we view patients, the understanding that sometimes health care and illness can be traumatic, and the belief that we have a responsibility to care for the whole person.

In the end, managing the psychological impacts of medical trauma is a shared responsibility. From health care and mental health professionals, administrators, researchers, and innovators to patients and their families, we all have a part to play in ensuring that whole people who enter the health care setting for treatment leave as whole people—not as shells of their former selves with no clear path for reclaiming self, emotional health, and well-being. Untreated medical trauma can rob us of our humanity, and therefore, it is up to each one of us to ensure that every patient receives care that honors and values *all* that makes them human. When health care and mental health professionals work together using the tools of innovation and a disposition of compassion— they can successfully manage the psychological impacts of medical trauma.

REFERENCES

Council on Patient Safety in Women's Health Care. (2015). *Safety Action Series: Obstetric hemorrhage drills.* Retrieved from http://www.safehealth careforeverywoman. org/downloads/SAS-OB-Hemorrhage-Drills-111814-Final-Slideset-for-Posting.pdf

Garland, E., & Howard, M. (2013). Mindfulness-oriented recovery enhancement reduces pain attentional bias in chronic pain patients. *Psychotherapy and Psychosomatics, 82,* 311–318. doi:10.1159/000348868

GlobalData. (2012). *mhealth: Healthcare goes mobile.* Retrieved from https:// healthcare.globaldata.com/media-center/press-releases/medical-devices/ mhealth-healthcare-goes-mobile

Goelen, G., De Clercq, G., Huyghens, L., & Kerckhofs, E. (2006). Measuring the effect of interprofessional problem-based learning on the attitudes of undergraduate health care students. *Medical Education, 40*(6), 555–561.

Gupta, M. (2013). Review of somatic symptoms in post-traumatic stress disorder. *International Review of Psychiatry, 25*(1), 86–99.

Husarewycz, M., El-Gabalawy, R., Logsetty, S., & Sareen, J. (2014). The association between number and type of traumatic life experiences and physical conditions in a nationally representative sample. *General Hospital Psychiatry, 36*(1), 26–32.

Institute of Medicine. (1972). *Educating for the health team.* Washington, DC: National Academy of Science.

Kabat-Zinn, J. (1982). An outpatient program in behavioral medicine for chronic pain patients based on the practice of mindfulness meditation: Theoretical considerations and preliminary results. *General Hospital Psychiatry, 4*(1), 33–47.

Liu, X., Wang, S., Chang, S., Chen, W., & Si, M. (2013). Effect of brief mindfulness intervention on tolerance and distress of pain induced by cold-pressor task. *Stress and Health, 29*(1), 199–204.

Ludwig, D., & Kabat-Zinn, J. (2008). Mindfulness in medicine. *JAMA, 300*(11), 1350–1352.

McFarlane, A. (2010). The long-term costs of traumatic stress: Intertwined physical and psychological consequences. *World Psychiatry, 9,* 3–10.

Stempniak, M. (2014). Technology: Key to engagement at the individual level. *Hospitals and Health Networks, 88*(6), 40–44. PubMed PMID: 25102622.

Titzer, J. L., Swenty, C. F., & Hoehn, W. G. (2012). An interprofessional simulation promoting collaboration and problem solving among nursing and allied health professional students. *Clinical Simulation in Nursing, 8*(8), e325–e333.

Ussher, M., Spatz, A., Copland, C., Nicolaou, A., Cargill, A., Amini-Tabrizi, N., & McCracken, L. (2014). Immediate effects of a brief mindfulness-based body scan on patients with chronic pain. *Journal of Behavioral Medicine, 37*(1), 127–134.

VanKuiken, D., Schaefer, J. K., Hall, M. F., & Browne, F. R. (2016). Integrating interprofessional education into the curriculum: Challenges and solutions for a university without a medical center. *Journal of Interprofessional Education and Practice, 2,* 5–11.

Workman, T. A., deBronkart, D., Quinlan, C., & Pinder, J. (2014). *What do patients and families want from patient engagement?* Washington, DC.

World Health Organization. (2010). *Framework for action on interprofessional education and collaborative practice.* Geneva, Switzerland: Author.

Zeidan, F., Emerson, N., Farris, S., Ray, J., Jung, Y., McHaffie, J., & Coghill, R. (2015). Mindfulness meditation-based pain relief employs different neural mechanisms than placebo and sham mindfulness meditation-induced analgesia. *The Journal of Neuroscience, 35*(46), 15307–15325. doi:10.1523/JNEUROSCI.2542-15.2015

Zeidan, F., Grant, J. A., Brown, C. A., McHaffie, J. G., & Coghill, R. C. (2012). Mindfulness meditation-related pain relief: Evidence for unique brain mechanisms in the regulation of pain. *Neuroscience Letters, 520*(2), 165–173.

APPENDICES

A TRAUMA RESOURCES

WEBSITES

ORGANIZATION	WEBSITE
Centers for Disease Control and Prevention	www.cdc.gov
Health Care Toolbox: Your Guide to Helping Children and Families Cope With Illness and Injury	www.healthcaretoolbox.org
Mayo Clinic	www.mayoclinic.org/diseases-conditions/post-traumatic-stress-disorder/basics/definition/con-20022540
National Child Traumatic Stress Network: Pediatric Medical Traumatic Stress Toolkit for Health Care Providers	www.nctsn.org/trauma-types/medical-trauma
National Institute of Mental Health	www.nimh.nih.gov/health/topics/post-traumatic-stress-disorder-ptsd/index.shtml
Somatic Experiencing Trauma Institute	www.traumahealing.org

(continued)

WEBSITES (continued)

ORGANIZATION	WEBSITE
Substance Abuse and Mental Health Services Administration (SAMHSA)	www.samhsa.gov/nctic/trauma-interventions
Trauma Informed Practices and Expressive Arts Therapy Institute and Learning Center	www.trauma-informedpractice.com
U.S. Department of Veterans Affairs	www.ptsd.va.gov
World Health Organization	www.who.int/en

BOOKS

AUTHOR(S)	TITLE/PUBLISHER
Suzette Boon, Kathy Steele, & Onno van der Hart	*Coping with Trauma-Related Dissociation: Skills Training for Patients and Therapists (Norton Series on Interpersonal Neurobiology).* W. W. Norton.
John Briere & Catherine Scott	*Principles of Trauma Therapy: A Guide to Symptoms, Evaluation, and Treatment.* SAGE Publications.
Elizabeth K. Carll (Ed.)	*Trauma Psychology: Issues in Violence, Disaster, Health, and Illness (Volume 2, Health and Illness).* Praeger Publishers.
Judith Herman	*Trauma and Recovery.* Basic Books.
Bessel van der Kolk	*The Body Keeps the Score: Brain, Mind, and Body in the Healing of Trauma.* Penguin Books.
Ulrich F. Lanius, Sandra L. Paulsen, & Frank M. Corrigan (Eds.)	*Neurobiology and Treatment of Traumatic Dissociation.* Springer Publishing Company.
Lisa Lopez Levers (Ed.)	*Trauma Counseling: Theories and Interventions.* Springer Publishing Company.
Peter A. Levine	*In an Unspoken Voice: How the Body Releases Trauma and Restores Goodness.* North Atlantic Books.
Peter A. Levine	*Healing Trauma: A Pioneering Program for Restoring the Wisdom of Your Body.* Sounds True, Inc.
Sheela Raja	*Overcoming Trauma and PTSD: A Workbook Integrating Skills from ACT, DBT, & CBT.* New Harbinger.
Babette Rothschild	*The Body Remembers.* W. W. Norton.
Robert Scaer	*The Trauma Spectrum: Hidden Wounds and Human Resiliency.* W. W. Norton.

SECONDARY 7–LIFESTYLE EFFECTS SCREENING (S7-LES)

INSTRUCTIONS

The S7-LES is a self-administered screening tool to help assess changes in many areas of your life as a result of your medical procedure or diagnosis. Please check the response that most accurately reflects your experience at this point in time.

	YES	NO
Developmental		
1. Since my medical procedure/diagnosis, I have had to alter my life plan or have been unable to reach important milestones (e.g., delayed graduation or marriage, relocation)		
2. I am experiencing emotional difficulties as a result of this (e.g., stress, anxiety, or depression)		
Intrapersonal (Self)		
1. Since my medical procedure/diagnosis, I feel more negative about myself and/or my abilities (e.g., self-confidence, feeling worthwhile)		
2. I am experiencing emotional difficulties related to these changes (e.g., stress, anxiety, or depression)		

(continued)

© Michelle Flaum Hall and Scott E. Hall

(continued)	YES	NO
Relationships		
1. Since my medical procedure/diagnosis, I have noticed strain on my relationships with others (e.g., friends, family, significant others, coworkers)		
2. I am experiencing emotional difficulties related to these changes (e.g., stress, anxiety, or depression)		
Career/Occupation		
1. Since my medical procedure/diagnosis, I have noticed negative effects on my career/educational performance (e.g., competence in duties, ability to advance)		
2. I am experiencing emotional difficulties related to these changes (e.g., stress, anxiety, or depression)		
Existential		
1. Since my medical procedure/diagnosis, I struggle with thoughts about what it all means for me and my life (e.g., endings, lack of meaning, limited freedom, or loneliness)		
2. I am experiencing emotional difficulties related to these changes (e.g., stress, anxiety, or depression)		
Avocational/Leisure		
1. Since my medical procedure/diagnosis, I have noticed changes in my ability to do things I once did for fun/health/relaxation (e.g., leisure activities, hobbies, or civic involvements)		
2. I am experiencing emotional difficulties related to these changes (e.g., stress, anxiety, or depression)		
Spiritual		
1. Since my medical procedure/diagnosis, I have noticed changes in my spiritual beliefs or practices (e.g., belief or relationship with God or a higher power, spiritual activities such as religious service attendance)		
2. I am experiencing emotional difficulties related to these changes (e.g., stress, anxiety, or depression)		

INSTRUCTIONS FOR USING THE SECONDARY 7–LIFESTYLE EFFECTS SCREENING TOOL

FOR CLINICIANS ONLY

The S7-LES assesses the presence of negative or maladaptive responses (secondary crises) to medical events, illnesses, and procedures in relation to seven life domains. The tool is a self-administered checklist that can be completed by patients in a provider's office after a medical procedure, hospital admission, life-threatening diagnosis, or any other circumstances deemed appropriate by providers.

The S7-LES can be used as a screening tool to detect areas in which patients struggle and to help determine when a referral to a mental health professional may be necessary. It is important that you consider any "yes" response to indicate that follow-up with a mental health professional could be helpful in preventing serious emotional consequences of medical trauma. By referring patients to mental health professionals to address psychological/emotional changes and crises in life domains, health care providers can work collaboratively to ensure overall health and well-being.

Suggested administration intervals: 2 weeks, 1 month, 3 months, 6 months

This copy is for individual use only—not for duplication, distribution, or institutional use.
For more information about using this tool, please contact:
Michelle Flaum Hall, EdD, LPCC-S
E-mail: hall@hawthorneintegrative.com
Phone: (937) 545-7392

C | MEDICAL MENTAL HEALTH SCREENING

1.	I have had previous traumatic experiences in my life	Yes	No
	Sexual trauma		
	Physical trauma or injury		
	Trauma from medical experiences or illnesses		
	Witness to traumatic event		
2.	I have experienced depression at some time in my life	Yes	No
3.	I currently struggle with depression	Yes	No
	I am being treated		
	I am NOT being treated		
4.	I feel I have a high level of stress in my life	Yes	No
	Family/relationship stress		
	Work or school-related stress		
	Health-related stress		
	Other:		
5.	I do not have healthy coping strategies for handling stress	Yes	No
6.	I experience anxiety about a lot of things in my life	Yes	No
7.	I do not have adequate social support to help me handle stress	Yes	No
8.	I use distraction and avoidance to cope with stressful situations	Yes	No

(continued)

© Michelle Flaum Hall and Scott E. Hall

(continued)			
9.	I have been diagnosed with PTSD (current or past)	Yes	No
10.	I am fearful about receiving medical treatment	Yes	No
	I have a fear of pain		
	I have a fear of needles or IVs		
	I have a fear of blood		
	I have a fear of being out of control		
11.	I worry about an upcoming medical procedure or diagnosis	Yes	No
	I worry about being under anesthesia		
	I worry about how I will cope with pain or discomfort		
	I worry about how my family will cope with my illness or procedure		
	I worry about the outcome of my procedure		
	I worry about how my procedure will affect my life		
12.	I have been diagnosed with stress-induced physical conditions	Yes	No
	such as irritable bowel syndrome (IBS), ulcers, or high blood pressure		
13.	I tend to be pessimistic about many things (e.g., the future, my health)	Yes	No
14.	I have a difficult time trusting people	Yes	No
15.	I use substances (e.g., alcohol, cigarettes, drugs) to help me manage stress	Yes	No
16.	I have close family members who have been diagnosed with PTSD or depression	Yes	No
17.	I feel that my life or well-being could be threatened by my medical condition or upcoming procedure	Yes	No
18.	I have a difficult time coping with changes in my routine or environment	Yes	No
19.	I struggle to follow through with goals related to my health (e.g., diet, exercise)	Yes	No
20.	I do not feel very hopeful about many things in my life	Yes	No

INSTRUCTIONS FOR USING THE MEDICAL MENTAL HEALTH SCREENING TOOL

FOR CLINICIANS ONLY

The Medical Mental Health Screening tool assesses risk factors that can contribute to adverse psychological responses (specifically, traumatic stress responses) to medical events, illnesses, and procedures. It is a prescreening tool and should be used as a means of flagging risk factors and intervening appropriately in order to prevent or minimize adverse emotional reactions to medical care.

The tool is a self-administered checklist that can be completed by patients *during preadmission* to the hospital for a scheduled procedure, *in a provider's office* prior to hospital admission, or in other circumstances deemed appropriate by clinicians.

It is important that you consider any items marked "yes" as potential risk factors for a traumatic stress response to a medical procedure or illness. Factors such as preexisting mental health conditions, past history of trauma (especially physical, sexual, and medical traumas), and personality factors (such as pessimism, general mistrust, difficulty with change) represent a potentially challenging recovery for the patient.

The following are subscales for the Medical Mental Health Screening tool. Add up the items marked "yes" under each subscale and note the instructions for addressing items in each subscale.

Note that multiple risk factors indicate greater potential for adverse emotional responses in patients.

Subscales and Follow-Up

Past Trauma History (1):___/1
Clinician notes past trauma history and ensures that care is patient-centered, sensitive, and caring. Note that if the patient is being admitted for greater than 24 hours, plan to administer the Experience of Medical Trauma Scale to screen for patient distress.

Medical Anxiety (10, 11, 17): ___/3
If any items are checked "yes" in this subscale, the clinician should consult with the patient prior to the procedure to determine a plan for addressing

specific fears or anxiety. Consultation with a mental health professional may be necessary to ensure proper management of anxiety.

Current or Past Mental Health Issues (2, 3, 6, 9, 16): ___/5
Clinician notes current or past mental health history and ensures that care is patient-centered, sensitive, and caring. Follow-up with a mental health professional may be necessary.

Personality Factors (13, 14, 18, 19, 20): ___/5
Clinician notes specific personality factors and ensures that communication is patient-centered, sensitive, and caring. Follow-up with a mental health professional may be necessary.

Lifestyle and Coping Factors (4, 5, 7, 8, 12, 15): ___/6
Clinician notes lifestyle and coping factors and identifies specific resources that may be helpful upon discharge (i.e., stress management resources, mental health referrals).

This copy is for individual use only—not for duplication, distribution, or institutional use.
For more information about using this tool, please contact:
Michelle Flaum Hall, EdD, LPCC-S
E-mail: hall@hawthorneintegrative.com
Phone: (937) 545-7392

SUPPORT ORGANIZATIONS FOR CHRONIC ILLNESS: CANCER, CARDIAC DISORDERS, AND DIABETES

CANCER	
ORGANIZATION	**DESCRIPTION**
American Psychosocial Oncology Society	A national association that provides patients with a hotline and list of mental health providers who specialize in the psychosocial aspects of cancer; promotes research and education for professionals.
Website	**www.apos-society.org**
Cancer Support Community (CSC)	This nonprofit organization is dedicated to providing free and personalized direct services such as education, wellness activities (e.g., nutritional education and yoga), and support for mental and emotional health to its members. CSC has a presence in all 50 states in hospitals, cancer treatment centers, and stand-alone locations within the community to serve its members.
Website	**www.cancersupportcommunity.org**

(continued)

CANCER (*continued*)

ORGANIZATION	DESCRIPTION
CancerCare	This organization based in New York offers online education and information, referrals for mental health services from oncology social workers, support groups in a variety of formats (in-person, phone, or online), and community programs for patients living in New York, New Jersey, or Connecticut.
Website	www.cancercare.org
American Cancer Society (Support Services Locator)	The American Cancer Society's website has a wealth of information about cancer, including the psychosocial impacts of living with cancer. There is also a database of support programs and services that can be searched by zip code or city and state.
Website	www.cancer.org/treatment/ supportprogramsservices/app/ resource-search

CARDIAC DISORDERS

ORGANIZATION	DESCRIPTION
Mended Hearts	A national and community-based nonprofit support organization with volunteers and support groups in 48 states and partnerships with over 460 hospitals nationwide. Offers in-room hospital visits from peer volunteers, and "online visiting" and "phone visiting" to provide support and encouragement for those recovering from heart-related medical procedures.
Website	www.mendedhearts.org

(continued)

CARDIAC DISORDERS (continued)

ORGANIZATION	DESCRIPTION
WomenHeart: The National Coalition for Women with Heart Disease	This nonprofit advocacy organization provides education specific to women living with heart disease and other cardiac disorders. The WomenHeart site includes information on prevention and heart health, as well as a database of support groups for women, searchable by state.
Website	**www.womenheart.org**
American Heart Association	This well-known, national nonprofit is dedicated to empowering patients who live with heart-related illnesses by providing education, resources geared toward prevention, and a database searchable by state and zip code to find the nearest branch office. A robust online support site features opportunities for patients to connect and patient stories and blogs.
Website	**www.supportnetwork.heart.org/home**

DIABETES

ORGANIZATION	DESCRIPTION
American Diabetes Association	A national nonprofit organization dedicated to advocacy, education, research, and patient empowerment, with branch offices and online education and support tools. Under the tab "Living with Diabetes," patients can explore mental health implications of living with diabetes, including "diabetes distress."
Website	**www.diabetes.org**
Diabetes Hands Foundation	A nonprofit organization that focuses on advocacy and promoting social connectedness among people living with diabetes through its two online social networks (including one in Spanish) with over 50,000 members.
Website	**http://diabeteshandsfoundation.org**

E | MINDFULNESS RESOURCES

WEBSITES

ORGANIZATION	WEBSITE
American Mindfulness Research Association	www.goamra.org
Mindfulness: Taking Time for What Matters	www.mindful.org
Mindfulnet.org: "Everything you need to know about mindfulness on one website"	www.mindfulnet.org/index.htm
Palouse Mindfulness: Free MBSR Training	www.palousemindfulness.com/selfguidedMBSR.html
MBSR Training from University of Massachusetts Medical School	www.umassmed.edu/cfm/stress-reduction
Center for Contemplative Mind in Society	www.contemplativemind.org
Heart Math/Inner Balance	www.heartmath.org
National Center for PTSD	www.ptsd.va.gov/professional/treatment/overview/mindful-PTSD.asp
Sounds True, Inc. (collection of books and resources)	www.soundstrue.com/store

BOOKS

AUTHOR(S)	TITLE(S)
Burdick, D.	*Mindfulness Skills Workbook for Clinicians and Clients*
Emerson, D., & Hopper, E.	*Overcoming Trauma Through Yoga*
Farrarons, E.	*The Mindfulness Coloring Book*
Follette, V., & Briere, J.	*Mindfulness-Oriented Interventions for Trauma*
Forsyth, J., & Eifert, G.	*The Mindfulness & Acceptance Workbook for Anxiety*
Gunaratana, B.	*Mindfulness in Plain English*
Hanh, Thich Nhat	*Peace Is Every Step: The Path of Mindfulness in Everyday Life*
Kabat-Zinn, J.	*Wherever You Go, There You Are: Mindfulness for Beginners* *Full Catastrophe Living*
Langer, E.	*Mindfulness: 25th Anniversary Edition*
Orsillo, S., & Roemer, E.	*The Mindful Way through Anxiety*
Santorelli, S.	*Heal Thyself: Lessons on Mindfulness in Medicine*
Williams, M., & Penman, G.	*Mindfulness: An Eight Week Plan for Finding Peace in a* *Frantic World*
Williams, M., & Teasdale, J.	*The Mindful Way through Depression*

APPS

- **Buddhify:** Mindfulness and Meditation for Modern Life
- **Calm** (www.calm.com)
- **Headspace** (www.headspace.com)
- **Meditation Timer**
- **Relax With Andrew Johnson**
- **Mindfulness**
- **Inner Balance** (with sensor from HeartMath: www.heartmath.org)
- **Mindfulness Daily**

(continued)

APPS (*continued*)

- Stop, Breathe, & Think
- Mindfulness Coach
- **Omvana**—Meditation for Everyone
- **Mindfulness**—Everyday Guided Meditations
- Mindfully Me
- Insight Timer

F | RECOGNIZING SIGNS OF ACUTE STRESS DISORDER IN POSTPARTUM WOMEN IN THE HOSPITAL SETTING

SYMPTOM	BEHAVIORAL SIGNS
Intrusion symptoms (Memories, dreams, flashbacks)	A woman can reexperience a birth trauma by having *involuntary* recurrent images, thoughts, illusions, dreams/nightmares, and/ or flashbacks related to the event. Intrusive symptoms can be a cause of sleep difficulty and can exacerbate symptoms of anxiety and depression (such as poor concentration, hypervigilance, exaggerated startle response, and negative mood). Signs can include agitation upon waking and fitful sleep.

SUPPORT NEEDED

- **DO:** If you suspect your patient is experiencing intrusive symptoms, consult with a mental health professional. Ask sensitive, open-ended questions about her current state, such as "I noticed you tossed and turned in your sleep last night. How was your sleep?"

- **AVOID:** Being insensitive, dismissive, or judgmental. Do not say things such as "It's over, just don't think about it," or "Try to think happy thoughts before you fall asleep."

SYMPTOM	BEHAVIORAL SIGNS
Distress with exposure to stimuli	While still in the hospital, a postpartum woman who has experienced birth trauma will be surrounded by stimuli related to the event. Signs of distress can be physical (tachycardia, perspiration) or can manifest as irritability, fear, or unwillingness to comply with requests. Can show an exaggerated startle response to stimuli. Stimuli that can trigger distress include alarms/beeping or other sounds, medical instruments, medical professionals who were present during the trauma, family members who were present during the trauma, the baby, bright lights, odors, and procedures.

SUPPORT NEEDED

🕯 **DO:** Recognize that your patient has experienced a jarring medical event and that it could have been traumatic for her. Many aspects of the hospital environment were present during her traumatic event, and she is still in this environment. Pay close attention to tachycardia as a sign of emotional distress, and ask your patient how she is feeling emotionally.

Be sensitive and use a warm tone of voice when providing instructions, and so on. Administer the Subjective Units of Distress Scale (SUDS) or Acute Stress Disorder Scale (ASDS) and share results with a mental health professional.

🕯 **AVOID:** Forcing any procedure, or saying things like "You just need to comply — it's for your own (or your baby's) good." Do not force any intervention. If patient shows signs of significant distress, contact a mental health professional.

SYMPTOM	BEHAVIORAL SIGNS
Negative mood	Inability to experience positive emotions. The patient may show little to no joy during time with her baby or family. She may be detached or seem numb to the events happening around her; aloof; withdrawn.
	Women who have experienced birth trauma can feel a flood of different and sometimes conflicting

(continued)

(continued)	
SYMPTOM	**BEHAVIORAL SIGNS**
	emotions, including: fear, sadness, terror, guilt, disappointment, happiness, anger, elation, joy, sorrow, embarrassment, and confusion. She may express these different emotions at times, or be overwhelmed by them and express nothing, seeming numb, cold, or detached.

SUPPORT NEEDED

- ❧ **DO:** Gently "check in" with your patient, inquiring about how she is feeling (not only physically, but emotionally). Ask her if she would like to speak to someone about her feelings, and try to normalize this for her (sometimes a woman might refuse because she feels a stigma for talking to a counselor). A woman can benefit from verbalizing her thoughts, feelings, and experiences about the trauma—if she feels safe in doing so.

- ❧ **AVOID:** Saying things like: "Cheer up!" "Put on a happy face!" or "You should be glad or grateful that you survived/your baby survived or is healthy/that the bad part is over." Also, do not give empty reassurance such as "This is so rare—it won't happen if you decide to have another baby in the future." These only minimize the patient's feelings, and could shame her into staying silent about her inner experiences.

SYMPTOM	**BEHAVIORAL SIGNS**
Dissociative symptoms (Altered sense of reality or disturbance in memory)	When dissociation occurs, it can seem like your patient is "out of it" or spacey, dazed, robotic, or confused about basic facts or her surroundings. Sometimes people lose concept of time (which can easily happen in the hospital setting). Some women might speak of an "out-of-body" experience, like floating above their own body or seeing the procedures happening to them. When patients experience flashbacks, they may have significant distress after seeing images, reacting as if the event were actually occurring.

SUPPORT NEEDED

- ✎ **DO:** Be calm and clear with your communication, and be accurate when adding psychosocial comments in her records. Pay attention to her behaviors and document them appropriately. Dissociative symptoms exist on a continuum: Your patient can seem a little dazed, or at the extreme, she can lose complete awareness of her surroundings. It is important to consult with a mental health professional immediately if you see signs of dissociation.

- ☞ **AVOID:** Minimizing or ignoring these symptoms, or trying to distract your patient from these experiences by suggesting she "just watch TV to get her mind off of it." Do not mistake dissociation for normal, compliant, or agreeable behavior, or assume that behaviors are the effects of pain medication. These are serious symptoms that need to be addressed by a mental health professional.

SYMPTOM	BEHAVIORAL SIGNS
Avoidance symptoms (Avoiding distressing memories/thoughts/feelings or external reminders of the event)	Women who have experienced birth trauma may attempt to avoid any memories or discussion about the birth experience, or may try to avoid reminders of the experience. She may refuse certain procedures, parts of the hospital, people who were present during the trauma, and at the extreme she may want to avoid spending time with the baby.

SUPPORT NEEDED

- ✎ **DO:** Be sensitive to your patient's feelings, recognizing her current context. Stay focused on providing excellent care, and be calm and direct when requesting compliance. While it is important to be supportive, it may also be necessary to challenge your patient to follow her plan of care. You may need to consult with a mental health professional.

- ☞ **AVOID:** Forcing your patient to comply, or to "face her fears" regarding specific reminders of the trauma. Statements such as "There is nothing to be afraid of!" or "You just have to do it!" are not supportive of your patient.

SYMPTOM	BEHAVIORAL SIGNS
Arousal symptoms (sleep disturbance)	Insomnia is common following a trauma. Signs of high arousal following a birth trauma can include fitful sleep or inability to go to sleep, which can indicate nightmares or an overly active sympathetic nervous system.

SUPPORT NEEDED

- **DO:** Ask her how she slept, and if she is having any problems with both the amount and the quality of her sleep.

- **AVOID:** Assuming that because her eyes are closed, she is resting comfortably. After a birth trauma, your patient may often need to lie quietly with her eyes closed—with as little stimulation as possible.

SYMPTOM	BEHAVIORAL SIGNS
Poor concentration	Because of the intense stimulation and activation of the sympathetic nervous system that occurs during a birth trauma, a woman may have difficulty concentrating on cognitive tasks or stimuli. She may ask you to repeat information or instructions several times or seem aloof with health care professionals or family/friends.

SUPPORT NEEDED

- **DO:** Be patient if you need to repeat information or instructions, recognizing her current emotional state. Ask her if she is having any difficulty concentrating, and if there is anything you can do to help. Provide important instructions in writing so that she can consult them when necessary.

- **AVOID:** Taking it personally, or getting agitated/impatient if you have to alter your communication to meet her current needs.

SYMPTOM	BEHAVIORAL SIGNS
Hypervigilance and exaggerated startle response	Because of a birth trauma, a woman can become hypersensitive to stimuli around her. As a result, her behaviors can become exaggerated in an attempt to detect threats in the environment. Her sympathetic nervous system was likely activated for an extended period of time during the trauma, and her instinct is to protect herself at signs of threat. A traumatized individual can react instantly to stimuli that might not bother others, such as sudden noises or movements. Signs of exaggerated startle response include jumping, flinching, shaking, and accelerated heart rate in response to stimuli such as sudden speech or movements by others, noises from hallway, alarms or beeping, and physical connection.

SUPPORT NEEDED

- **DO:** Keep your movements careful. If you notice hypervigilance and an exaggerated startle response in your patient, you should slow down your pace and be mindful of noise, bright lights, and effects of physical touch. Ask her about preferences, and make accommodations if possible. This may include turning down alarms/monitors or dimming the lights. If you notice these symptoms, consult a mental health professional.

- **AVOID:** Doing "business as usual" when your patient is clearly negatively impacted by stimulation. Do not make offhand remarks such as "Wow! Aren't you jumpy today!" or any other statement that would minimize her current state. Recognize if there are patterns in tachycardia, such as a rise in heart rate during physical examinations or discussions with medical professionals.

This copy is for individual use only—not for duplication, distribution, or institutional use.
For more information about using this tool, please contact:
Michelle Flaum Hall, EdD, LPCC-S
E-mail: hall@hawthorneintegrative.com
Phone: (937) 545-7392

G EXPERIENCE OF MEDICAL TRAUMA SCALE

The Experience of Medical Trauma Scale (EMTS) is a questionnaire completed by health care professionals to assess factors that contribute to a patient's distress while in the hospital setting and that can exacerbate a traumatic stress response to medical care. Such factors are distributed in the following categories: communications with clinicians, physical discomforts, environmental discomforts, and emotional discomforts.

INSTRUCTIONS TO CLINICIAN

The following questionnaire should be administered by a clinician (*nurse, physician, or mental health professional*) in the acute care setting following a severe event, sentinel event, or in any circumstance in which a patient may have experienced trauma due to the nature of the illness, procedure, or unique circumstances.

For any items scored a 2 or above, clinicians should create a plan for improvement that includes consultation with the patient. For Emotional Discomforts items scored a 1 or above, plan to consult a mental health professional (clinical mental health counselor, clinical social worker, or psychologist) immediately.

In the event that a mental health professional is not accessible while the patient is at your facility, ensure that a referral for follow-up mental health care is included in the patient's discharge plan.

	NOT DISTRESSING/ NOT EXPERIENCED	SLIGHTLY DISTRESSING	MODERATELY DISTRESSING	DISTRESSING	EXTREMELY DISTRESSING
	0	1	2	3	4
Communication					
Interactions with medical staff (assistants and technologists)					
Interactions with nurses					
Interactions with physicians					
Interactions with surgeons					
Communications too detailed/technical					
Communications too quick/confusing					
Communications too vague					
Communications too infrequent					
Communications too frequent					

Plan of Action to Ameliorate the Patient Experience

For **Communications** items scored 2 or above:

Patient Remarks: _____

_____

Provider Response and Plan: _____

_____

_____

© Michelle Flaum Hall and Scott E. Hall

	NOT DISTRESSING/NOT EXPERIENCED	SLIGHTLY DISTRESSING	MODERATELY DISTRESSING	DISTRESSING	EXTREMELY DISTRESSING
	0	1	2	3	4
Physical Discomforts					
Medication side effects					
Pain					
Medical procedures					
Experience of body in stressful positions					
IV placement and sensations					
Restriction of movement					
Uncomfortable gown/bedding					

Plan of Action to Ameliorate the Patient Experience

For **Physical Discomforts** items scored 2 or above:

Patient Remarks: _____

_____

_____

Provider Response and Plan: _____

_____

_____

	NOT DISTRESSING/ NOT EXPERIENCED	SLIGHTLY DISTRESSING	MODERATELY DISTRESSING	DISTRESSING	EXTREMELY DISTRESSING
	0	1	2	3	4
Environmental Discomforts					
Restriction of food					
Restriction of water/ fluids					
Limited personal hygiene					
Limited privacy					
Exposure to sounds (monitors, alarms, etc.)					
Exposure to lights (i.e., fluorescent overhead lighting)					
Exposure to odors					
Observing other sick/injured patients					
Threat of germs, infection					
Lack of personal clothing					
Lack of personal space					
Lack of typical routine/schedule					
Lack of typical diet					
Exposure to needles					

(continued)

(continued)

	NOT DISTRESSING/ NOT EXPERIENCED	SLIGHTLY DISTRESSING	MODERATELY DISTRESSING	DISTRESSING	EXTREMELY DISTRESSING
	0	1	2	3	4
Exposure to blood					
Experience being monitored (heart rate, blood pressure, etc.)					
Experience of private areas being touched					
Experience of private areas being seen by staff					
Exposure to temperature					
Experience of being confined to bed					

Plan of Action to Ameliorate the Patient Experience

For **Environmental Discomforts** items scored 2 or above:

Patient Remarks: _____

_____

_____

Provider Response and Plan: _____

_____

_____

	NOT DISTRESSING/ NOT EXPERIENCED	SLIGHTLY DISTRESSING	MODERATELY DISTRESSING	FAIRLY DISTRESSING	EXTREMELY DISTRESSING
	0	1	2	3	4
Emotional Discomforts					
Feeling disoriented					
Feeling isolated					
Fear for own well-being					
Fear for own life					
Feeling anxious					
Feeling powerless					
Feeling vulnerable					
Concern about quality of medical care					
Feeling numb or detached					
Feeling depressed					

Plan of Action to Ameliorate the Patient Experience

Emotional Discomforts items scored 1 or above? _____ YES _____ NO

If YES, consult Mental Health Provider: _____ *Name*

Patient Remarks: _____

_____

_____

Provider Response and Plan: _____

_____

_____

Additional Notes/Comments:

_____
_____
_____
_____
_____
_____
_____
_____
_____
_____
_____
_____
_____
_____
_____

Administered By   *Date*

This copy is for individual use only—not for duplication, distribution, or institutional use.
For more information about using this tool, please contact:
Michelle Flaum Hall, EdD, LPCC-S
E-mail: hall@hawthorneintegrative.com
Phone: (937) 545-7392

H

NEW ROLES FOR MENTAL HEALTH PROFESSIONALS BEFORE, DURING, AND AFTER SEVERE MATERNAL EVENTS

PROTOCOL FOR PATIENT, FAMILY, AND STAFF SUPPORT

Due to the intense nature of severe maternal events (e.g., postpartum hemorrhage, venous thromboembolism [VTE], severe hypertension) and the ensuing emotional reactions of patients, their families, and even providers, it is imperative that we look to integrated teams that include mental health professionals to help manage the psychological impacts of this type of medical trauma. While mental health services have sometimes been viewed as an afterthought when considering the acute needs of women during such events, given the steady rise in maternal morbidity and increasing awareness of the benefits of integrated care, it seems timely to consider new roles for mental health professionals within this treatment context.

The following outlines roles and tasks for mental health professionals (e.g., clinical mental health counselors, clinical social workers, and clinical/counseling psychologists) before, during, and after a severe maternal event.

During Pregnancy

At OB/GYN office:

- In the last trimester (or sooner, if necessary), OB/GYN screens for pregnancy risk factors for severe maternal event
- OB/GYN or other clinician administers the Medical Mental Health Screening to assess mental health risk factors that can complicate patient coping and recovery

- If pregnancy risk factors AND mental health risk factors are present, OB/GYN should refer patient to a mental health provider prior to childbirth

With a mental health provider:

- Review the Medical Mental Health Screening

- Provide resources for stress management and anxiety reduction that are customized to pregnancy risk factors and mental health risk factors

- Explain process of integrated teaming to patients, including mental health provider's role during and after childbirth

- For high-risk patients, provide coaching to learn stress-management skills (e.g., mindfulness-based stress reduction) and create a stress-management plan to use during the birthing experience and plan for follow-up mental health care

During a Severe Maternal Event

During the event, a mental health professional will serve on the interprofessional treatment team and will:

- Provide ongoing assessment of mental health status of patient

- Administer the Experience of Medical Trauma Scale (EMTS) and coordinate a plan for resolving factors contributing to patient distress

- Provide emotional support for patient and family

- Coach patient in stress management techniques

- Be a skilled communicator; take emotional "temperature" in the room and convey accurate assessment of psychological state to nurses for charting

- Be a witness to events, which can help during debriefing

- Call a huddle with providers to update on mental status and discuss necessary steps to ensure emotional safety (see TeamSTEPPS resources for interprofessional teaming resources; teamstepps.ahrq.gov)

Follow-Up Care

When patient is stabilized:

- Assess mental health status and screen for traumatic stress response (use screening tools: Breslau's Posttraumatic Stress Disorder [PTSD] Scale, Impact of Events Scale)

- Provide emotional support for patient, family

- Schedule meeting with patient/family/providers for debrief prior to discharge
- Consult with providers to ensure that follow-up mental health care is suggested

At discharge:

- Provide resources to patient and family to educate about the psychological effects of severe maternal events (including Understanding the Emotional Effects of Your Childbirth Experience tool)
- Connect patient/family with aftercare, as needed
- Schedule postdischarge follow-up meeting with patient, as needed
- Conduct assessment/follow-up with providers to screen for vicarious traumatization, if necessary

NOTE: This protocol requires the collaboration among members of an effective interprofessional team. It requires that hospitals have a staff of mental health professionals trained to meet the unique needs of women experiencing birth trauma. Training for OB/GYNs, nursing staff, and mental health professionals in a team-based communication curriculum such as TeamSTEPPS is strongly suggested to enhance patient safety and provide the best possible care. Integrated care throughout a woman's pregnancy, especially if she is high risk, can help the patient and family by ensuring that both physical and mental health needs are being addressed. Mental health professionals who could be cross-trained to perform such tasks include clinical mental health counselors, clinical social workers (master's level), and psychologists (PhD or PsyD). Training in crisis management and interprofessional teaming are a suggested requirement for mental health professionals. For hospitals that do not have adequate mental health professional staff, consider contracting with mental health professionals from the community and/or contacting nearby universities with graduate training programs in clinical mental health counseling, clinical social work, and professional psychology.

For more information about integrating mental health professionals into treatment teams for managing the psychological impacts of severe maternal events, contact:

This copy is for individual use only—not for duplication, distribution, or institutional use.
For more information about using this tool, please contact:
Michelle Flaum Hall, EdD, LPCC-S
E-mail: hall@hawthorneintegrative.com
Phone: (937) 545-7392

UNDERSTANDING THE EMOTIONAL EFFECTS OF A DIFFICULT CHILDBIRTH EXPERIENCE

Your recent childbirth experience was a difficult one, and now that you have been discharged from the hospital, you will begin the journey toward healing. While it is certainly important that you follow your provider's recommendations regarding your physical healing, it is equally important that you address your mental and emotional health in the days and weeks to come.

The physical signs of your childbirth experience are obvious to you: You may have scars, lingering pain, limited energy and strength, and possible physical changes as a result of the birth experience. What may be less obvious are the emotional impacts, so it will be helpful to pay attention to your thoughts and feelings, and to watch for signs of depression and anxiety.

Childbirth and caring for a new baby can bring on so many different emotions. While women and their families often expect to feel joy following the birth of a child, when childbirth brings unexpected challenges—and even trauma—feelings can become quite complicated. The following are just a few of the more difficult emotions you may experience following the birth of your child.

Sad	Vulnerable	Worried
Confused	Fragile	Terrified
Disappointed	Defeated	Numb
Fearful	Helpless	Irritable
Angry	Jealous/Envious	Disoriented
Grief-stricken	Shocked	Disconnected
Relieved	Hopeless	Disillusioned
Lost	Detached	Panic-stricken

While many of these emotions are quite normal following a difficult childbirth, it will be important to watch for signs of more serious mental health concerns in the weeks and months ahead.

Signs of depression include feeling sad, low, deflated, "blue," hopeless, helpless … these are just a few examples of the emotional experience of depression.

Depression can also cause a lack of interest in things you normally like, and it can even cause you to feel apathy toward your baby, children, and family. Depression can also cause low energy, difficulty concentrating, and disruptions in your sleep and appetite. At its most severe, depression can cause scary thoughts of harming yourself and even shocking thoughts about harming others, including your baby. It is important for you to seek the help of a mental health professional if you experience any of the symptoms of depression.

Remember that the healing process is a time of transition, and that you need the support of others to help you regain your footing as a woman, mother, partner, family member, and friend. It helps to express your thoughts and emotions, and to remember that an extreme event such as your childbirth experience can lead to extreme reactions.

Signs of an anxiety disorder such as posttraumatic stress disorder (PTSD) include feeling excessive worry and panic, numb, depressed, irritable, and spacey or dazed. Signs of PTSD can also include insomnia, having an exaggerated startle response (e.g., jumping at sudden movements or sounds), having nightmares or flashbacks about the childbirth experience, feeling detached from one's body, and avoiding reminders of the experience (e.g., avoiding doctor visits). It is important for you to seek the help of a counselor if you experience any of these symptoms.

As you continue to heal from your childbirth trauma, you may experience difficulties in different areas of your life, such as in your relationships, career, identity, and spirituality. When people experience trauma, there can be a ripple effect through every part of their lives. The following are some possible effects of your childbirth trauma. If you notice these, consider contacting a mental health professional who can help guide you through your journey toward emotional healing.

RELATIONSHIP CONCERNS

The trauma of your childbirth experience was likely difficult to endure, not only for you, but also for those who love you. While it is not uncommon to experience stress in relationships as you heal, there are some signs that may indicate a more serious concern, such as:

- Difficulty talking with your partner and family about your experience, or for your partner to listen to you share your thoughts and feelings
- Isolation from your partner and/or family and friends
- Eruptions of anger or chronic irritability that contribute to significant tension in the relationship
- Difficulty with or lack of interest in physical closeness
- Fear of sexual intimacy (after you have been cleared to engage in intercourse)
- Feeling numb toward others and/or disinterested in social contact

In order to maintain healthy relationships during this challenging time, try to communicate as clearly as you can. Good communication can help both you and your loved ones cope with the ups and downs of this time.

OTHER CONCERNS THAT MAY ARISE

In addition to mental health concerns and relationship issues, a difficult childbirth can also lead to challenges in other areas of life. Women who experience birth trauma can struggle to make sense of the event and what it all means to them; it can be difficult to accept that their childbirth experience was so fearful, chaotic, or at the very least, disappointing.

Women who endure life-saving medical interventions resulting in permanent physical changes (e.g., hysterectomy) can struggle to regain a healthy identity and can grieve their inability to give birth in the future. Birth traumas can also lead to a questioning of all areas of life, from a belief in a higher power to career and lifestyle choices.

How Family and Friends Can Help

- Take time to listen. It is not uncommon for women to need to talk about details of their childbirth experience, perhaps numerous times. Remember that your role as a listener is to simply be present, with a caring attitude.

- Do not try to problem solve. One thing that gets in the way of active listening is a need to solve problems. When women share their thoughts and feelings about the birth experience, listen without interrupting or giving suggestions of action steps.

- Communicate clearly and patiently. Due to the many emotions and physical challenges women face following a difficult childbirth, it can be difficult to communicate effectively. Slow down and make an effort to listen and share your own thoughts and feelings clearly and concisely.

- Do not try to rush the healing process. While it can be tough to get through this difficult time, it is important to have empathy for women who have experienced a birth trauma and to give them space to heal in their own time and in their own way.

- Ask how you can help. Sometimes women can feel very alone as they try to heal from a traumatic childbirth experience, and they may not ask for help from others or know exactly how others can be helpful. Check in and ask how you can assist in the healing process. Does she need to talk? Help with the baby or other children? Time alone or with others?

- Suggest talking with a counselor. Sometimes women do not recognize when they might be experiencing more serious emotional effects of a difficult childbirth. If you are seeing signs of depression or anxiety, express your concerns in a respectful, gentle manner. Talk about additional options for support, including speaking with a mental health professional.

- Take care of yourself, too. Family and friends of women who experience a traumatic childbirth often work hard to support the healing process. While being a caregiver and support person is an extremely important role, it can also be exhausting—both physically and emotionally. Make sure you are taking care of your basic needs and that you also have the emotional support you need in order to stay healthy during the healing process.

CONTACT A MENTAL HEALTH PROFESSIONAL

It is not uncommon for women who experience a birth trauma to seek the help of a mental health professional, such as a clinical mental health counselor, psychologist, or clinical social worker. Even when people have supportive family and friends, sometimes it can be helpful to talk with someone who is neutral and unbiased—and who is there to listen and empower you to achieve greater emotional well-being. Mental health professionals can provide support and guidance, as well as diagnose and treat mental and emotional disorders such as depression and anxiety. To find a mental health professional in your area, you can ask your health care provider for a referral, contact your insurer for a directory of providers, or visit the website www.psychologytoday.com to view profiles of therapists in your area.

INDEX

AAMC. *See* Association of American Medical Colleges
accidents, 75–77
Accreditation Council for Graduate Medical Education (ACGME), 110
ACGME. *See* Accreditation Council for Graduate Medical Education
ACS. *See* acute coronary syndrome
acute coronary syndrome (ACS), 73
acute medical trauma
  at discharge, 234–236
  ignoring, 237
  managing, 236–237
  screening for risk factors of, 232
acute stress disorder (ASD), 70, 227
  recognizing signs of, 227–228
ADEs. *See* adverse drug events
adverse drug events (ADEs), 115
Agency for Healthcare Research and Quality (AHRQ), 171, 172, 219
agreeableness, 51
  low in, 51
AHRQ. *See* Agency for Healthcare Research and Quality
alexithymia, 81
allied health professionals, 217
Alzheimer's disease, 83

American Psychiatric Association (APA), 227
  trauma definition, 18
American Psychological Association (APA), 70
anxiety, 37
APA. *See* American Psychiatric Association; American Psychological Association
ASD. *See* acute stress disorder
Association of American Medical Colleges (AAMC), 110
asthma, 80–81
autoimmune disorders, 81–83
avocational/leisure crisis, 42

behavioral health/mental health, 8
Big Five personality traits, 32, 47–52
biopsychosocialspiritual medical trauma, 22–23
birth traumas, 71
Body Remembers: The Psychophysiology of Trauma and Trauma Treatment, The, 124
Breslau Scale, 227
Bronfenbrenner's ecological model, 29